Europe's Balkan Dilemma

Europe's Balkan Dilemma

Paths to Civil Society or State-Building?

Adam Fagan

I.B. TAURIS

LONDON · NEW YORK

New paperback edition published in 2012 by I.B.Tauris & Co Ltd
6 Salem Road, London W2 4BU
175 Fifth Avenue, New York NY 10010
www.ibtauris.com

First published in hardback in 2010 by I.B.Tauris & Co Ltd

ISBN: 978 1 78076 406 1

A full CIP record for this book is available from the British Library
A full CIP record is available from the Library of Congress

Library of Congress Catalog Card Number: available

Typeset by Swales & Willis Ltd, Exeter, Devon

Contents

Acknowledgements

This monograph is the product of extensive fieldwork undertaken in Bosnia-Herzegovina, Serbia and Kosovo between 2004 and 2008. I am most grateful to the British Academy and the Nuffield Foundation for generously funding the research and also to the Department of Politics, Queen Mary, University of London for facilitating the endeavour. The completion of this research monograph would not have been possible without the generous support of New York University in London and Professor David Ruben.

I am eternally grateful to the numerous officials, employees and activists within the civil society and NGO sectors who provided me with invaluable data and submitted to requests for interviews and information. I also have appreciated the help of EU Delegation staff within the region. Again, too many people to name, but I would like to thank Vladimir Pandurević (Sarajevo), Jelena Miloš (Sarajevo), Zorana Ivanković (Belgrade) and John White (EAR Belgrade) for their time and support. I was also fortunate to obtain considerable help from senior staff at DG Enlargement in Brussels. In particular, the help of Mose Apelblat, Louis Hersom and Juri Laas was absolutely invaluable and much appreciated.

I would also like to thank Toby Vogel, Lejla Somun-Krupalija and Sonja Biserko for their comments, advice and encouragement. Liz Friend-Smith at I.B.Tauris deserves mention here for her considerable patience and positive encouragement. I am also very grateful to Indraneel Sircar for his assistance with aspects of the manuscript and for his insights into developments in Bosnia-Herzegovina.

However, I am in no doubt that the book would not have been written or researched without the support, love and patience of Julie, Ella, Molly and Noah Taylor. It is to you, and the memory of my dear Mother, that this book is dedicated.

Introduction

Sat in the ubiquitous pavement cafés of Belgrade, Sarajevo or Pristina, surrounded by gold star-emblazoned EU-livery advertising the latest Commission-funded development initiative, construction or pledge, it is quite easy to forget that when the European Economic Community (EEC) came into existence in 1957 it was to advance the economic interests of post-war capitalist European liberal democracies and that, until the end of the last century, external relations and foreign policy were rather minor aspects of EU activity. From the perspective of the Western Balkans in 2009, the EU looks and acts like a multilateral development agency: it funds road-building, railways and hospitals; it trains police officers, civil servants and doctors; supports community development, NGOs and substitutes for the absence of state and market provision in the realms of welfare and education. If you are a Bosnian or a Serb requiring credit or a loan to start a business, or for cancer screening or employment training the chances are the service will be delivered as part of an EU-funded scheme or programme.

How and under what circumstances did this transformation in the EU's role occur? Is the current intervention in Bosnia-Herzegovina (BiH), Serbia and now Kosovo simply an extension and refinement of earlier democracy assistance measures dating back to the late 1980s? What is the EU trying to achieve in these Western Balkan states, how effective are the strategies, and what specific challenges is the Commission's[1] enlargement strategy confronting in this region of weak states, post-conflict reconstruction and limited democratisation? This book does not attempt to answer all such questions. What it sets out to do is consider the impact of development assistance channelled through non-governmental organisations and civil society associations in terms of realising broader political and economic objectives. The book is primarily interested in whether such intervention is helping to lay the foundations of good governance, a critical component of Europeanisation and a significant test of the EU's enlargement strategy.

The EC (European Community) initially became involved in the region as part of broader international efforts to bring peace to the successor states of the former Yugoslavia in the early 1990s. However, it is widely acknowledged that EC/EU peace and mediation initiatives for Bosnia – in particular the 1992 European Community peace conference led by Jose Cutileiro and Peter Carrrington which called for the ethnic division of the territory, and later initiatives proposed by David Owen – were entirely unsuccessful and contentious. From 2000 onwards the EUs role changed. Drawing in part on its successes as provider of emergency relief and reconstruction aid during and immediately after the war, the EU has subsequently engaged with the successor states in the context of the Stabilisation and Association process (SAp), with the ultimate aim of assisting the new states towards eventual membership. In essence, once the wars of Yugoslavia's succession ended, EU intervention and assistance in the region was deployed in the spirit of Article 2 of the Treaty of Rome: 'to promote . . . a continuous and balanced expansion, an increase in stability, an accelerated raising of the standard of living and closer relations between the states belonging to it'.

It barely needs stating that the requirements of membership represent an enormous challenge for the Western Balkan states. From the perspective of pro-EU commentators, political elites and citizens within the region, EU intervention and the requirements of the Commission are broadly perceived as necessary to transform weak states and mitigate the political, economic and social legacies of conflict and socialism. For advocates, meeting the rigid requirements set by the Commission is about Europeanisation via enlargement; it is hoped that the strategy will deliver democratic governance and ultimately membership of the EU in much the same way that it did for the Central and East European States.

Regardless of whether membership for the states of this region is desirable or the intervention appropriate, it cannot be denied that the role of the European Union in assisting the political reconstruction of Serbia and Bosnia-Herzegovina has been, and continues to be, a particularly bold and largely unprecedented endeavour. The €2 billion of aid that has been poured into Kosovo, a land of 2.4 million people, plus the proposed assistance package designed to deliver supervised statehood to the province, represents an even more ambitious assistance package, taking EU intervention in and assistance for the region to new heights. The Mission to Kosovo (EULEX), once fully operational, will confirm the Commission's status as the main development agency in the Western Balkan region and represents the most ambitious and costly foreign policy adventure in the EU's 50-year history. Indeed, not only does the scale and remit of EU assistance in these states surpass the Commission's previous intervention in the post-socialist states of Central and South Eastern Europe, it also extends significantly beyond the provision of development aid delivered by the Commission to transitional and failing states globally.

But it is not simply the scale of the assistance that is contentious. For critics, whether these states can progress towards sustainable change and transformation will stand as the ultimate test of Europeanisation in the East; a bold endeavour since the early 1990s which has arguably 'not only crowded out other sources of institutions and policies, but also achieved rule adoption where other organisations had failed' (Schimmelfennig and Sedelmeier 2005a). Not only is the general transformative power of Europe at stake, but so too is the EU's capacity to intervene in weak, post-conflict or contested states.

The framing of aid for these states in terms of accession, and the discourses of democracy promotion and Europeanisation immediately suggest continuity with earlier enlargements; such a discursive arguably distorts the focus of the intervention and obfuscates the development realities on the ground. Yet the post-conflict states of the Western Balkans under examination in this study have had difficult transitions and can only barely be considered as consolidated democracies: Serbia has experienced a protracted and turbulent regime change; Bosnia barely functions as a single state and its future as a stable liberal democracy hangs, according to sceptics and even the more moderate commentators, in abeyance or at least is dependent upon significant further intervention to trigger the necessary constitutional reform; and the universal acceptance of Kosovo's sovereignty remains in dispute. In each case the rule of law, respect for human and minority rights and the capacity of the state to deal with corruption, implement policies and ensure compliance with European standards are far from certain and are not fully institutionally entrenched. Whilst depleted state authority combined with the legacies of state socialism do indeed represent continuity with Central and Eastern Europe, ethno-nationalism and war during the 1990s, plus the absence of any experience of sovereignty or *stateness*, immediately distinguish these fledgling countries from Slovakia, Bulgaria and Romania, not to mention the Czech Republic, Poland and Hungary. But it is perhaps within the realm of the economy where the contrast with the rest of post-socialist Europe is most acute and the EU faces the greatest challenge. Kosovo aside, market reforms have yet to be fully implemented in BiH and Serbia and standard macro-economic indicators – poverty, growth, foreign direct investment, inflation and unemployment – suggest serious difficulties that are likely to be exacerbated by the current global financial situation.

The focus of EU assistance for these Western Balkan states reflects the political and economic realities of the region and the intervention is also indicative of the EU's broader ambitions to become a key player in the 'high politics' of global security and conflict management (Glasius and Kostovicova 2008: 84). The key development conditions that Western Balkan applicant states must achieve, outlined in the Stabilisation and Association process (SAp), the framework through which the EU negotiates with candidate and potential candidate states, are: building state capacity, security and stabilisation, law enforcement and regional co-operation and integration. This marks a distinct contrast with the more vaguely defined democratisation criteria of the early 1990s. Despite employing a not dissimilar rhetoric, the Commission, in its dealings with Serbia, BiH and now Kosovo, places primary emphasis on post-conflict reconstruction and state capacity; civil society development is a somewhat subordinate objective, prioritised in the context of building the political and institutional capacity of states rather than specifically in terms of democratic consolidation.

Research questions and hypotheses

From the perspective of discrete short-term project assistance channelled predominantly through local non-governmental organisations (NGOs) in BiH, Serbia and Kosovo, the book poses a number of fundamental questions:

- What are the objectives of this aspect of EU assistance?
- How effective is the assistance in realising the EU's specific and more general objectives?
- What other outcomes are discernible?
- To what extent is the assistance generating a shift towards multi-level governance, increasing the capacities of state as well as non-state actors, and leading to the formation of pro-reform coalitions?
- How does the assistance for these states differ from the provision for the Central, Eastern and South-Eastern European states that entered the EU as part of the fifth enlargement of 2004 and 2007?
- What specific challenges does this aspect of EU intervention pose for the strategy of Europeanisation via enlargement?
- What lessons, if any, can and have been learnt for Kosovo from the experience of assistance provision in BiH and Serbia?

The core objective of this research monograph is to evaluate the impact of measures introduced by the EU as part of the CARDS (Community Assistance for Reconstruction, Development and Stabilisation), EIDHR (European Instrument for Democracy and Human Rights) and IPA (Instrument for Pre-accession Assistance) assistance programmes to develop and build the capacity of non-governmental organisations (NGOs). At a very basic level this aid is designed to extend democratic pluralism and the existence of a multiplicity of non-governmental and civil society organisations (CSOs) as a consequence of EU funding is seen as a positive outcome. However, the objectives of the provision is both more ambitious and specific: it is designed, in principle at least, to build and strengthen multi-level governance and engage state and non-state sectors in sustainable partnerships in the context of policy development, institutional reform, enforcement and regulation. Although the EU provides additional development aid, delivered directly and bilaterally through government and state agencies, the optic of recipient NGOs and the arena of project grants is used here as the basis for judging aims, impact, outcomes and rationale of the Commission's development assistance.

Evaluating the impact of NGO-delivered assistance

In seeking to scrutinise the link between EU project funding channelled through NGOs, and broader, quite significant development objectives for BiH, Serbia and Kosovo, *Europe's Balkan Dilemma* is pitched within the midst of several contentious methodological and conceptual issues. This section will provide a short summary of the general methodological and normative difficulties at stake in trying to judge the effectiveness of such funding, particularly with regard to evaluating the extent to which such intervention is leading to the emergence of governance partnerships between NGOs and the state.

Despite a huge increase in the development programmes and assistance projects run by national and international NGOs over the past three decades, to the extent that far more aid is administered by the non-governmental sector than by official aid agencies, measuring the impact of donor assistance channelled through NGOs remains replete with difficulties and fraught with contention (Burnell and Calvert 2004; Crawford 2003; Green and Kohl 2007; Riddell 2007a). Whilst several of the limitations of NGO-delivered assistance and the extensive critique of their activities in the context of transitional and developing states are explored in Chapter 2, it seems necessary from the outset of this book to highlight the complexities involved in trying to measure the impact of EU development assistance being channelled through NGOs and CSOs in the Western Balkans, and to inject a degree of caution with regard to the findings of the research: this study has focused on a sample of recipient

NGOs administering EU aid over a specific period of time. A more long-term analysis looking at the activities of different organisations may well generate contradictory findings.

The main criticism levelled at NGO-delivered assistance, whether large global NGOs or local nationally registered organisations such as those operating in BiH, Serbia and Kosovo, is that discrete projects do not deliver a great deal in terms of services to the community and the immediate impact may be short-term. The concern is three-fold: (1) the impact and outputs of discrete projects tend to be narrow, benefiting a small targeted section of the community; (2) once the funding runs out then initiatives will tend to cease and there will therefore be little or no sustainable benefit from the aid; (3) it is difficult to disentangle and measure the exact impact of an NGO project from the effects of other initiatives and changing social and economic circumstances. This is not helped by the fact that there is a tendency for NGOs to exaggerate the impact of their development role and to claim credit for change.

From a methodological perspective, measuring the impact of NGO interventions and quantifying the successfulness of discrete projects is fraught with difficulties. This is partly due to the fact that the available data is limited to what NGOs decide to publish and produce. Indeed even the larger transnational organisations have only in recent years published more detailed summaries of their activities. Even when reporting is comprehensive, the focus tends to be on illustrating the extent to which project outputs have been realised rather than on an assessment of broader social impact.

There is also a more fundamental normative contradiction regarding the role and function of NGOs, which serves to exacerbate the methodological difficulties concerning the measurement of impact referred to above. Critics, including political scientists in particular, are often dismissive of the service provision function of NGOs and the donor assistance that privileges such activities over and above policy advocacy and a more overtly political/ democratic/civil society role for recipient organisations. As this study illustrates, it is the case that a substantial amount of EU assistance results in service provision outcomes rather than political or policy-related advocacy. Whilst this is a critical concern for this study, which aims to measure the governance interaction that EU assistance generates, it is also a fundamental tension within any assessment of NGO impact. Other commentators, framing their analysis more in terms of political development, remain adamant that this aspect of assistance is critical insofar as NGOs running services in communities, providing training and skills development raises awareness and the capacities of recipients and therefore builds civil society from the grass roots level (Riddell

2007). Others argue that funding NGOs to deliver services in lieu of the state or the market does little to stimulate the transformation of state capacity, drive the process of regime change, or augment the *political* capacities of recipient organisations as representations of civil society (Ottaway and Carothers 2000). From the latter perspective, the emergence of governance as a consequence of assistance is dependent on NGOs being supported not just as agents of implementation and enforcement, but also as policy actors with the power to influence the development of laws and to counter the influence of the state and the market.

A further set of concerns about NGO development assistance stems from the efficiency of this mode of aid delivery and intervention. Some of the issues, such as the replication of initiatives, are discussed in detail in Chapter 2, but it ought to be noted at this stage of the study that critics have rightly questioned the extent to which efforts to build the institutional capacities of NGOs in order to improve the administration and efficiency of assistance are worthwhile, or whether this in fact siphons off scarce resources that could otherwise benefit the poor. It is indeed difficult to ascertain the extent to which institutional and management training benefits the organisation over and beyond providing an advantage to individual employees. The nature of NGOs is that staff turnover is high and that institutional memory is easily fractured as individuals take the knowledge and capacities with them when they move on to jobs in the private sector or to other organisations. Thus, however desirable it may be in terms of the long-term sustainability of the sector to divert donor resources towards building the organisation itself, rather than into specific development projects, this is usually greeted with suspicion.

Using NGOs as a conduit for donor aid is often justified on the basis that the non-governmental or voluntary sector does things more quickly and cheaply than governments and official aid agencies. This research, in tune with many other studies of NGO assistance, illustrates the extent to which this is largely true, particularly with well-conceived and executed projects. However, the concern is that the scarcity of resources, the complexity of assistance objectives, and the increased demands on NGOs to manage and report their activities serve to make the provision less efficient as organisations are compelled to invest more and more in management, auditing and public relations.

In reaching any judgement as to the effectiveness of aid channelled through NGOs, several points need to be borne in mind. First, NGOs rarely define their impact solely in terms of the narrow and specific objectives of individual projects. Most frame their contribution to the development of weak states and regions in terms of changing opinions, empowering communities and providing skills and increased capacity – all of which remain extremely difficult to measure and quantify. For example, a project that has provided training for unemployed women in a socially deprived region of Serbia or Bosnia may be deemed to have succeeded in delivering its objectives by providing the planned number of trainings. However, the women may not find employment for several months or years after the completion of the project, some may leave the area, or the employment opportunities will be dependent on investors not the actions of NGOs. Yet, the project run by the NGO may well have improved the skills of the local workforce, raised aspirations and encouraged women in the community to at least seek employment. The occurrence of the project may also stimulate the local authority to offer further training or to introduce initiatives in the area to stimulate employment and investment. In other words, the sustainable legacy of the project may be that it acted as a catalyst for change, it empowered beneficiaries to go on and engage with issues affecting their communities, prompted government authorities to take action, and led to other donors becoming involved in abating the issue.

Second, whilst NGOs may be rather cavalier in their claims to have helped the poorest of the poor, the implicit, if not explicit, assumption regarding NGO-channelled assistance is that 'introducing a process of development change . . . will require other, complementary inputs from both inside and outside the beneficiary community' (Barclay 1979). In other words, it is easy to be dismissive of NGO input on the basis that it is assumed that donor-driven projects should be able to change the world. Despite the specific focus of this study, NGO assistance should not be judged in isolation or seen as a substitute for other forms of intervention; states, the market and other agencies need to play a role if the assistance is to be effective and sustainable. As Riddell observes, 'the majority of NGO projects have probably delivered tangible benefits, but many have probably made only a small contribution to improving the lives and enhancing the well-being of the beneficiaries' (Riddell 2007).

Related to this point is the fact that the sustainability of NGO-driven projects is often criticised for being dependent on additional or new sources of funding. Again, such a criticism stems perhaps from a misconception about what NGOs can actually be expected to achieve. From the outset, 'most NGO projects are not financially sustainable without the continued injection of external funds' (ibid.: 281), and it is perhaps the short-term nature of most donor aid and the emphasis on tangible, measurable outcomes delivered within the duration of the project that fuels the misconception that NGO projects will achieve long-term development goals in two years for €100,000 without the government making an investment, resources from other donors, or the injection of private sector funds.

EU assistance and NGOs: a contentious development strategy

As already stated, the core objective of this book is to evaluate the impact of EU assistance on building and developing the interaction between state and non-state actors as a measure of both good governance and civil society development. But EU aid channelled through NGOs has been, and continues to be, allocated with a more specific and fundamental aim: to help national elites meet the criteria and conditionality associated with enlargement. Whilst EU-supported NGOs may well be successful or unsuccessful in providing social services and welfare, and whilst such provision may serve to empower citizens, enrich pluralism and democracy, such intervention may not necessarily be triggering sustainable partnerships and positive interaction between NGOs and the state; nor is the provision necessarily contributing to the development of pro-reform coalitions within recipient states. Though such a specific focus enables the analysis offered in this book to transcend some of the normative contentions referred to above, some of the more general difficulties relating to NGOs as conduits of aid still remain and will be discussed in more detail below.

Supporting, strengthening and developing the capacity of local NGOs has, since the early 1990s, formed the cornerstone of EU intervention in acceding or candidate states. Indeed, the provision by the EU of project grants for NGOs has become the most salient expression of EU assistance. Many, if not all, of the core objectives of the EU for the region involve funding and building the capacity of local NGOs to work on issues ranging from environmental protection to minority rights and refugee return. It is important also to remember that developing civil society organisations has, in itself, long been a key objective of the Commission, both as part of the Poland and Hungary: Assistance for Restructuring their Economies (PHARE) programme in the 1990s and more recently as part of the European Initiative for Democracy and Human Rights (EIDHR).[2] The Commission has sought to develop strong and efficacious NGOs as part of its commitment to strengthening democracy and human rights across the post-socialist region, and also specifically in the post-conflict states of the Western Balkans. From the Commission's perspective, establishing a tier of professional NGOs, with developed capacity and expertise, operating at elite level and within the orbit of national (EU-inspired) policy development, is not just a means to deliver more effective policy outcomes, but also the first stage in building a pluralist and democratic civil society. The logic employed here is that the knowledge generated and obtained by EU-funded NGOs will then be disseminated amongst smaller, local and community-based associations and campaign networks. In other words, developing NGOs is the first stage in a longer-term process of seeding civil society. Despite the extensive nature of the EU's role in the region and the commitment of significant resources, there has yet to be a comprehensive empirical and comparative assessment of exactly what impact the intervention is having on recipient non-state actors, and the effect of aid on the interaction between government or state actors and NGOs. Local Delegations of the European Commission in Belgrade, Sarajevo and Pristina do, of course, undertake assessments of projects, but they do so in terms of checking that project outcomes have been realised; data is compiled and reports drafted outlining the extent to which recipient organisations have delivered on their stated outputs, information which is then included in country progress reports submitted to Brussels. Audits undertaken by the enlargement directorate of the Commission also occur, but do so infrequently and again the focus is to check that funding has been allocated according to the rules and procedures, and that objectives have been achieved. What does not take place in either Brussels or in the local Delegations is an evaluation of the sustainable impact of the funded initiative, whether a project continues beyond the duration of the grant, whether it delivers tangible benefit beyond the target group of citizens, and how effectively the particular outcome contributes to the advancement of macro development objectives. In other words, assessment of projects is conducted from a purely project management perspective.

As already noted, the assumption which this book sets out to assess is that assistance delivered through NGOs is a cost-effective, efficient and viable means of realising a multitude of different micro and macro enlargement-related objectives, ranging from the development of policy knowledge, formation and implementation; bureaucratic, institutional and infrastructural reform; the augmentation and reform of state capacity, as well as the construction of good governance and pluralist democratic politics. The explicit assumption of the Commission is that developing the managerial capacity of NGOs will foster inclusive and engaged civil societies and will also help to construct stable and democratic states that are sufficiently legitimate, effective and sovereign to be considered for EU membership.

EU donor intervention, like democracy promotion in general, is based on the premise that aid will be empowering and that without such assistance an outcome would not otherwise have been achieved. This is immediately prob-lematic, both philosophically and empirically. Whilst the *overall* impact of EU intervention in post-socialist states can be measured in terms of compliance and engagement with new laws, regulations, institutions and processes on behalf of the applicant states, the impact of *specific* initiatives and projects is extremely difficult to gauge and disaggregate, not least because it cannot be assumed that a particular development would not otherwise have occurred. It may be, of course, that another donor would have implemented the particular scheme or provided the resources, or simply that the government would have introduced the reform, or created the institution or policy.

A major problem in measuring both outputs and outcomes is the extent to which initial objectives were clearly articulated, and the degree to which proj-ect or programme outputs were connected to and developed in the context of broader developmental goals relating to democratic governance (macro) objectives. Not surprisingly, international donors have found it extremely dif-ficult to demonstrate causality and to quantify the extent to which micro-level projects contribute to the realisation of macro-level objectives. The solution is perhaps for donors to focus instead on what might be termed 'middle-level objectives'. The German Agency for Technical Co-operation (Deutsche Gesellschaft für Technische Zusammenarbeit (GTZ)) has recently moved 'towards . . . middle-level objectives such as the establishment of a new crimi-nal code, rather than narrow outputs of training a number of defense attorneys or broad outcomes such as improving the rule of law' (Green and Kohl 2007). SIDA, the Swedish Agency for International Development Co-operation, has moved away from evaluating the impact of individual projects towards an assessment of the theories, logic and assumptions that guide the project. Such an attempt to measure the qualitative rather than the quantitative impact of a project is also being considered by the EU. The issue for many donors is per-haps that providing funding for NGOs seems to be the easiest way to support democratisation and civil society development; it represents non-partisan intervention and offers a route into a country that does not involve negotiating state or governmental processes directly. Whilst most donors will acknowl-edge that demonstrating a linkage between micro outputs and macro develop-ment objectives is important, there is overriding benefit to be gained from funding small discrete projects that deliver tangible outputs over a short time-period, and also openly benefit recipient organisations by providing them with, albeit temporary, resources and engaging citizens in community projects.

This brings us to a further set of considerations when attempting to measure impact: whilst donors may be able to acknowledge a plurality of objectives and rationales guiding their funding, they may be less aware of unforeseen or unpredicted outcomes and outputs. The unintended outcomes generated by assistance are often difficult to identify and it is crucial to recognise that whilst a project might have resulted in certain positive outputs, there may also be countervailing negative developmental consequences, perhaps unrelated to the project area, that ought to be borne in mind when making an overall evaluation of impact. For example, a project designed to develop state capacity in a particular area may succeed in delivering specific outputs, but if in achieving such output experts leave their jobs in the state sector in order to work in an NGO, this may ultimately weaken state capacity and result in a negative impact. Most donors engage in a variety of programmes, running concurrently, across sectors and issue areas.

A widely voiced criticism of donor aid to NGOs is that the objectives of the various projects and initiatives are inevitably likely to clash and there is often little sense that the individual donor or group of donors have an overall perspective of the aid being provided. Recent academic analysis as well as policy studies reports emphasise the importance of coherence of objectives, both in terms of donors working with other donors, but also with regard to ensuring that donor programmes are interconnected and that impact is measured across programme areas (Ottaway 2000, 2002; Picciotto 2005). Yet, as noted above, it is far easier for donors to judge tangible short-term benefits than it is to measure and identify longer-term impact. Green and Kohl refer to the problem of 'low-hanging fruit' to describe the tendency of assessments to latch on to obvious benefits and visible outputs without delving much further (2007: 5). The difficulty here is that many donor initiatives stress such short-term obvious benefits and devise their assistance around the deliverance of such goals rather than overtly connecting short-term outputs to strategic development goals. Whether, for example, an educational programme, an environmental initiative, or a community facility is still functioning effectively after two, or five, years is arguably the real test of successful output, but it is difficult for donors to delay assessment for such a period of time, not least because the data may no longer be available and key personnel may have moved on, but also because donors themselves are accountable to their corporate funders.

Perhaps the most important consideration when measuring the impact of development aid is to recognise that the endeavour is invariably a tool of foreign policy and external relations, or in the case of the EU, a cornerstone of external governance. In other words, any assessment of the objectives of particular programmes and the auditing of outcomes, or particular framing discourses of human rights, the environment or democracy promotion, has to be placed in the context of the broader goals of the particular multilateral or bilateral donor agency. In the case of the pre-accession and enlargement agendas assistance has long been geared towards a country meeting the requirements of the *acquis*. Decisions to continue funding a particular project, or to suspend certain programmes in favour of others, will be taken on the basis of a country's progress towards accession and may well override such imperatives as cost-effectiveness, reliability of partner organisation, or popular concern or support for a particular issue. With regard to the EU's intervention in BiH, Serbia and Kosovo in particular there is potentially a disincentive for the EU to engage in overt criticism of projects and the deployment of its resources lest this fuels suspicions of inefficiency, thereby providing ammunition for those within existing member states that oppose further intervention or indeed future enlargement.

It is frequently argued that the greatest shortcoming of donor programmes and democracy assistance is that the objectives are not set locally and that local input is limited or somewhat tokenistic. Indeed, as donors generally operate in a number of countries and contexts, initiatives tend to take on a generic character despite the fact that specific structural realities can determine the success of failure of initiatives. One obvious way of mediating the impact of this is for local experts, community leaders and elites to set agendas based on what issues are perceived by them to be important, but also for them to conduct evaluations of impact. However, the problem with local evaluations and input, that is often overlooked by academics and critics, is that local experts may 'have limited knowledge of a donor's overall interests and priorities' (Green and Kohl 2007), not necessarily have a sense of how the project fits in with broader political and developmental objectives and agendas, and may not necessarily be able to evaluate projects in terms of strategic importance. There is also no guarantee that local experts and practitioners will be sensitive to and accommodating of country-specific legacies. In reality, evaluations offered by local experts and agents tend to rely on generic and generalised criticisms, such as the need to increase amounts of funding, that donors expect results too soon, time-frames are too short, resources should be targeted more towards institution-building, and that greater consideration should be given to local culture and contexts without being more specific. Alternatively, local experts can be too deferential and, fearful of upsetting the donor agency, reluctant to criticise the project assistance too emphatically.

There is also a more fundamental problem relating to both local evaluations and to assessments carried out by the donor agency itself, which is particularly relevant to BiH, Serbia and Kosovo, namely, a lack of capacity to undertake effective scrutiny. In terms of relying on local experts, Green and Kohl point out that 'the pool of quality local research expertise can be extremely limited in many countries, particularly post-conflict countries' (2007: 4). The same problem affects donor agencies, particularly the EU, whereby the capacity to monitor and evaluate is dependent on resources and internal management structures. For instance, a programme may be devised and administered by a particular office, but a completely separate department or section of the agency will carry out the monitoring or audit. In the case of the EU, it may well be that the evaluation is carried out by the local Delegation who will have responsibility for the management of the country projects, but will not have control over the design and the setting of overall objectives. Much then depends on effective communication and a shared sense of objectives and a framework of evaluation, not just between 'centre' and 'periphery', but also between local Delegations.

The methodological difficulties identified above are extremely significant for a study such as this. The extent to which the Commission has addressed, for example, the issue of linking outcomes and outputs, or the use of local experts in the assessment of projects will be revealed throughout the course of the book. But it must be acknowledged from the outset that several of the methodological difficulties reflect deep-seated conceptual debates and contentions regarding foreign donor assistance, intervention and democracy promotion.

Contents of the book

The book will begin (in Chapter 1, The EU and the Western Balkans) with a detailed analysis and review of the EU's enlargement strategy for the region and for Serbia, BiH and Kosovo in particular. The Commission's bespoke Stabilisation and Association process (SAp) framework for candidate and potential candidate countries will be examined in terms of previous enlargements (2004, 2007), and in the context of the evolution of development priorities, terms of conditionality and intervention strategies employed by the Commission since 1990. The overriding aim of the chapter is to provide the reader with an overview and analysis of EU relations with the states under examination, and to provide a commentary on the logic and rationale of EU assistance. The key points to emerge from the discussion are that whilst there are continuities with previous assistance and enlargement processes, the potential candidate countries are being dealt with differently, with a far greater emphasis on capacity-building and building interaction between state and non-state actors. The discussion also highlights the importance placed by the Commission on developing regional co-operation, and the extent to which economic realities affecting these states (low levels of foreign investment, unemployment, lack of market penetration of the economies) are potentially critical factors in determining the impact of assistance, but also thwart efforts to foster co-operation and will ultimately determine the pace of enlargement.

In Chapter 2 (Theorising EU assistance and intervention in Serbia, BiH and Kosovo) a theoretical and conceptual framework is constructed for examining EU assistance and intervention, and to examine the key concepts – governance and civil society development – that are routinely employed by the Commission, practitioners and scholars to characterise and legitimise the pro-vision of assistance. The two core arguments of the chapter are: first, that the construction of good governance, as defined in the public policy and interna-tional relations literatures, depends not only on the capacity of non-state actors, but also on the strength of the *state* sector to implement and orchestrate policy development and the co-ordination of different governance actors. Second, that supporting NGOs as an expression of civil society, with all the lib-eral democratic connotations that this conjures up, represents a distraction from the reality that these organisations are supported and nurtured in order to provide services in lieu of the state and the market, to improve the content and implementation of policy, and if they happen also to be linked with civil soci-ety networks, this is *incidental*. In other words, the objective and impact of EU assistance requires demystifying; we need to move beyond the narrative of civil society as a means of critiquing assistance, and to assess EU intervention from the perspective of the extensive critique of international intervention designed to strengthen and build the capacity of what are perceived to be weak states. Although capacity-building is invariably linked within the development litera-ture to democracy promotion and support for civil society, the conflation is contentious (Leftwich 1994). For many the two are entirely separate and should not be confused; the very notion of democracy being introduced and nurtured by exogenous forces is contradictory (Ottaway and Carothers 2000). For other critics the issue is a far more fundamental one: Ottaway's assertion that 'external intervention has met in general with only partial success' (2003: 246) reflects a deep suspicion amongst academics regarding whether interven-tion channelled through NGOs under the guise of civil society promotion or capacity-building compromises national sovereignty and fails to deliver signif-icant benefit, regardless of whether the intention is democracy promotion or effective state development. The chapter provides an extensive summary of the literature critical of such donor intervention, much of which focuses on post-socialist states (which constitutes a key part of the broader critique of intervention) (Hann 2002; Quigley 2000).

Some analysis of the impact of donor assistance on NGOs and CSOs in the Western Balkans and the successor states of the former Yugoslavia has been undertaken (Deacon and Stubbs 1998), though there is little evidence of sustained and detailed empirical analysis looking at project outcomes and the impact of funding on individual organisations and networks. This is also true of studies of governance and the engagement of state and non-state actors, carried out largely by international relations scholars and critical theorists who invariably produce thorough critiques, but who do not substantiate their assertions with qualitative or quantitative empirical data (Belloni 2000; Chandler 1999).

With regard to constructing a conceptual framework for considering the extent to which EU assistance is delivering civil society development, one cannot avoid traversing the vast literature that exists to define and conceptualise civil society. The main focus here will be on conceptualisations of civil society held by donors and international development agencies, and to consider the extent to which the rather ubiquitous institution of 'NGO' is in fact an embodiment of the ideals and functions of 'civil society'. In other words, to challenge the embedded assumption of donors that NGOs equal civil society and that the success of the latter can in some way be measured by the proliferation of the former.

The chapter will also include a detailed analysis of the notion of 'capacity-building'. Most assistance to NGOs offered by donors such as the EU is framed in the language of 'capacity-building' or 'capacity assistance', and this has been a feature of the development literature since the 1950s. However, the notion of building national capacity to deal with development issues, as well as the specific notion of 'environmental capacity-building' gained momentum at the UN Conference on Environment and Development held at Rio in 1992, and more generally around discussions of sustainability and globalisation (Grindle 1997). The implicit assumption underpinning capacity-building programmes is that such assistance is *technical* rather than *political* and that 'knowledge' is both quantifiable and transferable. In its focus on EU development aid this study directly confronts the impact of 'capacity-building' assistance, both theoretically and empirically. In examining the extent to which aid channelled through NGOs is strengthening civil society and the representation of community interests, the chapter considers whether assistance delivered to NGOs is in practice privileging the development of policy 'knowledge' and constructing an epistemic community of compliant experts willing and able to assist in EU policy development.

The remaining chapters of the book provide an exposition of the empirical data gathered in Bosnia-Herzegovina (Chapter 3), Serbia (Chapter 4) and Kosovo (Chapter 6). In addition to an extensive elaboration and analysis of the interview data and qualitative research on EU-funded projects and NGO activities, each chapter will also offer a detailed analysis of the state's relations with the EU, an overall narrative account of EU assistance to the country since the collapse of Yugoslavia, as well as a summary of key political developments. Drawing on the quantitative research undertaken for this study – codification of interview data – the fifth chapter (Quantitative analysis of EU assistance to Bosnia-Herzegovina and Serbia) provides further exposition and details of the impact of EU assistance on NGOs in both states.

The final chapter of the book (EU assistance and intervention in Kosovo: lessons learnt?) offers the first detailed account of the impact of EU assistance administered by the European Agency for Reconstruction (EAR) and European Commission Liaison Office (ECLO) channelled through local NGOs in Kosovo and examines the extent to which the EU has changed or modified its approach in light of the distinct challenges facing the new state.

1

The EU and the Western Balkans

The EU and Post-Socialist Europe: assistance, association and accession

Since the fall of the Berlin Wall and the revolutions of 1989, post-socialist Europe has been configured and re-configured by EU enlargement and integration. Conditionality, phases of enlargement, regular reports, and pre-accession negotiations, aid and assistance have not only become the *lingua franca* of the post-socialist world, they have imposed a political and economic rationale on the group of states that were, during the Cold War era, referred to as 'Eastern Europe', or that constituted Yugoslavia. For the post-socialist states of this diverse region, it is a rationale that extends far beyond foreign policy or external relations; the accession agenda is all embracing and has become the defining political and economic imperative for countries that have now joined, are about to join, or that seek membership at some as yet unspecified point in the future. It is perhaps no exaggeration to claim that, just as Soviet-style socialism imposed a political, social and economic homogeneity on the East European nations between the late forties and 1989, the enlargement agenda has harmonised and standardised what is, after all, a rather disparate group of post-socialist and post-conflict states.

In its dealings with applicant states the Commission has adopted what has been described as a 'regatta approach' to enlargement (Smith 2005: 127). In practice this has meant that, based on their political and economic progress in meeting set criteria, the more successful post-socialist states have been able to propel themselves forward in the membership race. Others, after initially gaining pace, have lagged behind and faced relegation (Albania); in other cases (Slovakia) promotion to the first round of entrant states was quite rapid once political reforms began in earnest (Henderson 2002). Though in many respects the regatta approach is the only viable strategy for stimulating progress and development, it has nevertheless added to the fragmentation of the post-socialist bloc and contributed to a sense of uncertain demarcations. With regard to the former Yugoslav republics of the Western Balkans (Serbia, Croatia, BiH, Macedonia, Montenegro and Kosovo) in particular, the approach seemingly runs contrary to the key EU objective of strengthening co-operation and fostering regional coherence. Whilst the decision not to necessarily grant membership to all CEE states at the same time mobilised pro-EU reformers in Slovakia and brought about significant political and economic change (Henderson 2002), injecting a degree of competition between the candidate countries and potential candidate countries, in the context of the Western Balkans, may yet prove divisive and act as a powerful disincentive for progress and reconciliation.

The EU in the Western Balkans:
entrants, candidates and potential candidates

The particular states under examination in this study – Bosnia-Herzegovina (BiH), Kosovo[1] and Serbia – are part of the group of countries referred to by the EU as *potential candidate countries* (PCCs); former Yugoslav or South East European/Western Balkan states (Albania) to whom the Commission has 'promised the prospect of EU membership as and when they are ready'.[2] It is important to acknowledge that such delineation is the product and consequence of the EU accession and enlargement agendas as it has unfolded in recent years, rather than being bound to precise political, geographic, historic or cultural rationalities. The Commission's decision to include and exclude, to relegate, to set specific conditions, and to create distinct assistance packages is what has led to the grouping of these states (plus Albania and Montenegro) as *potential* entrants as part of a future and as yet unspecified enlargement. Of course, the EU and its accession agenda cannot be blamed entirely for such delineation: the Yugoslav crisis of the 1990s, differentiated development during the socialist period, varying resources, diverse political cultures and historic legacies have configured the region, and this group of countries in particular, since the somewhat forced homogenisation that both Sovietisation and Titoism attempted to instil upon the region in the four decades after the Second World War.

The designation of BiH, Serbia and Kosovo by the European Commission as 'potential candidate countries' (PCCs) – placing them behind Turkey, Croatia and Macedonia in terms of possible future membership – requires

some careful consideration in order to grasp fully the implications of such cat-
egorisation. As it stands, there is not a category of post-socialist states assem-
bled behind, nor any notion of a subsequent expansion beyond the four
'potentials'. This immediately suggests that these states are at the bottom of the
EU's pecking order of post-socialist countries with which it seeks an engagement concerning possible membership. It also has to be acknowledged that as
of late 2009 there is no planned enlargement involving a large group of countries entering at the same time. The reality therefore for individual PCCs is
entry according to the pace of reform and the realisation of what amounts to
extremely rigorous standards and conditions, but in the context of a global
recession and declining enthusiasm for further enlargement amongst EU
member states.

However, assuming that the process of moving through the various stages
from 'potential', to 'candidate', to 'acceding' is a linear and progressive one,
then the entry of Bulgaria and Romania in January 2007 means that Croatia,
which began accession negotiations with the Commission in October 2005,
and Macedonia, which signed a Stabilisation and Association Agreement
(SAA) as early as April 2001, are now next in line for accession, assuming a
future accession takes place. This has, in theory at least, implications for the
membership prospects as well as the *process* of potential entry for BiH and
Serbia (Kosovo, as noted in note 1 below, is more complex). Assuming Croatia
and Macedonia follow the accession route of Bulgaria and Romania (a Europe
Agreement, signed with both states, will provide a framework for accession),
they will nevertheless do so by a distinct route compared to the path trodden
by the post-socialist states that entered in 2004 or even 2007. They will have
entered the EU in the context of, and according to, a distinct contractual relationship with the EU, involving the Stabilisation and Association Agreements,
established in 1999, and Stabilisation and Association process (SAp), plus the
more recent European Partnership (EP), launched in March 2004. Their path
of entry will thus essentially provide a blueprint for the 'potential candidate'
states. Thus, the accession experiences of the Czech Republic, Slovakia,
Poland, Hungary, Slovenia, and even Romania and Bulgaria are of limited relevance to the Western Balkan states in the sense that they are negotiating with
the EU in an entirely different context, with more stringent conditionality, and
with far greater emphasis placed on stabilisation and dealing with the specific
legacies of conflict and ethnic fracture. If and when Croatia and Macedonia
enter, they will therefore be providing a road map for Albania, BiH, Serbia,
Kosovo and Montenegro that implicitly acknowledges that SAp and the EP
route does lead to eventual membership.

Europeanisation

One of the more oblique questions posed by this study is whether or not EU assistance is contributing to the *Europeanisation* of BiH, Kosovo and Serbia, and the extent to which assistance channelled through NGOs in particular is fostering 'European' values, norms and modes of behaviour. With such an endeavour in mind a definition of *Europeanisation* is required. Radaelli offers the following:

> Europeanisation consists of processes of (a) construction (b) diffusion and (c) institutionalisation of formal and informal rules, procedures, policy paradigms, styles, 'ways of doing things' and shared beliefs and norms which are first defined and consolidated in the EU policy process and then incorporated in the logic of domestic (national and subnational) discourse, identities, political structures and public policies. (2003: 30)

It is immediately apparent that Europeanisation is a multi-faceted concept involving rule formation and enforcement based on shared values. But according to Radaelli's definition, the concept also has implications for the interaction between state and non-state actors, new behaviours and means of conducting policy-making and enforcement. Much like the related concept of *integration*, Europeanisation is broader than and somewhat distinct from enlargement, and as a process of transformation is likely to occur both before and after accession. Thus, a country under consideration for EU entry may well display lower levels of Europeanisation than anticipated whilst still having met the conditions of enlargement and having successfully adopted all tenets of the *acquis*.

Such considerations notwithstanding, the concept of Europeanisation remains important to this study insofar as it offers a framework for measuring both 'soft' as well as 'hard' impact; a means of assessing change in 'ways of doing things' as well as in formal rules and procedures, transformation in 'styles, and shared beliefs and norms' (Grabbe 2006: 46). Whilst the measurement of progress and the focus of conditionality tend to initially at least be the enactment and implementation of policy and the harmonisation of laws ('hard' impact), this book is interested primarily in the impact of EU assistance on civil society and the extent to which aid channelled through NGOs is triggering good governance, cultivating interaction between formal/state and informal/non-state actors ('soft' impact).

What constitutes evidence of Europeanisation and how can it be measured?

It has already been ascertained that evidence of Europeanisation should not necessarily be seen as an indicator of successful reform or the completion of a particular enlargement condition or objective. Indeed, the influence of EU capacity assistance may well deliver degrees or aspects of Europeanisation without necessarily realising the specific enlargement outcome for which the aid was intended. For example, an EU-funded environment-related project may serve to get NGOs working with government without dealing with the particular pollution issue that the project was intended to address. Moreover, conditionality and external intervention are likely to generate certain unintended consequences, particularly when the intervention engages multiple actors and agencies and where objectives are perhaps less than clear and concise. In other words, Europeanisation must be distinguished from progress towards accession, can look very different across states, manifest itself in various ways, and generate differentiated outcomes and consequences. Some candidate countries will borrow norms and patterns of interaction from the EU without being compelled to do so; others will need to be offered extensive assistance and be subjected to considerable pressure. Certain aspects of political and economic life in a particular state may well appear Europeanised without the country making progress towards realising accession conditions (Schimmelfennig and Sedelmeier 2005a).

Equally important is to avoid assuming that all change in the region is occurring as a consequence of EU influence. As Grabbe notes in the context of CEE states, there was a tendency on both the part of the EU and the candidate country to exaggerate the degree of Europeanisation for political purposes. The EU obviously is keen to portray itself as 'the principal driver of most reforms' (Grabbe 2006); the government of the candidate state is equally concerned to demonstrate the extent of its compliance, but also 'to blame the EU for unpopular reforms'. It is important also to remember that the EU's political legacy on the CEE states has been largely an *indirect* rather than *direct* one: the EU did not directly bring about democratisation in these states, it merely responded to dynamics and processes already underway. It is also fair to say that the commitment on behalf of the CEE governments to Europeanisation was unanimous and largely unwavering, expressed at the time of the democratic revolutions in terms of a 'return to Europe' (Hyde-Price 1996). As will become evident from this study, the situation is somewhat different in BiH, Serbia and Kosovo.

A more important reason for not attributing all reforms and change to the EU in post-conflict states is the over-arching and significant presence of the

UN, the OSCE and various other American and European development agencies, working either separately or in conjunction with the Commission, but fulfilling specific peace and state-building roles. Although the EU has undoubtedly become in recent years the most significant single donor and agent of external governance across the region, it remains difficult to disaggregate the exact impact of the EU, and even harder to measure Europeanisation. The factors likely to impact on Europeanisation are: 'goodness-of-fit' between the EU objective and the existing institutional or behavioural reality, the extent to which there is political will to enact new policy or build new partnerships within a particular area, the actual reform or objective itself, as well as the discursive framing and particular politicisation of the issue (Börzel 2003).

Several of the methodological difficulties in measuring the 'soft' impact of EU assistance on NGOs and the extent to which good governance is being triggered were referred to in the introductory chapter of the book. The most appropriate and reliable method adopted for this study, is, broadly speaking, to use a functionalist approach focusing on the specific interaction between actors, in the context of specific EU assistance programmes and initiatives, and to measure outcomes and outputs, both during the designated project tenure and beyond, that is, to also evaluate the interaction beyond the terms of the project. In addition to the emergence of sustainable partnerships emerging between state/government and non-governmental actors as a consequence of funded projects, actual policy change brought about by NGOs, or their role in the development of new policy frameworks would be a significant measure of impact or effect. A more subtle and nuanced indicator of positive impact would be the empowerment of reform-minded elites who, by engaging and forming partnerships with pro-EU NGOs, are able to use EU conditionality and assistance to bring about substantive change, by bypassing obstructive national political and administrative processes and by engaging NGO networks in the formation and enforcement of EU-compliant policy. The somewhat optimistic premise on which the research is based is that as established conduits for transnational assistance and development aid, NGOs in BiH, Serbia and Kosovo are theoretically well placed to facilitate linkage between national political actors and the EU. As Grabbe observes, this is not to imply that Europeanisation is resultant in a decline of national sovereignty; in fact

> membership of the EU has been an integral part of the reassertion of the nation-state as an organisational unity, with the integration process strengthening the ability of national actors to develop bundles of domestic policies to satisfy coalitions of political interests. (Grabbe 2006: 14)

The legacy of previous enlargements: external governance and conditionality

As noted by the Commission in a recent communication regarding future integration capacity, 'enlargement has been at the heart of the EU's development over several decades. The very essence of European integration is to overcome the division of Europe and to contribute to the peaceful unification of the continent.'[3] However, each enlargement has been distinct, involving different strategies, conditionality and assistance. The reason for this is broadly twofold: even amongst the post-socialist states that entered during the fifth enlargement (May 2004 and January 2007) significant differences in terms of political reform, economic progress and state capacities necessitated bespoke approaches and refined strategies. Secondly, whilst the overriding sense is of enlargement strategy becoming more refined and developed, and the fine-tuning of the process, recent enlargement have also been shaped in large part by the capacity of the EU to increase in size further, and to successfully integrate new members (Hughes et al. 2004).

It should also be noted that whilst the Commission has made political and macro-economic stability conditions of accession for all post-socialist states, the decision to open negotiations with Bulgaria and Romania in 2000 seemed to have been driven more by security and foreign policy considerations than by a sense of these states having made significant progress. Bulgaria and Romania had both supported the Kosovo military operation in 1999 and commentators saw the opening of negotiations as a reward. Indeed, in the case of Romania the EU's decision actually coincided with the Regular Reports, undertaken by the Commission, pointing to a worsening of the economy and the political situation having certainly not improved (Grabbe 2006). Despite exercising a degree of pragmatism, the Commission subsequently stuck quite rigidly to political and economic conditionality in dealing with the two states in the run-up to their entry in January 2007, even going as far as to add additional criteria as the basis for judging readiness (Grabbe 2006).

Enlargement for all post-socialist states has primarily been about the importation of EU norms and the development of a particular mode of 'network governance' (Peters and Savoie 2000). The model of external governance employed by the EU for the CEE and SEE states has broadly been the *external incentives* model, whereby 'the EU sets its rules as conditions that (post-socialist states) have to fulfil in order to receive EU rewards . . . ranging from trade and co-operation agreements via association agreements to full membership' (Schimmelfennig and Sedelmeier 2004: 663). The EU's negotiations with all post-socialist states has involved the Commission exerting significant influence over policy development, the restructuring of domestic institutions, political, legal and social reform, and economic transformation (Schimmelfennig and Sedelmeier 2005a, 2005b). The extent and nature of such external governance stems from the Accession Partnerships that, established in 1997, provided a clear list of objectives that had to be met by potential applicants. They also re-orientated aid and assistance towards countries meeting the conditions for accession. Prior to 1997 PHARE aid had been geared rather loosely towards economic reform and democratisation and had been somewhat demand-driven. Thereafter the focus of assistance was tightened and targeted at CEE states meeting the third Copenhagen condition, the obligations of membership. The Accession Partnerships, negotiated separately with each contender state, marked a significant juncture in EU external governance (Schimmelfennig and Wagner 2004). They were based on the EU exerting profound influence over regulation and, to a lesser extent, redistribution which, as Grabbe points out, 'both . . . are normally policy preserves of the nation-state' (Grabbe 2006: 24). Reflecting the EU's role at the time within existing member states – which was to encourage governments to strengthen their enforcement capacity – the pre-accession strategy placed increased emphasis on establishing regulatory control and implementation rather than simply enacting policy frameworks. The Commission set objectives and left it to the CEE states to devise the legislative means to achieve the prescribed ends. As Grabbe observes, 'the emphasis at this stage was on having coherent policies and functioning institutions, rather than the EU specifying prescriptions for policy content' (2006: 24). However, in the realm of the economy the Commission was far more *dirigiste*, specifying neo-liberal economic reforms, such as privatisation, reduction in state expenditure and intervention in the economy. Considering the variations of European capitalism, the Commission imposed a rigid and distinctly 'Anglo-Saxon' model, placing little or no emphasis on industrial policy, and no overt consideration for social networks within the economy (Grabbe 2006: 24).

Whilst the Commission initially lacked a coherent framework for dealing with the CEE states, and was somewhat slow in responding to the demands for accession coming from Poland and Hungary in particular (Hyde-Price 1996), once the EU had refined its strategy for dealing with the front-line contender states a considerable proportion of the reforms were pushed through quickly and, by the end of the 1990s, the Commission had become the main driver of political and economic reform across post-socialist Europe. Most controversial was the fact that the front-running CEE contenders (Poland, the Czech Republic and Hungary) were being put under intense pressure to implement policies, such as the Schengen agreement on border control, which had not even been introduced within existing member states. Even more contentious was the fact that the CEE states were handing over sovereignty to the EU in policy areas that existing member states were steadfastly holding on to, or in which they were at least resistant to extending EU control and influence. For example, the pre-accession strategy involved judicial reform and prison conditions, pension reforms, social security reform and even foreign policy (relations with eastern neighbours). The sovereignty of the post-socialist states was arguably being compromised as a consequence of quite aggressive external governance and control. However, such strict conditionality and the demand that applicant states fully meet political and economic criteria was in a sense a response by the Commission to levels of ambivalence amongst some member states regarding the benefits of enlargement.

Although it seems appropriate to characterise the relationship between the EU and all post-socialist states in terms of 'external governance', the nature of the Commission's intervention has in fact been more nuanced, pragmatic, and has varied according to the political context of the candidate country, not to mention the particular policy area or issue. For example, in dealing with the CEE states regarding democratic conditionality – institutional norms, liberal democracy and human rights – the EU had to exert relatively little pressure as these processes were already well-established and underway. As Schimmelfennig and Sedelmeier contend, 'in the democratic frontrunners, such as the Czech Republic, Hungary and Poland, EU governance was unnecessary for democratisation and democratic consolidation' (2004: 669). However, in its dealings with these states, the Commission made far-reaching pre-accession alignment with the *acquis* a condition for starting accession talks. In other words, conditions and the extent to which they have been enforced and made part of the negotiation process have varied according to the developmental progress of the country in question. The EU was very effective, for example, at making minority rights and social inclusion a core condition for CEE states such as the Czech Republic that had otherwise incorporated much of the *acquis* and had consolidated democracy but had yet to deal appropriately with the issue of Roma rights and minority integration (Vermeersch 2003).

Across South East Europe and the Balkans, where the pace of reform has generally been slower, external governance has had to be more stringent and intrusive. For example, in Slovakia and Romania democratic conditionality would have been insufficient to bring about effective institutional and procedural change and therefore the EU had to ensure political change and the emergence of new elites before the incorporation of the *acquis* could be pursued in earnest. Perhaps the greatest lesson learnt from the accession of Bulgaria and Romania in January 2007 was the importance of dealing with corruption and organised crime at an early stage, and to enforce such conditionality more rigorously. As late as May 2006 the Commission was still reporting concern in both states regarding judicial processes and corruption (COM, 2006/214).

EU priorities and conditionality in the potential candidate countries: a different approach and agenda?

Whilst there is still a strong element of 'reinforcement by reward' in the Commission's relations with BiH, Serbia and Kosovo (and indeed Albania and Montenegro), the EU intervenes far more in the implementation and enactment of reforms through local Delegations and, in the case of BiH, the Directorate of European Integration (DEI), which is 'charged with the task of preparing a strategy for European Integration (Chandler 2006: 37). Indeed, in BiH and Kosovo the EU's role is, according to critics, more about *direct* governance than *external* governance (Chandler 2006). Whereas in the CEE states the EU did not directly intervene in the pace of reform, nor seek to manage the cost-benefit assessment made by recipient governments regarding the domestic impact of implementing and enacting EU Directives, the Commission is far more interventionist in the post-conflict states of the Western Balkans. For example, in BiH the DEI directly drives legislative change, judges the success of reforms, and then administers the rewards. In the case of Serbia, 'uncertain borders (have) accentuated the need for the EU to act as a security actor in the region, while at the same time attempting to advance its enlargement agenda with various degrees of success' (Glasius and Kostovicova 2008: 90).

Though there are clearly continuities with previous enlargements, the adoption by the EU of a distinct framework for conducting its relations with the candidate and potential candidate countries (PCCs) of the Western Balkans is at once indicative of the political, economic and social differences between this group of countries and the CEE or SEE states. The key difference and distinguishing characteristic of the approach is, in a nutshell, the emphasis on stability and security. Whilst it is of course true that in the run-up to accession the Czech Republic, Poland, Hungary and Slovakia all had to deal with issues of sovereignty and aspects of state capacity-building, this tended to involve strengthening the regulatory and implementation capacity of functioning state bureaucracies: reforming and modernising administrative systems so that they could cope with and respond to the implementation demands of the new legislative frameworks being adopted. All such change was, of course, occurring against a backdrop of quite rapid policy change, economic transformation, and a political momentum for progressive reform. Indeed, the main obstacles faced by the CEE states along the path of accession stemmed from the legacy of an over-stretched and excessively bureaucratic Soviet-style state machine, and from restricted sovereignty as satellite states of the USSR. In many respects, the accession conditionality set by the Commission in the period between 1997 and 2004 reflected such legacies and realities. It is also worth emphasising that for the countries that entered the EU in May 2004, state functions and structures had not collapsed, and therefore political and administrative conditionality centred on restructuring and reforming aspects of the state, building certain capacities, rather than outright reconstruction. Fundamental political problems association with limited experience of political sovereignty and democratic rights were quickly overcome during the early 1990s in the CEE states, so much so, that EU assistance could by the second half of the decade be focused on the transfer of know-how, capacity-building and micro-level intervention in aspects of administrative responsibility (Grabbe 2006).

The issues concerning the role and function of the state in the potential candidate and candidate countries of the Western Balkans, and particularly in post-conflict states of the former Yugoslavia, have been altogether more complex and far-reaching. As Glasius and Kostovicova have argued, '(t)he state in the Balkans is weak in a structural as well as the political sense: it cannot provide public goods and it lacks political, national and social cohesion' (Glasius and Kostovicova 2008: 91). Wherever else the EU has become involved in supporting state development it has done so in the context of reforming the Soviet-era bureaucracies and strengthening the institutions of the state, rather than state-building as such. However, in the cases of BiH and Kosovo in particular, notions of sovereignty and the basic institutions and functions of the state are being built more or less from scratch under obviously difficult circumstances. In Bosnia, the task is hugely complicated by the legacies of ethno-nationalist conflict and by the Dayton constitutional structure; in Kosovo much hinges ultimately on the acceptance of the country's sovereignty by the international community. In building and restructuring the Serbian state the EU is negotiating several constraining legacies: in addition to the absence of legacies of political and structural sovereignty, the incapacities and contradictions of the socialist state model, there is also the corrosive legacy of nationalism and the political influence of Milošević.

Perhaps the most striking contrast between the PCCs and the CEE states is differences in their economies and the lack of significant reform, restructuring and foreign direct investment. Whereas the re-industrialisation, or, perhaps more accurately, the productivity of the CEE economies occurred relatively quickly after the initial recession of the early 1990s, this did not occur in the Western Balkans. Whilst GDP figures suggest a growth rate of up to 6 per cent for some states in the region, levels remain below those of pre-1990, that is, before the end of the socialist era (Sergi and Bagatelas 2004). Re-industrialisation is occurring in Croatia and Slovenia, but there is little sustained evidence of this elsewhere within the former Yugoslavia (Gligorov 2005: 13–15). Although there has been a recent increase in the export of services, mainly tourism and transportation, the region is still characterised by high trade deficits (Sergi and Bagatelas 2004). Even prior to the global economic downturn of 2008, which has resulted in a decline in EU investment in the region,[4] employment levels were declining, with unemployment either increasing or having reached a plateau that is relatively high compared to the CEE. In the Czech Republic, Poland and Hungary employment levels had, by the end of the 1990s, begun to increase after an initial drop, or had at least stalled, and the trend in unemployment was broadly a declining one (Schiff 2006). An explanation for the difference lies in the fact that CEE states experienced growth based on increased productivity, which then generated increased employment. In the Western Balkan states where the rate of increase in unemployment has slowed or declined (Albania), this has tended to be a consequence of high levels of outward migration (Gligorov 2005: 14). This would explain the slightly curious phenomenon, characteristic of the region, of the concurrence of low levels of employment and declining unemployment, i.e. the latter not a consequence of growth or increased productivity, but of people leaving the country (Schiff 2006).

The most significant differential between the Western Balkans and CEE is comparatively lower levels of foreign direct investment (FDI). The reality of FDI flows into post-socialist Europe over the past two decades is that capital investment tends to be extremely concentrated, benefiting countries where there is greater macro-economic and political stability, namely Hungary, the Czech Republic and Slovakia, and, more recently, Croatia, Romania and Bulgaria. Whilst the Western Balkan states generally receive low levels of FDI, patterns shift continually and the contrast between states can be considerable (Sergi and Bagatelas 2004: 9). For instance, in BiH, most foreign investment from abroad is multilateral or bilateral donor assistance and tends to be directed towards NGOs (Pugh 2002, 2005). For other states (Croatia and, more recently, Serbia) the situation has improved in recent years, but generally flows of FDI are slow, varying from year to year, with penetration and diffusion patchy across the region and within states. In the case of Serbia (and to an extent BiH), recent increases in FDI tend to involve Russian investment in the energy sectors of both states.

Whilst overall there has been a liberalisation of trade across the region since 2000, the absence of significant levels of FDI is unquestionably the critical difference between this region and CEE, and has significant implications for the success of EU-driven reforms. Across Poland, the Czech Republic, Hungary and Slovakia an in-flow of capital followed the liberalisation of the economy; this helped legitimise political elites responsible for privatisation, monetary reform and fiscal rectitude measures, but also the economic dividends of FDI quickly soothed the harsh impact of reforms and restructuring for many sections of society. It would also seem characteristic of the Western Balkan region that growth, where it has occurred, has not been export-led, but has occurred as a consequence of an increase in consumer demand driving an upsurge in imports (Pugh 2002). It can be assumed, therefore, that trade liberalisation with the EU has only partially stimulated growth, with countries of the region selling to each other, but buying from abroad.

Taking the potential candidate countries (PCCs) as a whole, the development of market economies has been hindered by the slow pace of liberalisation and investment, by the absence of institutionalisation and implementation of reforms, and low levels of export capacity, all of which are reflected in the structural problems within the economies. The EU country reports regularly confirm that the implementation of regulatory frameworks governing, for example, environmental standards, or measures to improve corporate governance, labour relations and compatibility of standards generally is slow or non-existent. The Commission has also repeatedly identified reform of public services as a major issue yet to be tackled. The problems here are huge, ranging from inefficiency and the absence of accountability, to corruption and the maintenance of a secondary economy. Compared to the CEE states, the private sectors in the PCCs are small, particularly in BiH and Kosovo. Whilst, according to the *European Bank for Reconstruction and Development* (EBRD), all states in the region have done well in terms of small-scale privatisations, there has been little or no progress in financial institution and infrastructure reform. There has also been insufficient progress made in terms of large-scale privatisations of state-controlled enterprises and utilities (EBRD 2002; Sergi 2004). Indeed, critics have argued that where privatisation occurs in the absence of competition policy this has involved the redistribution of assets rather than efficient allocation (Donais 2002; Pugh 2005). Although it might be argued that the PCCs have an advantage in terms of attracting FDI due to low taxation and labour costs (relative to the rest of Europe), it is likely that the over-concentration of product markets, plus the rigidity of labour markets, serves to dissuade foreign investors and therefore jeopardises progress towards meeting EU conditionality.

In CEE public expenditure tended to remain high during the 1990s, partly, though not entirely, due to the realities of political elites having to mitigate the impact of neo-liberal reforms. It was only in the period immediately prior to accession that significant headway was made in controlling public expenditure (Grabbe, 2006). However, in the Western Balkans certain countries have exceptionally high levels of public expenditure as a percentage of GDP (Croatia, Macedonia, Albania), but social services and welfare systems are woe-fully under-resourced. In the case of BiH, although levels of state expenditure on social services are low, the state machinery is itself very expensive and highly cost-inefficient, due largely to the elaborate Dayton constitutional structure (Pugh 2005; Zaum 2005).

The economic difficulties described above – lower levels of FDI, slow pace of fiscal reform, low productivity, employment and restructuring – pose partic-ular problems for the EU in terms of further integration and potential accession, but also with regard to formulating an effective assistance and development strategy. The experience of CEE states, and Slovakia in particular, suggests that economic progress is critical in driving political reform, with even the prospect of membership stimulating FDI and liberalisation. For Bulgaria and Romania this was certainly the case: whilst there were negative economic consequences of being excluded from the 2004 enlargement, a firm promise of membership and a clear entry timetable stimulated growth in the 18 months prior to entry. Even according to the most positive and optimistic assessment, full member-ship for Serbia, and indeed for BiH and Kosovo, remains in the distant future. If Croatia and Macedonia enter without the PCCs, as is currently predicted, then BiH, Serbia and Kosovo will require a firm commitment from the Commission on entry, over and above what is currently implicit within the SAp and European Agreements, in the hope of stimulating growth and investment.

The Stabilisation and Association process: a bespoke framework for EU–Western Balkan relations

Conditionality, the setting of clear and stringent goals by the EU that potential entrant states have to meet in order for accession–related negotiations to progress, has been the basis on which the Commission has engaged with all post-socialist states since the early 1990s. However, as already noted, in dealing with the Western Balkan states and, to an extent, with Bulgaria and Romania, the conditions have been far more explicit and extensive. As Anastasakis and Bechev observe, 'conditionality in the Balkans is omnipresent, multi-dimensional and multi-purpose, geared towards reconciliation, reconstruction and reform' (2003: 2). It has also functioned as an agent of differentiation, enabling some states to propel themselves further forward in the negotiations than their neighbours. However, the difficulty with differentiation, competition between states, and bilateral negotiations is that this contradicts the objective of the Commission to foster regional co-operation.

The specific conditionality for the Western Balkans began to emerge in the immediate aftermath of the crisis in Kosovo in 1999, with the launch by the Commission of the Stability Pact for South Eastern Europe, which included BiH, Serbia-Montenegro (as then was), Croatia, Bulgaria, Romania, Albania and Macedonia. However, it had been acknowledged before the Kosovo crisis that in fact the long-term stability of the Balkans required initiatives based specifically on dealing with the needs of the less stable Balkan states of the former Yugoslavia, plus the unstable and particularly weak Albania. It was recognised by the Commission from the outset that Bulgaria and Romania had different developmental needs and that they should be dealt with separately.

Since March 2002 the Commission has reported regularly to the European Council and the Parliament on the progress made by Western Balkan states. The main overriding framework governing the relationship between the EU and the five potential candidate countries (including Kosovo), and the two candidate countries (Croatia and Macedonia) is the Stabilisation and Association process (SAp). There was initially some uncertainty as to whether this process would deliver full membership for the Western Balkan states. Some clarification was offered by the Commission in 2003, when it was confirmed that the SAp framework is designed to lead to eventual accession, albeit via a more bespoke and lengthy route. However, the stated objectives of the SAp – to stabilise the region, establish a free trade area, and to deliver European integration – suggest that the process is geared primarily towards dealing with the specific legacies of the Yugoslav crisis of the 1990s. The critical difference between European integration and accession is not lost on the political leaders of the Western Balkan states: *de facto* integration of neighbouring states – referring to the diffusion and influence of EU political and economic norms – occurs long before accession becomes a reality. Indeed, the influence of EU norms on the CEE states prior to accession was so significant that it has been equated with the influence that the EU had over member states during the 1990s (Grabbe 2006: 41). In other words, integration is no guarantee of membership and anxieties regarding the extent to which there was a firm commitment on behalf of the EU to accession were intensified by the fact that administration of the SAp and relations with the Western Balkans was, until 2005, the responsibility of the Directorate for External Relations rather than the Directorate for Enlargement. In describing its aid and assistance for the PCC and Western Balkans, the Enlargement website refers to its relations with these states as 'a key external relations' priority for the EU', the aim of which 'is to promote stability and peace in the Western Balkans, not only on humanitarian grounds but also because the region's conflicts are at odds with the wider objective of security and prosperity across the continent of Europe'. There is no suggestion here of accession.[5]

The main component of the SAp is the Stabilisation and Association Agreements (SAA). Launched in 1999 and negotiated bilaterally with each individual state, the agreements are based on the Europe Agreements that governed relations with Bulgaria and Romania and the CEE states that entered the EU in May 2004. The SAAs were presented as new, and did indeed represent the first legal contractual relationship between the Western Balkan states and the EU. Due to the fact that they were conceived of by the Commission as intermediary agreements rather than as an actual stage in the accession process, the SAAs do not explicitly offer the prospect of full membership as an outcome. However, eventual accession is nevertheless implicit and the Thessaloniki Summit, held in June 2003, involving the EU and all the Western Balkan states, added further clarification: the SAAs were to be the first and final contractual agreement between association and membership. Once an SAA has been successfully implemented, then the accession process will begin. The contention that remains however, is that the SAp and component SAAs offer the prospect of membership requiring the PCCs to embark, for example, upon asymmetrical trade liberalisation (Western Balkan states gain access to EU markets, but are given time to liberalise their own markets), but without awarding these states pre-accession status. This lends credence to the view that no firm commitment has been made by the Commission, and the SAp countries are expected to make a stronger commitment to the process than the EU.

In addition to the liberalisation of trade, the SAAs are designed to enable states to meet the Copenhagen conditions, as well as dealing with specific issues relating to the post-conflict character of BiH and Serbia.[6] The Commission negotiates with each country separately regarding the SAA, and the agreement is signed after a period of lengthy negotiation during which

certain pre-conditions are met and specific contexts are taken into consideration by both sides. An SAA only becomes operational once it has been ratified
by all EU member states and by the European Parliament.

Specific conditionality and relations with individual PCCs

Although aspects of conditionality for the PCCs have been carried forward
from previous enlargement and pre-accession negotiations with the CEE
states, the Commission has negotiated bilaterally with the individual PCCs,
agreeing and identifying specific terms that reflect the particular issues and
areas for development. Specific conditionality that has formed the basis of the
negotiations with individual states will be explored more fully in subsequent
chapters of the book, however a brief overview of the key issues is offered
below.

A Stabilisation and Association Agreement was finally initialled and signed
with BiH in June 2008 after a difficult and protracted negotiation process. The
Commission initially published a feasibility study in 2003 that reviewed the
country's readiness to open negotiations on an SAA. It was concluded that
progress needed to be made in 16 key areas before negotiations could begin.
The key development issues were institutional reform, building administrative
capacity and the establishment of state authorities and institutions. The criteria
reflect the Commission's concern about constitutional realities in BiH and the
lack of legitimacy and sovereignty of state institutions, as well as the absence of
sufficient co-ordination between state and entity level agencies. Other areas
for development include reform of the banking sector, improvements in public finance and a reduction in public expenditure (which was 54 per cent of
GDP in 2003). In its Annual Action Programme for BiH (2005) the
Commission placed much emphasis on what it termed 'the limited social and
economic rights of BiH citizens', by which it was referring to levels of unemployment and the percentage of the population living below the poverty
threshold. Issues identified as having an impact on democratic stabilisation
included reform of broadcasting and media, and further progress on internal
refugee return. It was also noted that 'in some sectors, a persistent lack of
interaction between public authorities and civil society is still evident in the
decision-making process' (CEC 2005: 6).

The signing of an SAA with Serbia was no less protracted. After periods of
stalemate and a breakdown in relations between the two sides, an SAA was
finally initialled in November 2007 and signed the following May. Agreement
had essentially been thwarted by the failure of the Koštunica government to

fulfil the conditions regarding full co-operation with the International Criminal Tribunal for the former Yugoslavia (ICTY). The Commission had made it clear that once Serbia established full co-operation with the ICTY negotiations would resume. The formation of a pro-European government in May 2008 and the re-election of Boris Tadić as president a few months before have established new political footings on which negotiations with Serbia can take place.

Until February 2008, Kosovo's formal status was as a province of Serbia, but one whose external sovereignty was governed by the UN administration. Since the declaration of independence the EU's strategy for Kosovo in practice remains the same; it is one of 'standards before status' (Gligorov 2005: 12); the Provisional Institutions of Self-Government for Kosovo continue to gradually assume responsibility for internal sovereignty; the United Nations Mission in Kosovo (UNMIK) will gradually relinquish power and hand over what remains of its authority to the EU. In other words, the aim is to make Kosovo a stable, legitimate and functioning state in all but name, before finally handing over sovereignty.

As long as Kosovo is not universally accepted as a sovereign state, it remains difficult for the EU to negotiate a separate SAA with Kosovo. However, in view of the EU's strategy to strengthen internal sovereignty it was agreed at the Thessaloniki Summit to allow Kosovo to participate in the SAp via the so-called Stabilisation and Association Tracking Mechanism (STM), which is nominally the same as the SAp, but without the SAA (Gligorov 2004: 4). On 20 April 2005 the European Commission adopted the Communication on Kosovo to the Council, 'A European Future for Kosovo', which reinforces the Commission's commitment to Kosovo. Prior to the referendum decision in Montenegro, the EU had dealt with Kosovo through a European Partnership established with what was Serbia-Montenegro in January 2006, with specific reference made to the province as defined by UNSCR1244. However, in August 2006, the Provisional Institutions of Self-Government for Kosovo adopted an Action Plan for the Implementation of the European Partnership and this document forms the current working basis between the EU and the Kosovan authorities.

The European Partnerships

The notion of European Partnerships (EPs) was also introduced at Thessaloniki in 2003, essentially as another instrument within the SAp. In effect the EPs are simply a list of changes and reforms that the Western Balkan states need to introduce in order to move closer towards pre-accession, or to develop what is often referred to by the Commission as their European *perspective*. The introduction of the Partnerships marked a significant stage in relations between the Western Balkan states and the EU insofar as they represent a clear commitment for future membership. However, it is important to recognise that the aim of the EPs is to introduce some elements of the pre-accession agenda into the negotiations between the EU and the Western Balkans without the Commission making any of the more significant financial or institutional commitments associated with the actual pre-accession process. Though the emphasis is still on stabilisation and reconstruction, the EPs introduce aspects from the experience of previous enlargements, namely, the economic policy dialogue, twinning and monitoring, the publication of annual country reports (Gligorov 2004: 6). Insofar as the introduction of the EPs seems to reflect the desire of the Commission to gradually shift the emphasis of funding and assistance away from reconstruction towards institutional capacity-building, the Partnerships are currently most relevant to Croatia and Macedonia, where greater progress within the SAp framework necessitates a stronger focus and emphasis on pre-accession criteria and closer dialogue with the Commission. As noted above, for BiH, Serbia and Kosovo the priorities surrounding negotiation within the SAp framework are still focused squarely on basic institutional construction and fundamental administrative reform.

Such reservations notwithstanding, the partnerships have clarified the pathway for perspective membership for all the Western Balkan states. For all applicant states the difficulty remains that as progress through the SAp is made, the reforms necessary to meet the terms of the Partnerships and the SAA become increasingly costly and complex. In order to gain domestic political support for such reforms, political elites are increasingly inclined to request firmer assurances from the Commission regarding future membership. Indeed, the experience of the CEE states and Bulgaria and Romania suggests that as the costs of compliance increase, the quest for more commitment from the EU regarding accession increases. Moreover, an unequivocal commitment on behalf of the Commission that membership will occur acts as the greatest incentive and driving force for legislative compliance and institutional and administrative change (Grabbe 2006). In essence, the impact of the EPs is thus limited to the extent to which they instruct applicants to embark upon reforms the costs of which generate demands for a firmer commitment on eventual membership.

Building regional co-operation as a core EU objective

Historically the EU has enjoyed considerable success in fostering bilateral co-operation, most notably with regard to Franco–German relations in the 1950s. Indeed, the Union itself is founded upon regional co-operation and this remains, for many, its *raison d'être* (Inotai 1997; Preston 1997). However, it is perhaps recent success in building co-operation between the Central and Eastern European states in the context of enlargement that may be seen as offering the most tangible legacy for the Western Balkans. Yet it is important to acknowledge that not only did extending regional co-operation in the context of CEE prove to be 'the least spontaneous' aspect of enlargement and one that required continual EU pressure, but that the imperative to co-operate was, overall, a latent rather than blatant imperative in the Europe Agreements signed with the Visegrad states (Dangerfield 2004: 208–10). Indeed cross-border co-operation was only a specified objective in the Commission's negotiations with Slovenia and the Baltic states (Phinnemore 2003).

The EU is modelling its efforts to develop regional co-operation in the Western Balkans on its experience of fostering integration amongst the CEE states. Notwithstanding the obvious contrast between building regional co-operation in a region where sovereignty is uncontested, and the fractured post-conflict situation within the successor states of the former Yugoslavia, the use of economic incentives and conditionality as a mechanism for driving forward co-operation provides a viable framework, in theory at least, for fostering regional co-operation amongst the candidate and PCC states of the Western Balkans. In its dealings with the successor states of the former Yugoslavia, the Commission has, formally at least, made economic and financial assistance conditional on states co-operating with each other. Various core political objectives – democratic governance, respect for human and minority rights, refugee return, the rule of law, implementation of the Dayton Peace Agreement – identified by the EU as non-negotiable conditions for progress and the signing of SAAs, have been framed in the context of regional co-operation. Aside from the obvious political imperative, there are also critical economic and social dimensions to the Commission's support for regional co-operation, insofar as it is also linked to energy policy, environment and transport, and effective border control. As Delevic-Djilas notes, as early as the mid 1990s and the South East European states being able to access PHARE programme funding, 'establishing contractual relations with the EU was dependent on proven readiness to enter into good neighbourly and cooperative relations with neighbouring states' (Delevic-Djilas 2007) .

At the fulcrum of the EU's post-conflict integration strategy is co-operation with the International Criminal Tribunal for the Former Yugoslavia (ICTY). Croatia's early willingness to comply with the Court's demands has unquestionably shaped the pace of the country's candidacy; conversely, failure to fully comply with the ICTY's requests resulted in the suspension of EU negotiations with Serbia, but subsequent co-operation and the new government's immediate handing over of Karadžić to The Hague has dramatically improved EU relations with Serbia.[7]

Regional co-operation and the SAp framework

The adoption of the SAp in 1999 formalised the stipulation for regional co-operation and made it both a central tenet of aid and assistance as well as a key aspect of conditionality. Both candidate and potential candidate countries were compelled to establish a formal framework for political dialogue at bilateral and regional levels. The SAp framework also specified the creation of free trade areas, social and civil society co-operation, as well as co-operation in the realms of education, science, technology, energy, environment and culture. At the Zagreb Summit of November 2000 the countries of the region agreed to a wide-ranging set of co-operation initiatives. The agreement was based on the EU offering these states, in return, the prospect of future accession and a pledge of assistance from the Commission to help support the progression towards membership. The final declaration of the Summit made it very clear that political and economic reform and assistance were indivisible from regional co-operation, stating that 'democracy and regional reconciliation and co-operation, on the one hand, and the *rapprochement* of each of these countries with the EU, on the other, form a whole'.[8] In practice this has involved regional governments establishing conventions and initiatives to deal with corruption, trafficking, organised crime, close co-operation in the field of justice, as well as establishing political dialogue and moves towards the creation of a free trade agreement. However, as this research demonstrates, EU assistance for NGOs has failed to trigger cross-border co-operation between state and non-state actors in contentious policy areas such as refugee return, or between civil society organisations working on similar issues in neighbouring states.

The Commission has also been extremely keen in its dealings with the post-conflict and weak states of the Western Balkans to build co-operation and interaction with existing member states, with the aim of modelling good practice and enabling a transfer of expertise. The European Partnerships from 2003 onwards introduced a greater degree of interaction between applicants and existing member states, as well as reinforcing the importance of regional co-operation by specifying tasks for improving interaction, in particular within the realms of justice, freedom and security, as well as in efforts to combat organised crime and trafficking.

How successful has the Commission been in building regional co-operation?

The EU funded regional co-operation in the period 2000–6 via the CARDS programme, with €4.65 billion of core community aid allocated after the Zagreb Summit of 2000. The introduction in 2007 of IPA as a new assistance framework placed even greater emphasis on regional co-operation. Indeed, *Cross-border Co-operation* and *Regional Development* compose two out of the five components or financial envelopes of the IPA framework. Whilst CARDS and IPA funding have largely been administered at the national level, regional co-operation has been a stipulation that each local Delegation or office of the European Agency for Reconstruction (EAR) has had to address. In addition, the Commission allocated 10 per cent of the overall CARDS budget to a specific regional co-operation fund – a 'regional envelope' – that was administered directly from Brussels. The purpose of this specific allocation was to enable countries in the region to realise the co-operation objectives of the SAp.[9] On the basis of the regular *Progress Reports*, the key monitoring tool for the Commission, the requirements of regional co-operation have become clearer and more stringent. What has also become apparent is that developing regional co-operation is not just about post-conflict reconstruction, but is also concerned with preparing these states for future co-operation within the EU if and when they gain entry. The challenge for the Commission has been to instil within the PCCs that co-operation with neighbouring states is an economic imperative, but also that co-operation is the basis of multi-level governance, which in turn is the cornerstone of prosperity, stability and eventual membership.

As to whether the EU has facilitated a level of economic and security co-operation between hostile states in a fractured region is not really in doubt. Rather, the critical issue is whether conditionality has also triggered a genuine momentum for co-operation amongst local elites and whether there is local and regional ownership of the momentum. In assessing the impact of EU attempts to strengthen regional co-operation and to use enlargement conditionality as a mechanism for improving the integration of the region, two key points must be borne in mind: first, there has been, since 1999, a significant expansion in the number of demands, as well as in the various aspects of co-operation, to the point where regional co-operation is fundamental to most, if not all, economic, political, environmental, judicial and social reform agendas. Second, regional co-operation in the Western Balkans is conceptualised and operationalised by the EU in much the same way as co-operation and interaction are conceived within the Union itself; that is, in terms of trade benefits, border control, energy and environment, and political stability, rather than as a mechanism for de-enmification. From the perspective of economic integration, in a region of such small and fledgling states, replete with economic difficulties, regional co-operation is absolutely imperative for the rebuilding of markets and the management of resources.

When EU initiatives to build regional co-operation in the Western Balkans began after 1999, they were conceived largely as a means of stabilising the region, ending violence, and as a mechanism for post-conflict reconstruction. The regional co-operation agenda has subsequently become the cornerstone of EU integration for the region and is now usually articulated and framed in the context of enlargement. In other words, a subtle shift has taken place from a political to an economic focus. However, ultimately the success of EU initiatives in the realm of regional co-operation is likely to depend on the extent to which the countries of the Western Balkans view regional integration as a critical security and development imperative, or merely as something they need to address in order to gain entry to the EU. The Commission has certainly made a concerted effort since the Zagreb Summit to emphasise the integral significance of regional co-operation, rather than to portray the issue in terms of merely one step amongst several on the road to accession.

Indeed, as Delevic-Djilas rightly observes, 'the countries of the region are today much more closely connected through various co-operation schemes than they were seven years ago' (2007: 5). The EU's tried and tested method of forging economic and political dependency as the basis for integration and co-operation, plus making progress towards membership conditional on regional integration, appears to be delivering a dividend, particularly with regard to trade agreements (Dangerfield 2004). The construction of an economic space incorporating all of these states has occurred relatively quickly, and the SAP report for 2003 noted that there had been an increase in the frequency and substance of multilateral and bilateral contacts in the region (Delevic-Djilas 2007: 4). Recent initiatives such as the Central European Free Trade Agreement (CEFTA), signed in Bucharest in December 2006, which will establish a free trade zone in the Western Balkans, and the Energy Community of South East Europe treaty, which will establish an integrated energy market, suggest an increased level of co-operation that will provide a foundation for political integration reminiscent of the European Coal and Steel Community initiative of the 1950s. The Regional Co-operation Council, the planned successor to the Stability Pact for South Eastern Europe, began operating in 2008 from its headquarters in Sarajevo with the aim of 'promot(ing) mutual cooperation and European and Euro-Atlantic integration of South Eastern Europe in order to reinvigorate economic and social development in the region to the benefit of its people'.[10] It is hoped that the RCC, which consists of 45 countries, international organisations and IFIs including all the PCCs, candidate countries, as well as the post-socialist states that entered the EU in 2004 and 2007, will further institutionalise and formalise economic integration.[11]

However, the emergence of a more integrated trading zone, whilst significant, is unlikely, in the short term at least, to overturn the huge political and economic disparities within the Western Balkan region as a whole, and amidst the PCC states in particular. Whereas the CEE countries that entered in 2004 were roughly similar (and became increasingly so as the accession process gained momentum) in terms of their GDP and their economic capacities as well as their political development, the economic differences between BiH, Serbia, Montenegro, Albania and Kosovo are significant and are likely to become more so. Whilst prospects for Serbia's economy are encouraging according to recent EU reports,[12] the potential impact of an EU-supported free trade zone have to be set in the context of the economic realities generated by the need for both BiH and Kosovo to move from aid dependent economies to self-sustainability.

Whilst tying co-operation to enlargement has arguably been successful in delivering economic progress, the varying pace of progress towards accession has undoubtedly served to fracture attempts at economic integration and cohesion. Early initiatives (pre-1999) to build regional co-operation, which involved all of the post-conflict successor states of the former Yugoslavia (Croatia, Macedonia, BiH, Serbia), as well as those neighbouring South East European states whose security was likely to be compromised by the absence of co-operation (Bulgaria, Romania, Albania), were fractured by the reality of the enlargement agenda. Once it became clear that Romania and Bulgaria were economically and politically more advanced than the rest, regional co-operation tended to involve the remaining five states, which was consistent with the Commission's general use of the term 'Western Balkans' to refer to BiH, Serbia-Montenegro, Albania, Croatia and Macedonia. However, by 2004 it had become clear that Croatia and Macedonia were likely to become candidate countries (rather than PCCs). This meant that, somewhat paradoxically, regional co-operation initiatives were being encouraged within a region that the pace and logic of enlargement and the terms of conditionality had effectively divided (Dangerfield 2004: 205).

Regional co-operation and the prospect of future enlargements

Any understanding or assessment of EU efforts to foster regional co-operation has to be set in the context of discussions relating to how the Commission will orchestrate future accessions. The fact that Croatia is by far the most economically successful state in the region suggests that a regatta approach – whereby states are considered individually for entry once they are ready – is initially likely and this will result in Croatia and possibly Macedonia entering together. Notwithstanding the case of Turkey, what happens thereafter is uncertain – if Serbia and/or Montenegro were to surge ahead economically then they may be able to enter separately from BiH and Kosovo, further fracturing the region. However, if the Commission decides that the PCCs can only enter together as a bloc with Kosovo once the latter is ready, then regional co-operation becomes of greater significance and is likely to gain momentum. The obvious advantage of this strategy is that it would prevent Serbia, as a member state, from vetoing and blocking the accession of Kosovo. It would also provide the Commission with a strong bargaining tool for mediating relations between Belgrade and Pristina. Whilst the signing of SAAs with BiH and Serbia, the latter's renewed co-operation with the ICTY, and the new pro-EU government in Belgrade may well serve to inject a new pace into the enlargement process, the Commission's official position remains that:

> there is no further enlargement with a large group of countries at the same time in view. The Western Balkans contains smaller countries at different stages on their road towards the EU. Further enlargements will go at the pace dictated by each country's performance in meeting the rigorous standards.[13]

The prospect of eventual EU membership has certainly been the key driver of co-operation and closer integration in the region. However, if certain states enter before others (which seems likely), and progress towards membership remains slow for those that remain as candidates, or if additional criterion are introduced and the EU decouples enlargement and co-operation, then regional co-operation is likely to suffer and achievements may even be overturned. For some commentators the two priorities – regional stability and EU integration – remain a mutually reinforcing continuum, with co-operation thus far having established a 'foundation course' for EU accession and laying the basic groundwork for Europeanisation. However, even the optimists acknowledge that ultimately 'a deep mutual integration will only be able to happen within an EU membership context' (Dangerfield 2004: 210).

The fundamental tension and contradiction at the heart of the EU's strategy is the antagonism between regionalism and bilateralism. In terms of the success of EU integration much depends on how effectively the EU is able to concurrently pursue regional agendas based upon co-operation, security and integration, at the same time as bilateral negotiations with individual states making progress at different paces. As noted already, the bilateralism at the heart of the SAp, SAAs and EPs will potentially lead to further differentiation amongst the PCCs, which will perhaps negate the critical objective of regional co-operation on which stability depends. At present the Commission is keen to negotiate separately with BiH, Serbia, Albania and Montenegro.

The ideal scenario from the Commission's perspective may well be to continue with a combined strategy of bilateralism and regionalism, and in a sense this appears to be the most logical way to proceed. However such a hybrid strategy is not without its complexities and contradictions. For example, delivering constitutional and political change in BiH may appear to be an issue to be dealt with through bilateral negotiations. But in fact the country's stability as a sovereign state is dependent upon the co-operation and integration of its neighbours: a re-devised constitutional framework based on a federal but single state model which preserves the autonomy of the ethnic entities will depend upon Serbia's co-operation and support. In turn, this will be easier to achieve the greater the prospects of membership are for Serbia. In other words, bilateral and regional strategies are inextricably linked and the dynamics are complex and incongruent.

Thus far the discussion has alluded to a number of critical issues regarding the EU's overall approach and highlighted some significant constraints on the impact of its assistance. The key questions that have emerged are: should the EU offer more short-term goals and rewards? Are the objectives of its intervention confused and contradictory? Is a regional approach appropriate, or should the Commission pursue bilateralism and focus more on negotiating separately with individual states? Can the two objectives be pursued concurrently? Is the entire approach still too closely oriented towards dealing with the legacies of the Yugoslav crisis? What capacity does the EU have for state-building, and are its strategies and approaches sufficiently coherent for such an endeavour? This study aims to consider theses questions from the perspective of EU assistance 'on the ground', from the vantage point of funding initiatives and processes in the recipient states, and to examine what the Commission is realising through its strategic intervention in Serbia, BiH and now for Kosovo.

EU Aid and Assistance 2000–6:
The CARDS programme

This final section of the chapter will provide a detailed overview of the actual aid and assistance programmes that have been delivered to the PCCs since 2000 in the form of CARDS (Community Assistance for Reconstruction, Development and Stabilisation) (2000–6) and IPA (Instrument for Pre-accession Assistance) (2007–13). The aim is to provide a framework for examining the impact that such assistance is having, and to gauge the extent to which CARDS and IPA have constituted effective mechanisms or frameworks for delivering development assistance.

Overall and through its various aid and assistance packages, the EU has committed approximately €6.8 billion to the Western Balkans since 1990. Prior to the introduction of the CARDS programme, aid delivered to these states was largely un-coordinated. Economic assistance was dispensed either via the PHARE programme (Council Regulation (EC) No. 3906/89) dating back to 1989, or as part of specific emergency and reconstruction aid provided for the former Yugoslavia (Council Regulation (EC) No. 1628/96) from 1996 onwards. This meant that the provision of assistance was subject to different conditions and procedures and no clear overriding objectives or strategic vision were identified. It also meant that there was the potential for considerable overlap both in terms of EU projects as well as with the initiatives of other multilateral and bilateral donors.

After discussions at the Helsinki Council meeting in December 1999, and the establishment of the SAA framework, the Commission decided, in the interests of efficiency, to establish a single legal framework for the provision of development assistance to the region, incorporating a single set of agreed objectives and aims. The new CARDS programme was adopted in December 2000 (Council Regulation (EC) No. 2666/2000) with the aim of developing and assisting regional participation in the SAp. The countries included were the Western Balkan states of BiH, Serbia-Montenegro, Macedonia, Croatia and Albania.

There was an initial commitment of €4.6 billion to be delivered to the region during the period from 2000 to 2006 specifically for investment, institution-building, and other measures to achieve four main objectives:

1. Democratic stabilisation, reconciliation and the return of refugees;
2. Institutional and legislative development, including harmonisation with European Union norms and approaches, in areas such as the rule of law, human rights, civil society and the media, and the operation of a free market economy;
3. Sustainable economic and social development, including structural reform;
4. Promotion of closer relations and regional co-operation among countries and between them, the EU and the candidate countries of CEE.

Regulation 2666/2000 identified the process via which aid would be delivered. A 'country strategic paper' initially for the period 2000–6 would 'set long-term objectives for assistance and identify priority areas', and emphasis was to be placed on drawing up short-term programmes linked to the priorities of the SAp, including detailed indicative budgets. Since its inception CARDS assistance has taken the form of either supply procurement notices, or calls for project proposals within a specified framework area. In the case of the former, tenders are invited for the provision of equipment and services, for example, in 2006, the Delegation of the European Commission to BiH announced a supply procurement notice inviting tenders for the supply of equipment for databases, scanners and other equipment for the state police force and courts. Tenders are usually open to foreign companies as well as domestic suppliers, but it is often local NGOs and companies that bid for and are awarded contracts. In the case of project proposals, which tend to focus on more political and social objectives such as building civil society, refugee return, or improving the environment, the Commission will issue a notice such as the following:

> The Delegation of the European Commission to Bosnia and Herzegovina is seeking proposals for strengthening democracy, human rights and rule of law in Bosnia and Herzegovina with financial assistance from the European Initiative for Democracy and Human Rights (EIDHR) micro-projects programme of the European Communities.

Organisations and groups of individuals will then submit, by a specified deadline, detailed project proposals that fall within the specified remit. In delivering aid to Albania the Commission has identified several specific areas – capacity-building in customs, fighting crime, fraud and corruption; strengthening public administration, supporting trade, education and transport; pollution monitoring; electoral reform – and it has announced calls for project proposals and tenders to deal with these developmental issues. Examples of projects funded include providing young Roma women with education and skills ('Proud to be Roma'), and tenders for specific pollution projects, including the cleaning up of an environmentally hazardous nitrate fertiliser plant near Fier in the south west of the country.

Critique of CARDS

The main criticism levelled at the CARDS programme and framework by the Commission's own evaluation[14] was that the mechanisms were overly centralised, with too little programming power delegated to local Delegations thus resulting in a slow allocation and agreement process. This led to significant delays in the allocation of funds to the extent that projects were only agreed and able to begin in 2008, two years after the termination of the CARDS framework. Further criticisms were that there was insufficient emphasis on regional co-operation and institution building, and that there was a duplication and crossover between CARDS projects and EIDHR initiatives, particularly with regard to gender and minority rights. The other significant criticism levelled at CARDS, and one that has been directly addressed in the IPA framework, was that there was no specific distinction drawn between candidate and potential candidates and that this resulted in the absence of a sufficiently sharp focus for either group of states.

Aid and assistance 2007–13: the Instrument for Pre-Accession Assistance (IPA)

In planning its external assistance and commitment of aid to the candidate and PCCs for the period 2007–13, and in light of the concerns noted above, the Commission proposed a new framework to replace the CARDS programme. The Instrument for Pre-Accession Assistance (IPA), which is described as 'a new financial tool for promoting modernisation, reform and alignment with the *acquis*', was presented by the Commission to the European Parliament and the Council and adopted in July 2006 (Council Regulation (EC) No. 1085/2006) as the single framework for EU aid to the Western Balkans for the ensuing period. IPA is best understood as the framework for providing financial assistance for modernising societies generally, as well as for enabling them to prepare for and implement the conditions of membership. Insofar as the core objectives of IPA are 'to support countries in their transition from potential candidates to candidate countries and through to membership of the EU',

the new framework confirms a potential linear progression to full membership.[15] Indeed, by incorporating both sets of states within one framework it
gives the clearest signal yet to BiH, Serbia, Albania, Kosovo and Montenegro
that accession is a realistic ultimate outcome. The IPA framework was also
designed to further 'streamline all pre-accession assistance' and bring together
and unite under one framework the various different aid programmes that previously existed (PHARE, ISPA, SAPARD, Turkey Instrument and CARDS).

In practice IPA means that since 2007, a single set of rules and procedures
has governed the allocation of EU funds which, according to the Commission,
will equal approximately €11.5 billion over the seven-year period for the
Western Balkans and Turkey. Insofar as it was the Commission's objective to
create a flexible instrument that would allow the level of assistance to increase
as and when countries made progress, the 'graduation' from PCC to candidate
status will involve a gradual transfer of responsibility and authority from the
Commission to the individual state. Indeed, what distinguishes the assistance
provided for the two groups of countries is that for potential candidate countries the Commission, as a contracting authority, manages the assistance
through either a branch of the European Agency for Reconstruction, or
through the local Delegations; for candidate countries the assistance is managed by the states themselves. The capacity to identify funding priorities and to
manage pre-accession assistance thus constitutes an important developmental
stage and represents a transformation in the relationship between pre-accession states and the Commission.

The single assistance framework IPA is designed foremost to enable recipient states to realise objective pre-accession standards. However, there is, in
practice, a strong bespoke element to the provision. Based on priorities set out
in the European and Accession Partnerships agreed with individual states,
assistance is then targeted to realise commitments made by the Commission to
a specific state as outlined in the agreed multi-annual indicative financial framework (MIFF), which details the actual amounts allocated per component. A
Framework Agreement, negotiated between the recipient state and the
Commission, forms the basis for agreeing the legal and institutional framework for allocating and managing IPA funds.

Though IPA consists of five distinct funding components ('Transition
Assistance and Institution Building'; 'Cross-Border Co-operation'; 'Regional';
'Human Resources'; ' Rural Development'), the PCCs receive assistance under
the first two categories only. Essentially, the key funding and aid priorities of
CARDS – strengthening democratic institutions and the rule of law; reform of
public administration; economic reforms; promotion of human and minority

rights, and gender equality; the development of civil society; regional co-operation; sustainable development; poverty reduction – are subsumed under 'Transition Assistance and Institution building'. As candidate countries, Croatia and Macedonia (and Turkey) receive assistance under all five components in order to help them prepare for the implementation of the Community's agricultural and cohesion policies and to adopt and implement the *acquis communautaire* (Council Regulation (EC) No. 1085/2006: 1.4).

Conclusion

The foremost aim of this first chapter has been to provide an exposition of the EU's framework for its negotiations and provision of assistance for the Western Balkan states in general, and for BiH, Serbia and Kosovo in particular. The discussion has attempted to highlight the dimensions and specific nature of assistance and interaction between the Commission and the Western Balkan states, whilst also setting the EU's approach in the context of previous enlargements and dealings with the post-socialist states of Central and Eastern Europe in particular. In other words, we need to know what is uniquely complex and different, but also to be able to identify continuities and similarities.

What emerges quite clearly from the discussion is the extent to which the Commission has come to place considerable emphasis on building state and administrative capacity and on regional co-operation. In principle at least, the focus of assistance is targeted squarely on recipient states realising the development objectives set out in the SAA and SAp, as well as in the regularly updated European Partnerships signed and agreed with individual countries. However, the Commission clearly places considerable emphasis on the capacity of states not just to be able to identify their development priorities, but also to be able to programme and manage funding appropriately and to enforce and implement outcomes is clearly a key objective that reflects the importance of bureaucratic reform and the development of good governance as hallmarks of readiness for membership.

Thus, prior to launching into a micro assessment of the impact of EU assistance in BiH, Serbia and Kosovo, we are now suitably armed with a clear understanding of what it is the Commission aims to achieve, what is in place to allocate and regulate assistance, and what lessons have been learnt from previous enlargements.

2
Theorising EU assistance and intervention in Bosnia-Herzegovina, Serbia and Kosovo

Introduction

The aim of this second chapter is to construct a conceptual framework for examining and evaluating EU intervention in the form of assistance channelled through local NGOs, in Serbia, BiH and Kosovo. The theoretical question being posed here is whether such assistance is designed to, and is resulting in, the development of civil society and thus promoting democratisation and regime change, or whether the aims of the Commission are better understood in terms of strengthening state and non-state capacity and the construction of *governance*, or more precisely, *good* governance. Whilst the two objectives – strengthening civil society and building governance – are somewhat analogous in the sense that governance implies a role for strong informal actors and associations emergent from civil society, as primary objective building governance may strengthen civil society only indirectly and somewhat incidentally.

Understanding the objectives of assistance and using an appropriate critical framework to evaluate the impact of initiatives is critical: for example, from the perspective of *civil society development*, EU assistance for elite-level NGOs in Serbia or BiH that apparently fails to mobilise and engage grass roots associations, or permeate enmeshed and submerged indigenous networks would be deemed to be deficient. However, from the perspective of *governance* – which prioritises building the capacity for partnership between formal and informal actors – the impact of EU intervention may be viewed somewhat differently and seen as effective insofar as engagement between the sectors is the critical measure of success.

Civil society development aid as a framework for
assessing EU assistance

Donors view building strong and efficacious NGOs as a means of strengthening citizen participation, holding governments to account, and enabling the representation of a plurality of interests; they also represent good policy partners and an efficient means of developing policy expertise. Thus, in practice, the normative democratic value and function of civil society is reduced to supporting professional NGOs.

As noted in the previous chapter, the most salient aspect of EU assistance to the Western Balkan states is undoubtedly the support channelled through local NGOs and civil society organisations and networks. Such assistance is delivered via short-term project grants, and the resources provided as part of the Community Assistance for Reconstruction, Development and Stabilisation (CARDS) programme, and from 2008 onwards, the Instrument for Pre-accession Assistance (IPA).

At first glance, such assistance appears to be the EU's version of the sort of democracy promotion assistance or civil society development aid delivered over the years by a host of American and European donors across post-socialist Europe. Indeed, developing civil society organisations as a vital expression of liberal democracy is, and has long been, a key objective of the accession/enlargement process dating back to the early 1990s and PHARE assistance to the central East European states. EU aid being channelled through local NGOs in BiH, Serbia and Kosovo thus appears typical of the bilateral and multilateral donor assistance that has flowed into the region since the mid 1990s.

Whilst EU assistance to the region does bear similarities to other donor intervention, the Commission's provision differs with regard to the over-arching emphasis placed on strengthening the capacity of civil society organisations (invariably NGOs) as vehicles for the realisation of various other core development objectives aligned to the Stabilisation and Association programme (SAp). Thus, for the Commission, supporting civil society is not just an end in itself, it is first and foremost instrumental in delivering policy development and implementation in the realms of environmental protection, minority rights and refugee return, welfare provision and employment services, as well as economic, political and social reforms required as conditions for accession.

Civil society development and its critics

An evaluation of EU assistance channelled through NGOs from the perspective of civil society promotion must situate itself within what now constitutes an extensive literature critiquing foreign donor assistance for civil society development. The critical literature, which draws heavily on the realities of foreign donor intervention in post-socialist states as well as the global South, offers this study a comprehensive critical framework for assessing the impact of EU assistance in BiH, Serbia and Kosovo.

The Commission's support for NGOs across post-socialist Europe has been influenced by the legacy of USAID and other bilateral American donors who have since the second part of the 1990s, if not before, channelled their civil society development aid through American-style advocacy NGOs. It is important therefore in assessing EU initiatives to fully grasp the rationale and normative assumptions guiding this form of intervention. The first thing to note is that whilst the impact and extent of such aid has tended to be exaggerated, professional NGOs competing for externally funded donor projects have become a ubiquitous and almost generic feature of post-socialism. The overall momentum is extensive and, for critics, pervasive (Quigley 2000; Sampson 2002). Whilst the EU is now the largest donor supporting NGOs in BiH and Serbia, various other European and American donors continue to target NGOs and civil society organisations. Indeed, for most multilateral agencies, philanthropic foundations and national donor organisations the provision of grants to NGOs is the cornerstone of their developmental aid to post-socialist Europe.

However, as Ottaway and Carothers point out, this was not the case in the early 1990s, or at least not to the same degree. Donors initially provided institutional support focusing on political party development and reform of state institutions. The shift towards civil society development coincided with the Clinton presidency and occurred in large part due to the limited success and complications associated with other forms of assistance and support (Ottaway and Carothers 2000). Channelling aid through NGOs and prioritising civil society development as a development strategy has considerable appeal for donors: apart from pandering to liberal and neo-liberal concerns about checking the power of the state and holding governing elites to account, it is relatively cost-effective – NGOs often deliver projects and services cheaply and efficiently, they tend to be non-bureaucratic and are highly professional in their operations. Most importantly, not only does such intervention engender broad-based support from across the political spectrum within donor states, but it also enables donors to circumvent resistant political elites within the recipient states.

It is this aspect of civil society development assistance that has courted most controversy: what purports to be politically significant assistance, designed to drive consolidation and genuine regime change, with lofty ambitions and loaded with normative overtones ('democracy', 'civil society', citizen participation etc.)

in practice seem to function as apolitical technical support. By side-stepping political elites and prioritising support for 'soft' institutions of power (i.e. NGOs) rather than driving institutional reform and challenging 'hard' power (corrupt elites, transnational networks resistant to democratic reform and liberalisation), donors have been criticised for ignoring critical disparities in power relations. Carothers argues that donors' tendency to purport that it is indeed possible to bring about change and improvement 'without grappling with the deep-seated interests of the actors involved' is not just a tacit admission of the failure of earlier interventions, but is also plainly wrong in its conviction (2002: 10). In other words, at worst democracy promotion ignores structural realities, fails to address the causes of corruption, anti-democratic practices and misuse of power; at best international donor efforts resort to framing their intervention in terms of apolitical technical assistance and measuring the impact in terms of the completion of discrete projects rather than an assessment of fundamental shifts in power, the formation of new institutions, or the behaviour of elites (Crawford 2003a).

The quite extensive critical literature that has emerged challenging such a rationale questions whether the NGOs supported and developed by donors are fulfilling the role and functions of civil society; critics pour considerable scorn on the assumption that a tier of professional elite-level NGOs should be seen as a hallmark of democratic consolidation (Fagan 2005; Sampson 2002). Fundamental questions have been raised concerning whether normative democratic notions of civil society can be equated with donor-dependent NGOs, or whether the organisations that donors support reflect the realities of civil society in established western democracies or indeed can be successfully transported beyond the specific context of established liberal democracies (Hann 1996; Kaldor 2003). Ottaway and Carothers (2000) contend that the NGOs favoured by foreign donors, including the EU, are 'set up along the lines of advocacy NGOs in the United States . . . with designated management, full-time staff, an office, and a charter or statement of mission'. Such NGOs will engage government through US-style advocacy and lobbying, but will not themselves seek political office; they will operate above the cut and thrust of party politics thus preserving the veneer of *non-partisan* donor activity. What this essentially creates is a sense of donor-funded NGOs pursuing a Rousseauvian public interest role, committed to civic values rather than divisive party politics. The role of such non-partisan organisations takes on additional relevance in post-conflict situations, both as a counterbalance to nationalist-ridden party politics, and as a means of driving civic education.

The problem for commentators would appear to be that whilst such advo-cacy organisations may well represent an aspect or component of civil society in Western European states, critics would hardly reduce civil society in its entirety to such manifestations. Indeed, studies of civil society in contempo-rary European democracies place great emphasis on the diversity of formal and informal organisational forms; on dispersed and opaque collectivities and enmeshed networks as the hallmark of democratic civil society (Hall 1995; Keane 1988). The 'civil society' envisaged by donors is trifurcated. The first ele-ment is a sector of advocacy organisations, schools for democracy in the Tocquevillian sense, that will, through their advocacy role, bring about a new culture of interaction and political engagement based on compromise, toler-ance and participation. The second consists of professional non-governmental organisations with policy knowledge and expertise, forming the basis of a new pro-EU epistemic community. The third component of donor-constructed civil society consists of service provider NGOs that may engage in low levels of advocacy but concentrate primarily on securing project grants to provide services such as labour force training, recycling and other such facilities, credit provision and other commercial services either in lieu of or conjunction with the state and the market.

Whilst seemingly the most benign aspect of donor funding for NGOs, this latter aspect is no less contentious. Critics argue that rather than helping to kick-start the economy and engage the state and the market in the provision of services, NGOs and voluntary organisations that assume core service provi-sion functions often weaken the capacity of both the state and the market to offer such services by luring professionals from the other sectors into the more lucrative NGO world, or by removing the incentive for state agencies to com-pete with donor-funded NGOs and provide sustainable public services.

The transition to democracy paradigm: a partnership interpretation of civil society

The vision of civil society envisaged by international donors, whether in post-communist Europe, Latin America or parts of the global South, has generally been the consolidation of a distinct arena of associations assisting in the devel-opment of public policy and the enactment of regulation (Carothers 2002: 6–7). At a liberal normative level, such intervention is often justified in terms of such partnerships between civil society and the state repairing the destruc-tion to natural bonds and moral codes wrought by late capitalism. According to Pearce and Howell, this 'partnership' interpretation of civil society 'draws on a particular history of the concept that makes it relevant to a problem solving agenda' (2001: 17). It is based on the premise that solutions are to be found within the context of the market through partnership with big business. Professional, policy-focused associations thus perform a key role in the neo-liberal scheme of transforming state power and freeing capital. As well as providing foreign donors with cost-effective mechanisms for the transmission of aid and tutelage, NGOs act as watchdogs for arbitrary regulation and, in the words of Larry Diamond, 'prohibit actions that offend interests within bour-geois society' (Diamond 1996).

Such an interpretation of civil society finds endorsement within the ration-ale-choice influenced transitions literature, the paradigm through which regime change and democratisation across post-socialist Europe is generally analysed and understood. For instance, Linz and Stepan's (1996) distinction between political, economic and civil society relegates the latter to an ephemeral arena of civic organisations which, if they do have political aspira-tions, are intent not on challenging or transforming the state, but in assisting or influencing its neo-liberal policy agenda. Political society is defined as elite-level political institutions (such as political parties); economic society relates to firms and corporate interests.

Civil society is not seen as a vehicle for serious political critique, for chal-lenging economic and political hegemony, or for transforming state–society relations. In essence civil society thus defined is highly compartmentalised – its remit is restricted to strengthening the status quo, assisting the neo-liberal reconfiguration of power, and enabling the state to transfer some responsibil-ity for regulation and social protection to the voluntary sector. Such a notion of civil society does not permit the questioning of the type of state institutions, or their effectiveness in regulating capital. All civil society can realistically do is to assume some of the discarded responsibilities of the state, shoulder the costs of the state's partial withdrawal from social protection, and facilitate the symbolic aspects of liberal democracy: freedom of speech and association.

In essence the promotion and development of NGOs as a representation of civil society is based either on the notion that such organisations are apolitical, offering technical assistance and policy solutions, or they are non-partisan institutions seeking to promote the public interest over and above narrow political and ideological interests.

NGOs as civil society in post-communist Europe: a critique

There exists a considerable and extensive literature critiquing donor-driven civil society development across post-socialist Europe. Beyond questioning the extent to which donor-funded organisations operate like their western counterparts, and whether in fact they could realistically be expected to do so (Bunce 2000; Hann 1996), scholars have gone so far as to question the extent to which the ubiquitous professionalised NGOs that exist across the region can in fact be considered to represent 'civil society' at all (Fagan 2008). Others have contemplated the 'uncivil' aspects of post-communist civil society (Kopecky and Mudde 2003), or issued warnings about its internal dynamics and questioned whether all aspects of post-communist associational activity were necessarily positive (White 1994). Such criticisms are particularly relevant in the context of BiH and Serbia, where questions arise as to who actually benefits from EU assistance, whether there is absorption capacity for the type of aid being offered, the somewhat oblique linkage between EU-funded NGOs and nationalist political factions and elites, and the longer-term impact of such assistance (Fagan 2006).

From the perspective of comparative studies and country case studies of women's organisations and environmental NGOs, scholars have observed low and declining levels of mobilisation, the absence of representation within the policy process, and popular suspicion of NGOs across post-socialist Europe despite significant donor efforts to promote civil society (Cellarius and Staddon 2002; Fagan 2006; Howard 2003; McMahon 2004). Concerns have also been expressed regarding the extent to which the new communities of NGOs do in fact represent or reflect the interests of society at large and the degree to which the narrow sector of increasingly professionalised NGOs acts as a critical space, relatively un-colonised by political and economic power (Baker 1999; Fagan 2006). Studies seeking to explain and better understand why such low levels of mobilisation persist have questioned whether donor resources have been appropriately deployed. To critics, donor funding has merely fostered dependency and displaced indigenous networks (McMahon 2004).

Studies of NGO development at the periphery of post-communism – the Balkans, Central Asia and the Former Soviet Union (FSU) – have gone so far as to question the extent to which post-socialist civil society needed to be professionalised, de-radicalised and institutionalised and whether the supplanting of new skills and knowledge has merely undermined existing informal networks and hierarchies. Scholars have variously concluded that the legacy of international assistance has therefore been disenabling and even counterproductive (Belloni 2000; Hann 2002; Sampson 2002). The core contention is that donor assistance is based on the assumption that civil society has to be constructed from scratch and that no positive legacies from the late socialist period exist or are worth salvaging in the quest to build civil society. Indeed, it would seem that donor assistance is founded on the tacit presumption that socialist states were totalitarian, with no societal interaction or informal networks existing. Whilst this may be more akin to what was the reality in Romania and Albania, it was certainly not what existed in CEE or the Balkans, or even parts of Central Asia (Weinthal 2002); the political, economic and social significance of informal and semi-legal networks have been well documented by anthropologists and human geographers (Hann 1996, 2002).

The aspect of donor assistance and NGO development in Central and Eastern Europe that has seemingly aroused the most controversy is the extent to which the transfer of know-how has been presented by western donors as non-ideological; a practical means of realising desirable ends, a technical solution for overturning the legacies of communism. Such assuaging of ideological content has obviated the divergence between civil society and NGO activity, and hindered attempts to locate the intervention within a broader context. For critics, the notion of civil society development espoused by donors is, of course, ideologically specific, drawing as it does on a particular interpretation of United States political history, and a somewhat subjective interpretation of how civil society emerged and operates in established capitalist democracies. In the context of post-communist Europe, the notion of civil society having gained concessions from the state and democratised the political realm in Western Europe is then interpreted through the neo-liberal paradigm of dismantling and restraining the state.

Through such an ideological prism, civil society's functions are cast as preventing the atomisation of commercial society, healing its wounds in order to nurture growth and stability and encouraging philanthropy. In terms of economic reconstruction in post-communist states, the latter becomes a critical function: as the state retreats, civil society's role in coaxing the private sector to 'give back' is vital in order to plug gaps in social welfare and to ensure cohesion. There is little sense here of the model of civil society being exported to post-socialist states reflecting the realities of civil society development in Western Europe: associational activity emerging and growing in conjunction with the expansion of the state, or indeed of the inherent social democratic legacy of what exists as civil society today, for example, in Britain.

Other critiques have focused more on the practical constraints on the effectiveness of this form of intervention. The most pressing concern raised is the capacity of the recipient state and non-state actors to absorb the aid being offered. Civil society development assistance is often designed to promote specific skills and develop particular capacities that indigenous organisations either already possess, or are too complex and advanced for fledgling organisations requiring very basic assistance. Resources are thus wasted because the provision is based on the assumption that existing capacities are either greater than they are, or the aid is wrongly targeted towards providing very basic skills training instead of more specific tutelage. A further criticism often voiced is that much duplication occurs with donors replicating each other's assistance agendas without any overall co-ordination of initiatives. The consequence of this is that either there are too many grants and project proposals in circulation for the number of NGOs able to meet the stringent allocation requirements, or the same core of organisations are repeatedly engaged in the same types of project without there being any serious evaluation of impact and sustainability. Put rather bluntly, there are only so many Roma rights campaigns or environmental education projects that can realistically and effectively be pursued.

Civil society promotion and donor assistance in the post-conflict successor states of the former Yugoslavia

The extensive donor involvement in the post-conflicts successor states of the former Yugoslavia since the mid 1990s has, not surprisingly, spawned a considerable critical literature. In particular, scholars have penned quite scathing denouncements of attempts by donors to prioritise NGOs and civil society as the solution to political, economic and social crisis in the region (Chandler 1999; Fagan 2006; Sorensen 2000).

Largely as a consequence of the violent conflicts of the 1990s it would seem as though all aspects of transition in Serbia, Kosovo and BiH hinge on civil society development and donor initiatives channelled through domestic NGOs (Belloni 2000). There is an implicit assumption that a vibrant sector of local advocacy networks can entrench democratic values, heal the wounds of ethnic conflict and facilitate economic growth, bringing an end to the international administration of Bosnia (Chandler 1999: 143; Deacon and Stubbs 1998; du Pont 2000).

In other words, a developed civil society will be the hallmark of successful state-building, the point at which the Bosnian state is able to be left to rule without the international community. Thus, to suggest that civil society development is anything less than central to the international community's state-building agenda would be an understatement. The situation is not entirely dissimilar in Serbia, where attempts to liberalise the post-Milosevic regime and to strengthen human and minority rights has been seen as the remit of civil society and donor assistance initiatives.

Practically every international NGO, foreign donor organisation and multi-lateral agency involved in the Western Balkan region states makes explicit reference to civil society development as a key objective of their involvement and as a means of legitimising their continued presence. But it is not just the international donors that have used the language of civil society promotion; local NGOs providing services within the community, running small education programmes or providing practical assistance to displaced persons, the elderly, or those with medical conditions, also express their objectives in terms of civil society (ICVA 2002). The term has thus become eponymous for almost every aspect of regime change; the *lingua franca* of governance and the interaction between international and local actors, formal and informal actors, politicians, agencies, citizens and commentators.

Whilst many aspects of what has emerged under the rubric of civil society are to be applauded, to view NGO development as instrumental in the envisaged transition to a democratic and multi-ethnic autonomous state exaggerates their capacity to deliver fundamental change. Whilst NGO activity in BiH crosses nationalist and ethnic boundaries, challenges the agendas of local elites, and does seem to be mobilising citizens to make use of democratic processes, the capacity of civil society to realise radical transformation is contingent upon more fundamental institutional and political change.

Despite the discourse of governance and partnership with the state, or the rhetoric of peace-building, in practice international donors have predominantly supported various service-provision initiatives, ranging from help for internally displaced persons, to education organisations, business services organisations and health care initiatives. Indeed, for many Bosnians, it is western-funded local NGOs or an international donor agency located in the country that provide, for example, credit and new technical skills, psychosocial support for women and children,[1] childcare,[2] medical training and access to breast cancer screening. For others, western-funded NGOs are a source of relatively secure and well-remunerated employment. In other words, the conceptual understanding of civil society employed by donors is as a mechanism for allocating their assistance and draws heavily on the notion of civil society as the third sector, a realm of voluntary non-profit organisations operating between the market and the state in order to compensate for the shortcomings of both (Salamon and Anheier 1997).

The existing analysis of civil society development in the Western Balkans has tended to echo the issues and constraints seen as limiting the political capacity of donor-created civil society in post-communist Europe, the former Soviet Republics of Central Asia and parts of the developing world (Cellarius and Staddon 2002; Mandel 2002; Quigley 2000; Sampson 2002; Wedel 2001). On the basis of research undertaken at the end of the 1990s, a host of British and American scholars charted the extent to which the donor-dependent sector of NGOs in BiH was characterised by low levels of citizen involvement, and an apparent separation from society at large (Chandler 1999: 151–3). The picture painted was of a small sector of NGO professionals, a handful of people, drawn mostly from the urban middle-classes, clustered predominantly, though not exclusively, in the towns and cities of the Federation (FBiH) (Freizer and Kaldor 2002). Typically, these people were involved in a multiplicity of different donor-driven initiatives, their sense of accountability and political focus being the international donors, NGOs and agencies that supply the funds and devise the projects. Though the role of international donors in terms of resource provision was acknowledged, the condescending nature of know-how transfer, of assumptions about Bosnian citizens lacking the capacity to engage with democratic procedures and institutions, and the political implications of donor intervention were noted and echoed in all the studies (Belloni 2000; Sorensen 1997).

In addition to the usual concerns – regarding the true benefactors of donor aid, the colonial nature of western intervention in NGO development, and the immeasurability of added value – the critique extended significantly beyond concerns about sustainability, dependency and societal linkage. It was argued that the new tier of NGO professionals had been encouraged by western donors to see their function and role as essentially technical and apolitical, distinct from the nationalist-dominated political sphere. Sorensen claimed that this separation led to the lack of an overall democratisation/civil society development strategy, and had resulted in the inability of the NGO community to challenge dominant political discourse or to mobilise significant political support (Sorensen 1997: 35), the contradiction here being that civil society was expected to achieve heady political objectives through apolitical means. The reality of the international community's confused efforts, it was claimed, was a divided and politically enfeebled civil society, which lacked the capacity to deliver the sort of political change envisaged by donors (Belloni 2000: 4).

Whilst so much was expected of the new NGOs in terms of achieving democracy and healing wounds, the main thrust of civil society development aid focused on grooming NGOs as service providers. The fact that 'civic groups and NGOs [were becoming] contractors for the provision of services commissioned by foreign donors' was seen by critics as a constraint on the political change dimension of civil society, and as a hindrance to the emergence of civil society as a vehicle for the articulation of local political agendas (ibid.).

It was claimed that western-funded NGOs trained in how to write project proposals and apply for donor funding were being drawn into substituting for the
state in areas such as social policy, fiscal reform and social and economic provision at the expense of a more politicised local advocacy role. Although less
controversial studies have explained the emphasis on service provision in
terms of a continuum with the communist period, others felt that devolving
services to NGOs within the existing political and economic framework of
BiH served only to maintain 'the fragmentation and multiplication of political
authority' (Deacon and Stubbs 1998). The overriding depiction was of NGOs
operating within the constrictions of the post-Dayton infrastructure: plugging
gaps, duplicating provision and generally trying to compensate for the absence
of state-level authority and a nascent market economy.

But the critique was actually more nuanced than the claim that NGOs were
propping up the status quo instead of acting as agents of change. It has been
suggested that western-funded and trained NGOs were, in fact, exerting a negative effect on the country's long-term sustainability and socio-economic
development in the sense that the sector siphoned off the intellectual elite and
those who would otherwise be engaged in the public sector and the local labour
market. That the professionalism and growth of the NGO sector occurred at
the expense of the public sector, civil service and state administration, not to
mention the expansion of the market, was a pretty devastating critique of the
international community's intervention when so much politically depends
upon the economic regeneration of both states.

Even more damning was the suggestion that by assuming functions such as
social provision, regulation, redistribution and education, NGOs allowed
nationalist elites to shun any responsibility for the misappropriation of funds
by local authorities, or for their failure to permit displaced persons to return to
their pre-war locations. NGOs thus stood accused of providing a smokescreen
for the feudalist, corrupt and ethnicised politics of the nationalist elites and for
actually preventing the empowerment of multi-ethnic state authorities (Belloni
2000: 6). It is woefully ironic that the NGOs championed as agents of democratic change were accused of foiling the contractual relationship between citizen and state that is so fundamental to democratic governance.

Capacity-building instead of civil society?

An alternative theoretical framework from within which to examine donor aid
channelled through NGOs in BiH, Kosovo and Serbia is the neo-functionalist

perspective of 'capacity-building', which evaluates the impact of assistance in terms of the augmentation of functional capacity of recipients – in other words, the extent to which donor assistance empowers and enables NGOs to perform various functions and tasks such as policy development, service provision or knowledge construction. Whilst proponents of capacity assistance do refer to the impact and benefit of capacity-building assistance in terms of *civil society*, this aspect or dimension is somewhat peripheral; if civil society organisations and community associations benefit from capacity assistance this is an added value of aid, but it is incidental and subordinate to the overall purpose of developing effective administrative and political processes, building the knowledge and abilities of a host of formal and informal actors engaged in policy development, service provision and the advancement of best practice generally.

The notion of capacity-building has been a core component of the development studies literature since the 1950s and the post-war wave of de-colonisation in Africa. As a conceptual framework it provides those studying post-authoritarian states with a set of benchmarks for monitoring change and progress and for building institutional and policy frameworks, whilst at the same time acknowledging the impact of constraining legacies from the imme-diate past. Capacity-building has become, since the mid 1990s, intrinsically linked to efforts by the World Bank, the IMF and other international financial institutions (IFIs) to develop 'good governance', usually as part of poverty reduction strategies in the poorest states across the world. The various aspects of capacity, as defined by international donors, has become an extensive and ever lengthening list, including the building of institutions, development of state functions and the interactions between state, market and civil society (Grindle 2004: 526). Although the more specific notion of 'environmental capacity-building' gained momentum at the UN Conference on Environment and Development held at Rio in 1992, and is deployed more generally around discussions of sustainability and globalisation, donor-driven capacity-building and development initiatives tend to be all-embracing and will focus on envi-ronmental reforms as part of poverty reduction strategies or in the broader context of institutional and state reform (Grindle 1997).

Referring specifically to environmental policy and practice, the OECD defines capacity specifically as 'a society's ability to identify and solve ... prob-lems' (OECD 1994: 4). Accidents and natural-resource endowment notwith-standing, capacity is determined and shaped by political actors and their decisions, the dimensions and appropriateness of policy, availability of techni-cal knowledge and expertise. In his discussion of the factors limiting a state's environmental capacity, Janicke includes 'lack of ecological, technological or administrative knowledge, lack of material or legal resources, the weakness of environmental organisations or institutions in relation to vested interests . . .' (Janicke 1997: 4). Analyses of a state's capacity tend to focus on the quality of public sector human resources, non-governmental organisations and state or quasi state institutions (VanDeveer and Dabelko 2001: 20). The environmental capacity of a particular country is not static: new issues and problems, plus the availability of new technology and approaches, can alter the assessment of a country's ability and success in dealing with environmental issues. Moreover, the focus of capacity-building can shift from one 'site' to another, with a country deemed to have developed sufficient capacity in some aspects of environmental management and yet not in others (ibid.).

Proponents of capacity-building as a tool of and conceptual framework for development are keen to emphasise that it is important not to reduce the dimensions of the concept to the formal policy process, legislation and the role of governments. Indeed, the OECD has, for example, cautioned against trying to explain the failure of environmental policy solely in terms of the wrong policy or the use of inappropriate regulatory instruments (OECD 1992: 4). In many ways the greatest virtue of the capacity concept is the stress placed on the objective limitations to successful intervention. The approach places emphasis on the 'complex interaction of influences' rather than on 'a single isolated factor, or a favourite instrument . . . or a single type of actor, condition or institution' (Janicke 1997: 5). In other words, analysis of capacity must look not just at the weaknesses of institutions, but at the causes of incapacity that may include the absence of shared objectives, or economic and social constraints on individuals within key organisations. Capacity is therefore determined not so much by the actors themselves, but by the structural context in which they operate. Similarly, capacity-building should not be about installing policies that may have worked elsewhere and are deemed to be best practice in Western Europe or the US, without considering the context to which they are being transferred. As VanDeveer and Dabelko observe:

> when efforts to build capacity fail, they often do so because of a lack of domestic concern in the recipient country about the policy objective . . . If technical assistance programs fail, it is likely to be the fault of program design, not the fault of recipients. (2001: 20)

By paying heed to both structure and agency, the capacity-building framework thus offers an apparently extensive and far-reaching set of criteria for explaining the constraints on the successful management of political, social and economic development, the interaction between state, non-state and market actors, as well as providing a theoretical basis for mapping change across a wide spectrum of variables.

Despite such rhetoric, the reality of donor-driven capacity-building initiatives 'on the ground' tends to be a disregard for long-term impact and sustainable solutions in favour of short-term and rather haphazard interventions, couched in somewhat technocratic language. As Vandeveer and Sagar observe, what is invariably absent from discussions of capacity-building is a sense of strengthening a society's 'capacity to recognise, analyse and define environmental problems and their causes' (2005: 3). They conclude that 'activities targeted purely towards assisting countries in the completion of specific tasks, or moving towards short-term goals, may not only fail to build local capacity, but may actually be counter-productive . . .' (ibid.: 6). Insofar as capacity-building invariably becomes conflated with notions of building 'good governance', the reality for developing states tends to be a plethora of donor-driven initiatives focusing on tangible outcomes and short-term objectives that reflect 'multiple priorities (and) an unrealistically long agenda' (Grindle 2004: 526).

In practice, most capacity development programmes involve either building the capacity of donor agencies to help in the implementation of specific programmes abroad, or funding projects to build capacity in recipient countries. With regard to environmental initiatives in particular, this involves integrating environmental considerations into donor programmes and developing the skills base of the staff in the agency, and building expertise in the fields of environmental economics and law, and developing monitoring tools in recipient countries. Overall this tends to be top-down assistance, such as building planning and administrative capacity in ministries. It also places great emphasis on developing the role of NGOs in policy forums, as providers of scientific knowledge, and as institutions for the collection of data and research.

But the providers of capacity assistance have themselves been critical of effectiveness and impact. In its 1999 review of capacity development for the environment (CDE) efforts, the OECD observed that most programmes had realised only limited success (OECD 2006). It was suggested that the reasons for this were largely to do with the conceptualisation of capacity held by donor agencies. Rather than top-down initiatives based around discrete projects decided on by development agencies, the OECD urged donors to:

1. Recognise, analyse and help define environmental problems and their causes;
2. Encourage joint decision and management processes (i.e. not imposed by donors);
3. Locate local initiatives in the context of global implementation capacity.

In an attempt to emphasise the importance of the social processes that need to occur for successful implementation, as well as the need for problems and solutions to be defined and identified locally, and also to shift the focus of capacity development away from recipient states simply being trained to implement internationally established environmental policy objectives, VanDeveer and Sagar (2005: 3) define capacity as consisting of three overlapping categories:

1. Capacity to recognise, analyse and help define environmental problems and their causes;
2. Capacity to jointly decide on appropriate management processes;
3. Implementation capacity.

The concern being expressed here is that in the context of Southern states, and no less so in post-socialist and post-conflict states, capacity initiatives have invariably meant little more than funding local NGO representatives to attend international meetings, or to finance technocratic training programmes with little regard to how such knowledge could then be used to good effect locally to deliver sustainable and long-term change. A more fundamental contention, and one that is an inherent problem within development more generally, is that capacity initiatives are based on the tacit assumption that there is no *in*capacity in the North, and that Southern states must learn everything from the 'successful' Northern experience. Related to this is the embedded assumption that within states receiving capacity-building assistance there is no existing capacity and that everything has to be built from scratch. This is particularly contentious with regard to post-socialist states, in which there are invariably high levels of scientific and technical know-how (Carmin and Jehlicka 2005). The assumption also encourages donors towards a 'scatter-gun' approach, whereby a host of capacity-building initiatives are launched simultaneously with little regard for what already exists in a particular state, and what measures should in fact be prioritised. Grindle has referred to this problem in terms of capacity and good governance programmes lacking any sense of sequencing (2004).

Perhaps the most fundamental contention, and one with specific relevance to the role of the EU in the Western Balkans, is the evident disconnection between the capacity programmes that donors advocate, and their concurrent commitment to the promotion of economic liberalisation, growth and consumption. For example, recent studies of environmental capacity in post-socialist Europe now acknowledge that, two decades since the revolutions of 1989, the massive increase in consumption that has occurred as a consequence of marketisation, rather than legacies from the socialist period, represents the most significant threat to sustainable development (Andersson 2002; Caddy and Vari 2002; Fagan 2001).

A *good governance* perspective on EU assistance

Examining the impact of EU aid in terms of developing *good governance* shifts attention away from the impact on NGOs themselves (as expressions of civil society), towards the interaction between state and non-state actors, formal and informal actors and institutions, and the partnerships that emerge between them. Indeed, the perspective combines emphasis on effective policy imple-mentation and building functional capacity, with concerns about inclusive decision-making and value of civil society and non-state actors.

From a governance vantage point, the impact and effectiveness of aid is therefore to be judged in terms of the extent to which it generates engagement between the state and non-state sectors and sparks interaction between diverse actors as the basis for good and inclusive decision-making, and the effective implementation of public policy.

Governance: a definition and critique

Not surprisingly, the ubiquity of the term 'governance' amongst practitioners and scholars has generated a high degree of contestation (Keohane and Hoffmann 1991; Pierre and Peters 2005; Schmitter 1991). Most development aid delivered by bilateral and multilateral donor agencies and international financial institutions (IFIs) – for example, the World Bank, USAID, DFID and the EU – is framed in the language of building 'governance', or more precisely, 'good governance'. Conceptual and theoretical contradiction tends to focus on why *governance* is being used instead of *government*; whether as an *explanatory tool* governance helps to locate or further obfuscate power; and the extent to which as *purposive activity* governance adequately identifies the deployment of power between politically engaged actors (Barnett and Duvall 2005; Rosenau 1995; Rosenau and Czempiel 1992). Governance thus 'consists of both structure and process' (Börzel 2007: 3).

The defining feature or common denominator of all interpretations of the concept is the emphasis placed on multiple locations of power, authority and control that are both institutionalised and informal, involve state and non-state actors; what Pierre describes as 'the conceptual or theoretical representation of co-ordination of social systems and, for the most part, the role of the state in that process' (Pierre 2000: 3), or what Mayntz refers to as institutionalised modes of co-ordination through which collectively binding decisions are adopted and implemented (2003). The definition offered by Mayntz captures the extent to which governance as process will take place in a structural context of institutionalised power and authority.

Such a definition and understanding of governance immediately conjures a rationalist notion of liberal interventionism and the construction of transnational institutions to deal with ever more complex collective action and to overcome the dichotomy between self-interest and the need to co-operate (Hurrell 2005: 33). However, implicit within all conceptualisations of governance is the embedded or latent neo-liberal notion that the dispersal of power involves both the retraction and reconstitution of state power *vis-à-vis* the market and the third sector.

The key normative difference between government and governance appears, therefore, to be in terms of scope: the latter is more encompassing, both in terms of actors involved in control or regulation, and in the sense of the number of activities being regulated. Rosenau provides perhaps the clearest illustration of the multiplicity of actors when he describes governance as 'encompass(ing) the activities of government, but . . . also includ(ing) the many other channels through which commands flow in the form of goals framed, directives issued and policies pursued' (1995: 14). In a similar vein Kooiman defines governance as 'all those activities of social, political and administrative actors that can be seen as purposeful efforts to guide, steer, control and manage societies' (1993: 2). Governance implies simultaneous regulation and control of various overlapping issues. However, whilst there is flexibility and variation, governance also involves 'order plus intentionality', with order consisting of 'routinised arrangements' (Rosenau 1992: 5). There is therefore within a model of governance significant scope for fluidity and diversity, for new actors, issues and institutions, but within established procedures and boundaries.

An important aspect of governance, identified by all scholars, is that relations between the various actors, whether international or sub-national, governmental or non-governmental, dependent or coerced, formal or informal, institutional or non-institutional, are 'temporary, ad hoc, conceived under pressure of events and voluntary' (Yanacopulos 2005: 251). Not only is political power portrayed as being widely dispersed across disparate formal and informal agents, such interactions are fluid and continually re-negotiated. In this sense the architecture of governance, in contrast to that of government, is far less fixed and may not be institutionalised or formalised.

However, whilst the plurality of actors and the co-ordination of diversity are integral components of the concept that characterise its distinctiveness and newness, in order to grasp the configurations of power and the interaction between actors there is a need to identify the contexts in which governance as a mode of co-ordination and decision-making is likely to occur. To this end, scholars distinguish between three broad ideal types of institutionalised rule structures: hierarchy, competition (market) systems, and negotiation systems (Börzel 2007: 4). The interaction between dominant and subordinate actors is referred to in the literature as 'coupling': in hierarchies a relationship of domination in which the power and inflence of subordinate actors in constrained, is referred to as 'tight coupling' (Scharpf 1997: 36–50). It is immediately apparent that potential for any significant deliberation and the involvement of non-state actors is possible only in the context of competition or negotiation systems; political hierarchies will restrict access to all but public actors.

In order to elucidate further what precisely constitutes 'governance' – what it looks like and where to find evidence of it occurring – a further distinction is made in the literature between the actor constellations occurring in negotiation systems and the level at which such negotiation is, or is not, likely to occur: *trans-governmental* negotiation systems (high-level diplomacy between states around, for example, international treaties or bilateral co-operation) tend to engage public actors in conventional, classic diplomacy; *intermediate* negotiation systems (inter-state policy development and sectoral co-operation) are most likely to engage non-state actors, including business and civil society representatives, and is thus the most probable location of 'governance', or 'new modes of governance' (Mayntz 2003; Rhodes 1997).

From public policy to international relations: the concepts of good governance and global governance

Whilst there are distinctly normative liberal overtones to the governance concept, it is deployed most often, and with perhaps the most clarity, in the realm of public policy. In this context, and in the interests of greater efficiency, the concept of *good* governance draws attention to the importance of incorporating within the equation of power actors with differing levels of legitimacy and empowerment. It re-focuses analysis on the core concerns of policy analysts: what *type* of actors and network coalitions are involved? What is the *nature* of the interaction? What *mechanisms* for resolving and managing conflict are employed? (Smouts 1998: 86). The dynamic imperative that has driven public policy scholars to engage with the concept of governance is a sense that government is inefficient, ineffective and lacking capacity. The perceived advantage of the governance concept thus lies in its potential to engage, identify and ultimately co-opt interests and sections of society that governments alone fail to reach, and to penetrate horizontal co-operation and self-organisation so as to maximise benefit for the community at large. In other words, within public policy, use of governance is rooted in concerns about the limits of governability and thus *good* governance represents increased efficiency and policy competence (Smouts 1998: 84).

Governance began to be used within international relations during the 1980s, with the shift in usage from public policy emanating from the broader critique of realist and neo-realist perspectives that refused to acknowledge the plethora of social actors involved in decision-making and regulation beyond the level of the state. In the hands of some scholars, particularly those interested in the emergence of *global* governance, use of the concept takes on idealistic dimensions of world government; for instance, Finkelstein's (1995) claim that 'global governance is doing internationally what governments do at home' suggests a very prescriptive application of the concept rather than using it to illustrate the complexities and obscurities of power beyond the state, and to address the issue of governability.

If the concept of governance as employed at the level of the state by public policy analysts emphasises efficiency and the involvement and participation of multiple actors in the formation of enforceable and legitimate policy outcomes, use of the concept of global governance tends to lack overt connotations of empowerment, transparency and accountability. Rather, it is used descriptively by Weiss (1998) to make sense of power in the post-Cold War era, to refer to the ever-changing distribution of authority and control within the international system, and the relative erosion of state authority *vis-à-vis* transnational NGOs, intergovernmental institutions and a host of non-state actors operating at supra-state level. Rosenau tries to counter this bias by emphasising that global governance is not just about the relationship between national government, the UN and supra-state negotiations, but should be used to discover overlapping systems of rule and control at every level of human activity – 'from the family to the international organisation' (Rosenau and Czempiel 1992). For Murphy (2000), global governance is 'what world government we actually have' and the concept therefore needs to be used to enable the UN, as defender of the poor, the exploited, the victims of conflict and the environment to play a bigger role in this unregulated and undefined terrain (Weiss 1998).

Governance and European integration

The shift from (national) government to (international or global) governance was encouraged by increased European integration during the late 1980s and 1990s and the scholarly literature on multi-level governance, which emerged from studies of policy-making and normative discussions regarding the distribution of power within the European Community (Jachtenfuchs 2001). The concept of governance provided scholars of European integration with a conceptual framework that allowed them to move beyond the dichotomy of nation states versus federal institutions (ibid.: 245). Multi-level governance can incorporate both within a descriptive account of control and regulation (Bernard 2002). The notion of governance at the core of EU negotiations with accession states is derived from such a model of multi-level governance, a conceptualisation that allows for an accommodation of power and sovereignty between the Commission and the governments of acceding states.

Governance and development

However, in evaluating EU aid to post-conflict and transitional states it is important to acknowledge the close association between the governance concept and its usage by International Financial Institutions (IFIs), such as the World Bank, in the context of political conditionality imposed on countries in receipt of financial assistance that are considered to be incapable of managing loans and making effective use of the revenue (Smouts 1998: 81–2). It is in such a context that NGOs in developing and transitional states are usually engaged in donor-funded 'good governance' initiatives, the primary objective being, despite the discourse of civil society and social capital, to build inter-sectoral partnerships and to strengthen state capacity.

With regard to the post-conflict successor states of the former Yugoslavia, in which state capacity is weak, and many of the development issues are indeed akin to those facing states of the global South, building 'good governance' involves the exportation of new public management and the transposition of a model of rule-making that seeks to legitimate the role of external actors (including transnational NGOs, the EU Commission) in policy-making, implementation and compliance. Governance initiatives launched by bilateral and multilateral donors since the mid 1990s (most notably USAID, EU, OSCE) have translated in practice to a series of reforms, both policy and institutional, in order to build the capacity of the region's weak and inefficient states (Kostovicova and Bojičić-Dželilović 2008). As with intervention in the global

South, whilst the provision of assistance is invariably framed in terms of build-ing accountable government, strengthening civil society, or nurturing social and ethnic integration, the imperative and the reality 'on the ground' is finan-cial accountability and the empowerment of internationally funded NGOs as regulatory watchdogs.

Whilst the outcome of such intervention is to potentially obfuscate power by transferring legitimacy and accountability away from the state and elec-torates, Smouts reminds us that the World Bank first employed the discourse of governance in the late 1980s to more effectively identify the location of power and control in African states in which solid state structures were not in place, and in an attempt to move away from discussions of power that focused only on location and on the character of decision makers (1998: 82). It is this contrast between earlier illustrative uses of the concept by development agen-cies, and its more recent prescriptive usage as a tool of structural adjustment and the neo-liberal transformation of state-market relations that has aroused controversy and led many to reject the concept (Harrison 2004).

Power, hierarchies and new modes of governance

Once it is acknowledged that in order to comprehend the dynamics of power, decision-making and control, whether at state level or beyond, we have to widen the scope of actor involvement beyond state and formal institutions, the key concern becomes the *distribution* of such power, accountability, trans-parency and legitimacy.

Governance scholars do, understandably, concern themselves not just with illustrating the diversity of power relationships and the emerging multi-layered nature of decision-making, but also employ the concept purposively to provide insight into the quality of outcomes (namely to identify instances of 'good gov-ernance') and to make a normative case for shifting the balance of power between actors. However, as already noted, this translates in practice either to the rather simplistic and visceral claim that efficient decision-making and 'good' policy is equated with multiple actor involvement, or the overtly ideo-logical premise that the power of the state has to decline relative to the market or non-state actors if efficient outcomes are to be delivered.

Such a deployment of the governance concept has led some scholars to reject the notion that there is value in using the concept other than to reflect the changing contexts and processes of governing. Smouts argues that 'the more seriously the notion of governance is taken, the less content it has' (1998: 81). In other words, it is essentially a concept of limited analytical value that can only be used objectively to describe the diversity and variation in political deci-sion-making and control; its core assertion being that there is a high degree of vagueness and fluidity, and that governance is little more than a set of regula-tion or control mechanisms operating in a sphere of activity, which function effectively even though they may lack formal authority (Rosenau 1992: 5). Used in the context of development politics as a prescriptive model for state and policy-making reform, its objective value rapidly diminishes: it cannot con-vincingly or effectively interpret the roles of actors, nor provide commentary on the asymmetries of power without either embedded neo-liberal assump-tions coming to the fore, or a normative premise that effectiveness is possible and that 'an issue (can) be managed, a problem resolved (through) an accom-modation of mutual interests' (Smouts 1998: 88). In essence, intervention in order to build governance capacity inevitably becomes ideological if it is about anything more than supporting a flexible infrastructure to accommodate the various actors likely to contribute to policy-making. Attempts to use it pre-scriptively as a means to fashion actor or policy networks in development con-texts either fail to unmask the asymmetries of power, or implicitly suggest that the power of certain actors – normally the state – should decline *vis-à-vis* that of others – usually the market or NGOs.

New modes of governance: post-socialist states and EU accession

If, as argued above, the main critique levelled at the governance concept is that it conceals an ideological attempt to dis-empower states and transfer regulatory authority to non-state actors, and that any attempt to use the term more pre-scriptively inevitably falls prey to neo-liberal assumptions about state interfer-ence and capacity, then recent scholarly analysis looking at the changing dynamics of state power in post-socialist states acceding to the EU have gone some way to challenge this perceived embedded bias. Scholars looking specifi-cally at the Central and Eastern European states have used the governance con-cept more prescriptively, both to locate submerged and unaccountable power, and to theorise the interaction between state and non-state actors in the context of regime change, whilst, critically, acknowledging the complex diffusion of power between the two. Rather than simply endorsing the neo-liberal assump-tions of the early 1990s regarding the need for the state to relinquish control and authority, recent work identifies the determinants of new forms of interaction that can potentially empower both state *and* non-state actors (Börzel et al. 2008).

Much of the 'governance beyond the state' analysis somewhat optimistically emphasises the extent to which non-hierarchical decision-making and co-ordination, involving private and civil society actors, states, multilateral agencies and a host of informal actors, has increasingly become the norm (Swyngedouw 2005), terming such interactions as either 'new governance' (Hix 1998), or 'new modes of governance' (Börzel 2007). Recent work across post-socialist Europe has questioned whether such non-hierarchical modes of governance do indeed deliver better public policy, and if not, why this is so (Börzel et al. 2008). Essentially, what is being questioned is the limited effectiveness of new modes of governance; whether this is due to a failure to move beyond old hierarchies and patterns of decision-making; whether such a shift is indeed possible; and if so what factors are likely to determine the outcome or effectiveness of new modes of governance.

Studies of the changing dynamics of power between government and non-governmental actors in the context of compliance and conditionality within accession states have sought to explain the non-emergence of new modes of governance and the predominance of conventional hierarchical patterns of decision-making in the states of CEE in terms of an absence of *governance capacity* on the part of both state and non-state actors. What has been observed is low levels of co-operation between the sectors, co-operation that rarely extends beyond consultation, and if it does occur at all, does so only in the context of EU policy frameworks, where public or civil society participation is mandatory or a requisite for funding and assistance (Börzel et al. 2008: 2). Drawing on Mayntz and Scharpf's notion of the 'shadow of hierarchy', Börzel (2007) argues that the critical driver for closer and more effective participation between state and non-state actors is the capacity of policy makers to hierarchically impose outcomes in contradiction, if necessary, to private actors and civil society. In other words, non-hierarchical deliberation and the open exchange of opinion is most likely to occur within a framework in which compliance will ultimately be pursued by state actors or a policy-making elite, who will exercise their authority to impose outcomes. Building non-hierarchical modes of governance in which state and non-state actors interact on an equal footing is therefore dependent on the fundamental capacity of elites. This is far removed from neo-liberal uses of the concept to lambaste the regulatory state, and is of immediate relevance to EU efforts to build good governance in the context of state weakness as well as the weakness of civil society in the Western Balkans.

Whilst measures to strengthen the capacity of non-state actors are, in principle at least, worthy, governance scholars and those studying the impact of Europeanisation on CEE states have argued that the critical driver of new modes of governance is mutual resource dependency: state actors need to become increasingly dependent on the resources of non-state actors to effect policy change and implementation, and vice versa (Rhodes 1997; Scharpf 1978). Establishing new modes of governance in transitional and post-conflict states, where state capacity is likely to be limited by depleted resources, is particularly crucial insofar as it allows for 'webs of relatively stable and ongoing relationships which mobilise and pool dispersed resources so that collective (or parallel) action can be orchestrated toward the solution of a common policy' (Kenis and Schneider 1991: 36). The core assumption here is that the greater the involvement in decision-making of affected non-state actors, the more likely the implementation and acceptance of policy outcomes, even if the interests of civil society actors have not been fully accommodated or are reflected in the final piece of legislation (Héritier 2003).

Drawing on transaction cost and principal–agent theories,[3] it might be assumed that governments and state actors in post-socialist and post-conflict states, with depleted state capacity, may be more inclined to engage non-state actors because of the additional value (knowledge, expertise) they can bring to decision-making and policy implementation. However, the flaw in this argument is essentially that when the state is *too* weak, and the capacity of the non-state/NGO sector is also undeveloped, neither side is provided with sufficient incentive to engage the other. Indeed, what is likely to emerge is 'agency capture' or 'problem-shifting' whereby authority becomes shared between state and non-state actors with both lacking sufficient capacity (Hellman et al. 2000). This raises a fundamental concern regarding the propensity of donor intervention to build the capacity of non-state and private actors to the point at which they have greater capacity and authority than state actors. The risk here is, first, that weak states are unlikely to recapture regulatory capacity once authority and power have been transferred to NGOs or the market, and second, over-empowering non-state or private actors, who are likely to bear the costs of compliance, can lead to 'lowest common denominator' policy decisions and solutions.

Under circumstances in which there is parity in the low level of capacity held by both state and non-state actors, donor-driven attempts to introduce and to stimulate new modes of governance can actually encourage the transfer of authority away from already demoralised and depleted states instead of fostering reform and effective public management. Thus, the discourse of good governance and cross-sectoral partnerships merely obfuscates a neo-liberal reform agenda. Weak states and a sector of weak, or only marginally stronger, NGOs exacerbate the threat of corruption and the persistence of unregulated political and economic spaces.

However it is not simply a question of donor assistance needing to focus instead on building the capacities of both state and non-state actors in situations where there is an absence of sufficient mutual resource dependency to stimulate new modes of governance. The capacity of the state to enforce policy outcomes is paramount and the outcome of intervention should not be to equate, or level, the capacity of both actors. Rather, the state needs to command a 'shadow of hierarchy' over non-hierarchical deliberations if policy effectiveness is to be augmented. If state actors perceive their role to be ephemeral and to be engaging with non-state actors from a position of weakness, then they are unlikely to engage positively in new modes of governance. Equally if there is a sense on behalf of state actors that interaction will result in loss of their agency and autonomy this will equally act as a disincentive for new modes of governance (Hellmann et al. 2000). Moreover, if non-state actors distrust the capacity of state actors to be able ultimately to enforce a mutually agreed decision, then this will also act as a disincentive for partnership and governance engagement (Mayntz and Scharpf 1995). Whilst the shadow of hierarchy will generate a desire on behalf of non-state actors to co-operate and engage in new modes of governance, and the degree to which state actors are capable of resorting to hierarchical modes of governance will increase such willingness, the reverse is also true for state actors: the greater their capacity for hierarchical policy-making, the less impetus there will be for co-operation with non-state actors (Mayntz 2003). This assertion is based on the rationalist claim that state actors seek to maximise or at least maintain their autonomy and capacity within policy processes, and will only relinquish a degree of autonomy to non-state actors if this delivers additional capacity. In other words, for state actors there has to be additional value derived from new modes of governance compared to the value obtained from hierarchical and more conventional forms of governance (Kohler-Koch 1996). As Börzel et al. note,

> state actors have to possess sufficient capacities in terms of both resources and autonomy in order to cast a credible shadow of hierarchy so that non-state actors have an incentive to co-operate, and state actors are not afraid of being captured. But ... these state actors must not be too strong in order to provide an incentive for state actors to seek co-operation with non-state actors. (2008: 6)

In terms of understanding why new modes of governance may not occur or flourish, scholars such as Migdal (1988), Weiss (1998) and Evans (1995) have argued that resources and autonomy alone are not sufficient variables for explaining why new modes of governance occur. Much will depend on the specific political culture and dominant attitudes towards state–societal interaction in particular. As Börzel (2003) notes, 'this is particularly true for countries with an authoritarian legacy and no sustained tradition of institutionalised state-society relations'. In post-socialist states the emergence of new modes of governance is also constrained by the fact that non-governmental organisations and other non-state actors are perceived by both the elite hierarchies and the masses to be unaccountable and therefore non-democratic and illegitimate policy makers and enforcers (Fagan 2006; Howard 2003; Sissenich 2007). In post-conflict situations (BiH, Kosovo) or in contexts in which state formation and sovereignty remain in their infancy (BiH, Kosovo and Serbia), the prospects for new modes of governance are even more remote.

Conclusion

This chapter has surveyed three broad and somewhat intermeshed conceptual frameworks for understanding and examining EU assistance channelled through non-state actors and NGOs in BiH, Serbia and Kosovo: civil society development; capacity-building; and governance/good governance. The argument constructed here is that to view such intervention solely in terms of civil society promotion or democracy assistance fails to capture the objectives of assistance, but also potentially distorts any assessment of impact – the primary objective of the Commission is not to support civil society organisations as a qualitative measure of democratic consolidation, but to engage NGOs with state agencies in the process of policy formation, implementation and control. The 'democratic' or 'civil society' dividend is thus somewhat incidental, the main goal being to build a sector of organisations with the capacity to partake in the process of governing and regulating the state and the market and in harmonising laws with EU norms. The capacity-building perspective shifts emphasis towards policy and implementation and locates NGOs within the context of other actors, policy development and enforcement. However, it does not adequately capture or seek to deconstruct the dynamics of the interaction between state and non-state actors, nor isolate the democratic value of civil society's role. In a nutshell, capacity-building is primarily technocratic rather than political in its focus. Scholars are concerned with good and effective outcomes in the context of socio-economic development; they are more than happy to endorse the importance of structural constraints and the imperative of looking beyond the state, but ultimately it does not matter how good outcomes occur or who is in the driving seat, as long as policy is drawn up, enacted and implemented and outcomes delivered.

On the basis of such a critique it was therefore argued that the most appropriate conceptual framework for examining EU assistance channelled through CSOs or NGOs was that of governance, and the emphasis governance scholars place on the interaction between the state and non-state actors; the existence within policy-making and enforcement of NGOs and the importance and legitimation of their role as partners of the state immediately casts new explanatory meaning on the efforts of the EU. What the analysis of the scholarly literature revealed, however, is the complexities in moving beyond a descriptive account of which actors are involved in the equation of power, and trying to identify dominance and the marginalisation of interests within the process. Two issues emerge as particularly problematic: first, the neo-liberal overtones at the core of both public policy and development usages of the concept and its covert deployment by those wishing to launch visceral acts on state power. Second, whilst some interpretations of the concept certainly move beyond neo-liberal attacks on the state, the importance of building the governance capacity of state as well as non-state actors, and the critical aspect of sovereignty are under-played. In other words, because the real value of the governance concept is its ability to identify multiple actors and legitimate the role of informal and non-state agents, there is a tendency to ignore the importance of state sovereignty – the so-called 'shadow of hierarchy' – and exaggerate the power and influence that NGOs can and should exercise. Such criticisms notwithstanding, the governance frame provides the most appropriate optic for examining EU assistance designed, in theory at least, to engage non-state and state actors.

3
The EU in Bosnia-Herzegovina

Introduction

This first empirical chapter will provide a detailed analysis and evaluation of EU assistance to BiH delivered in the context of the Stabilisation and Association Process (SAp) and the European Partnership, and committed under the remit of CARDS, EIDHR and, since 2007, IPA assistance. As in the following chapter on Serbia, the primary data on which much of the argument is based is drawn from empirical research into the projects funded by the Commission through its local Delegation in Sarajevo, the focus and outcomes of the assistance, analysis of the process of allocation, monitoring and evaluation, and the extent to which funding outcomes reflect broader EU objectives with regard to BiH. After briefly placing the current intervention by the EU in some historical context, the chapter will offer a discussion and analysis of the Dayton political framework and, critically, the shift in power and influence towards the EU that has occurred in recent years and is on-going. Indeed, the context in which the EU has become the main provider of development assistance and the driving force of Bosnia's post-Dayton reconstruction will be analysed in considerable detail.

The remaining sections of the chapter will address directly the key theme of this book, namely, the extent to which EU assistance is triggering governance, empowering the non-state sector, and the extent to which there is a symbiosis between the Commission's overall objectives for BiH, and the outcomes of its significant assistance delivered locally on the ground by the local Delegation in Sarajevo. To this end, the provision of development aid, the process of allocation, the absorption capacity of the NGO community, plus the various outcomes and outputs of projects will be analysed.

Bosnia's past and present: external development and intervention

The most cursory review of foreign intervention in BiH during the course of the past 200 years reveals the extent to which the current intervention of the EU – external intervention to strengthen state capacity – is, in both its objectives and operations, historically consistent. Bosnia's development, however patchy and imperfect, in the century prior to the collapse of Yugoslavia in the early 1990s had always been exogenous; imposed from above and invariably delivered by an external force (Malcolm 1994). Attempts at industrialisation and modernisation, whether under the Austro-Hungarian administration before the First World War, or the Yugoslav monarchy in the inter-war years, or under socialism, had occurred as a consequence of political diktat, external pressure or at least the instigation of outsiders. The international community's presence in BiH, and the role of the EU in particular, forms part of an ingrained and deep-seated tradition. It has been noted by many commentators that Bosnia's political elites, not to mention society at large, are accustomed to seeking solutions to their problems from outsiders, from neighbours, allies or at the behest of great powers.

The imperial authorities within the Austro-Hungarian Empire, seeking to legitimise their occupation of Bosnia-Herzegovina in 1878, claimed that the social and economic backwardness of the region was causing regional instability and therefore necessitated intervention. In particular, the Austrians identified rural underdevelopment and the need for land reforms as key priorities, which necessitated, they believed, strong and decisive government, something Bosnia lacked (Tomasevich 1955: 107). The Austrians promised 'first to raise the living standard of Bosnia-Herzegovina, then to concentrate on education, and finally to turn to political self-government' (Sugar 1963: 56). Though the Austrian administration did build roads and invest in the economy, an indigenous entrepreneurial class failed to emerge, with the greatest beneficiaries of Bosnia's natural resources – forestry, tobacco, salt – being foreign investors, who did little to invest in sustainable projects. In contrast to the earlier Ottoman period, during which time the elite tended to be Muslim landowners, the Austrian epoch saw the rise of an administrative class or bureaucracy, which encouraged the emergence of a small service sector in the largest urban centre at the time, Sarajevo. There is an immediate comparison to be made here with the current period, which equally has seen the exponential growth of an elite of public officials, whose well-paid positions and consumption of state resources has aroused considerable concern amongst commentators as well as ordinary Bosnians. Despite the concentration of political authority, the

Austrian elite failed to deliver on its pledges to raise living standards, develop education, or establish political self-government. Sugar's assessment of the Austrian legacy, that 'Yugoslavia inherited some good roads, a railway network, a few fully equipped and operating industrial plants, and several empty factory buildings' (1963: 67), acts as a potent warning for any foreign initiative or intervention in the country today.

As part of the Kingdom of Yugoslavia, during the inter-war years, Bosnia's economic development stalled; constitutional and ethnic wrangling became politically all-consuming and little was achieved in terms of dealing with social problems and underdevelopment. Indeed, on the eve of the Second World War, three-quarters of Bosnia's population depended on subsistence agriculture (ESI 2006: 72). This interlude of parliamentary democracy and elected government was short-lived and, after the Great Depression, was replaced by a royal dictatorship. For many Bosnians, much the same as for East Europeans in general, the legacy of this period was that liberal democracy had delivered little in the way of political and economic development, and was ill suited to their society.

The legacy of the 1990s, war, ethnic violence and socio-economic devastation, has, understandably perhaps, obscured other legacies, in particular the impact of four decades of socialist development. In terms of grasping Bosnia's current economic problems and development needs, the socialist period is a critical starting point. Whereas in the immediate post-Dayton period the international community's efforts in Bosnia were focused on peace-implementation tasks – security, demobilisation, reconstruction and return – the country's development issues over a decade later are predominantly social and economic. The international community, and the EU in particular, is today dealing less with the legacies of war, and more with the consequences of socialist modernisation and development under Tito.

Whilst certain aspects of the socialist legacy are immediately familiar to scholars of East European societies – over-employment, excessive emphasis on heavy industrial and military production, subsidised production and consumption – other aspects are unique and quite surprising.

Post-war Bosnia-Herzegovina: from Dayton to Brussels

Although the political configuration of BiH remains very much a legacy of the 1992–5 war and the Dayton peace settlement which formally ended the conflict in November 1995, it is important to acknowledge the extent to which EU influence and intervention can be credited with initiating various reforms of the constitutional and political architecture. In essence, the challenge for the EU has been, and remains, to strengthen the authority of the Bosnian state *vis-à-vis* the entities in order to deliver state-wide reforms and compliance, and to counteract the most potent legacy of the Dayton agreement, namely that the sovereignty of the Bosnian state is compromised by the existence of a state within a state. Not surprisingly, the process of building the authority of the federal state, largely at the behest of the EU, has been 'a painful and time-consuming process' (Juncos 2005: 92).

The Bosnian Constitution is Annex 4 of the Dayton-Paris Agreement (DPA). The document was drafted at the State Department and appended to the peace agreement in 1995 (Bose 2002). Although ostensibly a single state, political power and authority rest with the two separate entities, the Bosniak (Muslim)-Croat Federation and Republika Srpska. In reality, Bosnia is essentially a *consociational confederation* in which the three collectivities (Bosniak, Serb and Croat) are given primacy over individual citizens (Lijphart 1984). Indeed, at each level of government, there are stipulations to ensure that the three constituent groups can veto decisions and are represented in all levels of government. The over-arching Bosnian state is confederal in character, exerting virtually no authority; the federating units (the two entities) rather than the federal government are constitutionally empowered (Bose 2002). Though the central state is weak, it has been slowly acquiring competencies over the past decade, largely, though not entirely, as a consequence of EU pressure. However, today, as in 1995, power lies predominantly with the aforementioned entities (i.e. FBiH and RS), which are largely autonomous and can even conclude treaties (called 'special parallel relationships') independent of the central state. Whilst substantial power rests in the hands of the entity-level governments, the diffusion of power in the Federation is more opaque, as the territory is divided further into ten cantons delineated to reflect ethnic divisions within the entity, and enjoying extensive competencies, including housing, education and public services. Each canton elects its own government (and until recently its own prime minister), the aim being to allow political representation for the majority ethnic group within a specific territorial area.

The fragmentation does not, however, end at cantonal level. Substantial power is then devolved to local municipalities, again in an attempt to maximise political representation of ethnic communities. Within these local units, there are two 'special cases' where municipalities are agglomerated into 'cities' (i.e. Sarajevo and Mostar). The result is a political quagmire in which responsibility and accountability become blurred and overlap, with much confusion about the validity of legislation across the two entities and the status of state-level decisions versus entity-level laws.

In large part the international community, and the EU in particular, encourages reforms to create a 'normal' centralised liberal democratic state because the multi-tiered, highly decentralised configuration has proved costly and inefficient. In the context of pre-accession and the Stabilisation and Association process (SAp), the Dayton constitutional infrastructure is expensive, lumbering and out-dated; reaching Decisions and progress in enforcing Directives is extremely slow and complex (Juncos 2005: 93). But, not surprisingly, there is no consensus regarding constitutional reform: Bosnian Serbs tend to support the status quo insofar as it grants them a large degree of autonomy within 'their' territory of Republika Srpska, though support for secession is not insignificant. Most Bosniaks, who constitute the numerical majority in the state, support the process of building a 'normal' centralised state. The increasing economic and political detachment of the ethnic Croat population, numerically the smallest constituent group, has encouraged demands for even greater autonomy for what is seen as Bosnia's western 'third entity.' Whilst their demands for further autonomy or separation are muted somewhat by their relative prosperity and their close political and economic links with Croatia, Bosnian Croats certainly do not defend or support proposals to strengthen the authority of the centralised state. Indeed their attitude towards the Bosnian state is one of indifference at best, and contempt at worst.

Both critics and advocates of the Dayton architecture acknowledge that political power and influence in BiH rests with the international community in the form of the Office of the High Representative (OHR). The OHR, which was established in 1995 as a temporary measure but continues in existence despite plans over the years to close it down, is vested to mediate between the three divergent conceptions of Bosnia described above, and to facilitate continuing progress and to monitor reforms. The powers and responsibilities of the OHR were defined in Annex 10 of the DPA: it is stipulated that the High Representative is a citizen of an EU state selected by the Peace Implementation Council (PIC), the international body comprising representatives from more than 50 countries and organisations charged with implementing the DPA, monitoring the activities of the OHR, and tracking Bosnia's progress. Although the original interpretation of the role of the High Representative (HR) was as a facilitator, the 1997 Bonn PIC meeting redefined the role of the HR to be more proactive with executive powers. The PIC concluded that the HR could issue binding decisions, including passing of laws and removing intransigent office holders. The formal role of the OHR is to uphold democratic governance and intervene wherever and whenever the conditions of the peace accord are transgressed.

To critics, this represents a colonial power structure, which permanently weakens and infantilises the Bosnian government at all levels (Belloni 2000: 2). For others, the presence of the OHR and the international community is a transitory period designed to help nurture democratic institutions and 'on balance, has done more good than harm' (Bose 2005: 322). However, as David Chandler points out, the reality of power in BiH is that:

> in ten years since Dayton, not one piece of substantial legislation has been devised, ratified and implemented by Bosnian politicians and civil servants . . . the lack of political autonomy for Bosnian representatives, and of political accountability for Bosnian citizens, is possibly the most remarkable feature of the Dayton settlement. (2005: 308)

In reality much has depended on the particular incumbent, the specific issues and reforms they have had to deal with, as well as the particular political tensions of the day. Paddy Ashdown used the so-called 'Bonn Powers'[1] extensively, prompting Knaus and Martin to liken the OHR under Ashdown to a modern-day 'European Raj' (2003). For example, he imposed changes in the entity constitutions in 2002 to safeguard equal protections for constituent peoples. But Ashdown's willingness to remove elected officials, such as the exclusion of Dragan Covic when the HDZ leader refused to resign in March 2005, provoked concerns from critics that such intervention was delegitimating the fledgling democratic system and undermining local ownership of reforms (e.g. Chandler 2000).

Christian Schwarz-Schilling took over as High Representative from Ashdown in January 2006, but unlike his predecessor, the German politician saw his role as an advisor and was far more *laissez faire* than Ashdown. However, Schwarz-Schilling did not last for the whole two-year term, having been sharply criticised for being too 'hands-off' with intransigent politicians and for not facilitating the implementation of vital constitutional reforms agreed by Bosnian politicians in March 2006. The reforms, which included reducing the three-person rotating presidency to one president with two vice-presidents, were enacted by Schwarz-Schilling's successor, Miroslav Lajčák, a Slovak diplomat, who demonstrated a greater willingness to exercise the Bonn powers.

In terms of how one views the role of the OHR, and evaluates its function and mandate, much depends on the extent to which its existence is in fact temporary and the succession of power to domestic authorities. The fact that the OHR is still in existence so long after the DPA, and that its mandate has been extended on several occasions – a deadline set for its closure of June 2007 was postponed for 12 months – encourages cynics to conclude that the international community's presence in Bosnia is not a temporary phenomenon and that little progress towards genuine autonomy has been made. A decision taken by the PIC in February 2008 to make closure of the OHR dependent on Bosnia having met certain conditions and fulfilling certain objectives rather than there being continual extensions at least harnesses the debate about closure to clear and concrete developments. Whilst this clarifies the terms and conditions surrounding eventual closure of the OHR, it does not imply any change in the planned phase-out mechanism, which is to hand over some but not all power to the EU Special Representative (EUSR). The controversial powers to dismiss elected officials and managers of state-owned companies, to impose or revoke laws, or to penalise political parties will not be handed over to the EUSR and thus the transfer, when it does occur and regardless of other implications, will mark a significant shift in power away from the international community (Vogel 2008).

Bosnia and the EU

Despite the fact that the OHR still exists and a full transfer of power to the EUSR has yet to occur, the sustained increase in the power and influence of the EU is undoubtedly the most remarkable and discernible political development in BiH in recent years. From initially being involved in the implementation of civilian aspects of the Dayton agreement, the EU has, since 2000, assumed much broader influence. Indeed, according to Chandler (2006: 35–9), there has been, since the start of this decade, a shift in the focus away from strengthening 'Dayton' towards preparing for 'Europe'. The somewhat vague objectives of Dayton have been largely replaced by the much more specific and tangible objectives of the EU accession agenda. Since the PIC in 2000, the EU has framed its involvement in and assistance for Bosnia in terms of an entry strategy into the Union through the framework of the SAp. EU conditionality for BiH focuses not just on building functioning institutions and economic reforms, but also full co-operation with the ICTY, specific institutional reforms, sustainable return of displaced persons and human rights (Juncos 2005: 98). There is also much emphasis placed on the rule of law and building good governance as a means of ensuring regional stability as well as mechanisms for reducing the threat posed to the rest of Europe by trafficking, drug-smuggling and organised crime.

But aside from co-operation with the ICTY and the legacies of war, what undoubtedly complicates the EU's relationship with Bosnia is the constitutionally enshrined and manifest weakness of the state, the existence of a state within a state, and the contested nature and political limitations of the Dayton constitution. In general SAp negotiations are designed to engage states in the process of legislative approximation and reform; in BiH the competencies and jurisdictions of the federal state are minimal and where they do exist are contested. Thus, EU negotiations with Bosnia have focused in large part on transferring authority from the entities to the state and on building state capacity from scratch. This imperative is reflected in the specific conditions set out in the European Partnership for BiH, which stipulates various short-, medium- and long-term objectives regarding the transfer of power from entity-level to state-level ministries, or indeed in many instances creating state administration where currently no over-arching jurisdiction exists.[2]

The complications of Bosnia's constitutional design notwithstanding, the gradual shift towards European oversight and involvement has been significant and is reflected in the role and function of three institutions: the EUFOR mission took over from NATO's Stabilisation Force (SFOR) in December 2004 with an initial deployment of 7,000 troops. The current number of troops is just over 2,000, including personnel from 24 EU states (Malta, Cyprus and Denmark are not present), as well as contributions from Albania, Argentina, Chile, Macedonia, Norway, Switzerland and Turkey. Whilst EUFOR's mandate is to maintain the peace in Bosnia, it also assists in tackling organised crime and supports the work of the International Criminal Tribunal for Yugoslavia (ICTY). EUFOR also forms a part of the EU integrated approach to facilitate closer ties between Bosnia-Herzegovina and the EU.

The second relevant institution is the EU Police Mission (EUPM), which took over from the United Nations International Police Task Force (IPTF) in 2003 to ensure the rule of law in Bosnia-Herzegovina. Though the EUPM has no executive function as such (it can recommend, monitor and train) its mandate was extended in 2006 and changed to pursue three objectives: tackling organised crime with local police, ensuring police accountability and supporting the restructuring of Bosnian police forces. The third institution, the Office of the High Representative (OHR), has already been discussed above. The General Affairs Council (GAC) of the European Union meeting in February 2002 appointed the Bosnian High Representative as the EU Special Representative (EUSR) in Bosnia-Herzegovina effective from the start of

Paddy Ashdown's tenure in May 2002, since 'the EU sees the future of BiH lying in integration into the European structures'.

In February 1996, GAC suggested a 'regional approach' for consolidating peace in ex-Yugoslavia. Agreements between the EU and bilateral agreements with Former Yugoslav republics, and multilateral agreements between these states would lead to long-term economic and political development. The GAC established specific criteria for each country in 1997. For Bosnia-Herzegovina this included economic transition, institutional reform, but also co-operation with the High Representative and the unification of Mostar. The Operational Conclusions in May 1999 shifted the focus away from regional co-operation towards a more 'advanced relationship' between the European Union and the states in the Western Balkans. In other words, the incentive of European integration would drive economic and political reforms in these states, which was declared explicitly at the European Council meeting in June 2000: 'All the countries concerned are potential candidates for EU membership.'

As discussed in Chapter 1, the policy instruments prescribed in May 1999 by the European Commission comprise the Stabilisation and Association process (SAp) and include: a Stabilisation and Association Agreement (SAA) tailored to each potential candidate for the gradual implementation of EU standards; trade measures and financial assistance; assistance for the development of civil society; help for displaced persons; co-operation in justice; and the 'development of political dialogue'. The Western Balkan states declared support for these measures in November 2000.

In order to move Bosnia forward in terms of signing an SAA, as well as advancing the ultimate goal of EU membership, the European Commission established a specific 18-point 'EU Road map' in March 2000, which identified specific economic and political criteria that needed to be achieved. The Peace Implementation Council (PIC) declaration of May 2000 stipulated that reforms would be completed as a part of European and Euro-Atlantic integration and that this was of paramount importance to the PIC. Bosnia-Herzegovina completed the 'Road Map' at the end of 2002, so a Feasibility Study to start discussions on the SAA commenced. The Feasibility Study published in November 2003 identified 16 key areas that Bosnia-Herzegovina would need to tackle before negotiating the SAA, including full co-operation with the ICTY and police reform. In the meantime, the June 2003 European Commission General Affairs and External Relations Council (GAERC) in Thessaloniki agreed that part of a more 'enriched' process of European integration with Western Balkan states would be the conclusion of European Partnerships, akin to the Accession Partnerships. These Partnership agreements would outline the important issues to tackle and would be updated regularly according to the progress reports from the European Commission. The Council adopted a European Partnership agreement with Bosnia-Herzegovina in June 2004, but this was superseded in January 2006 after the Commission's 2005 Progress Report. The agreement was re-established in 2006 and the progress report of February 2008 contained, as noted above, a revised list of recommendations for constitutional, political and economic reform. In November 2005, the European Commission deemed that Bosnia-Herzegovina had made substantial progress in all 18 areas identified in the Road Map and recommended the start of SAA negotiations. However, as discussed in some detail below, progress on signing the SAA has been slow and complicated.

To facilitate the negotiation and implementation of agreements with the EU the OHR created the Directorate of European Integration (DEI), which some commentators claim has become Bosnia's main executive body (Chandler 2006: 37). Whilst this may be an overstatement of the role of the Director of the DEI – he or she does not have a vote in the state-level Bosnian Co-ordination Body for Economic Issues and European Integration[3] – EU conditionality and compliance has exerted a strong influence for change in other post-communist states, and the assumption is that the promise of future membership, confirmed at the Thessaloniki Summit in 2003, will help drive domestic reforms in BiH.

But the shift in power and influence, described above, has not been greeted positively in all quarters. Indeed, it has been portrayed by some critics as a deliberate de-railing of the original aim of gradually transferring power from the OHR to Bosnian politicians and the public. In acknowledging that 'in effect (the Directorate for European Integration) has become the key executive body in BiH', Chandler's contention is that the transfer of power to the EU represents an obviation of democratic processes and popular sovereignty (Chandler 2005: 343). The difficulty in terms of the EU's role and its relationship with Bosnia's political elites is that whilst on one hand the SAp agenda and the process of accession have served to construct a different type of interaction between the Commission and Bosnia, on the other hand the EU has assumed the role of enforcing constitutional change and thereby stands charged by critics of undermining the will of elected politicians, albeit in the interests of democratic state-building.

The limits of EU conditionality and reform: the political crisis of December 2007 and its aftermath

As acknowledged recently by Miroslav Lajčák, for closer ties with Europe to effectively drive domestic reforms then 'the right balance between sacrifices and rewards needs to be found'.[4] There are, broadly speaking, two discernible strands to the EU's policy and reform strategy for BiH: the first is to develop regional co-operation through economic and security co-operation (Juncos 2005: 96), and second, as noted above, to use the European perspective for BiH as leverage for domestic reform.

But the process of driving conditionality and moving Bosnia forward in terms of meeting the various criteria has not been easy. Such difficulties are starkly reflected in the political crisis that occurred towards the end of 2007. The EU's strategy of pushing political and constitutional reforms in Bosnia-Herzegovina ran into such difficulties that in December 2007 there was talk amongst journalists, academics and commentators of renewed ethnic violence in Bosnia and the collapse of the fragile state.[5] Illustrative of the fragility of ethnic consensus, the crisis also reflected the sensitivities and complexities in seeking to secure agreement on measures designed to strengthen the power of the state *vis-à-vis* the entities. For critics, the political row that erupted concerning police reform and attempts to strengthen state political institutions highlights the extent to which international intervention, and in particular the political conditionality of the EU, are based on a deep-seated confusion between 'wartime rights and wrongs and the requirements of state-building' (Loza 2007: 2). As noted, much of the EU reform agenda is based on transforming Bosnia into a 'normal' state; transferring power from the entities, weakening the ethnic veto, and centralising political and bureaucratic jurisdiction. Such endeavours are not just controversial, they are arguably an attempt to fundamentally reconstruct post-Dayton Bosnia and thus carry enormous risk.

The December 2007 crisis was initially sparked by a constitutional reform proposed by Miroslav Lajčák, the then High Representative, and also the EU Special Representative. In October 2007, using his significant legislative powers, Lajčák imposed a change in the law so that members of the Council of Ministers could hold sessions when there was not a majority present, and decisions made on certain issues when at least one member from each constituent people assents. By making it possible, in theory at least, for the Council to make decisions without ethnic consensus, this intervention challenged the foundation and core element of post-Dayton Bosnia. From Lajčák's perspective the reform was designed purely to streamline decision-making and speed up the reform agenda; as far as the Bosnian Serb leadership was concerned, the measure 'tipped the delicate ethnic balance' towards the Bosniaks as the largest ethnic group, and reflected an attempt to undermine the Serbs' political veto by shifting power away from the entities towards state-level decision making

(Loza 2007). The main political parties in Republika Srpska (SNSD, PDP and SDS) strongly opposed the changes and threatened to walk out of the government. The Chair of the Council of Ministers (effectively the prime minister of the federal Bosnian state), Nikola Spiric, a Bosnian Serb, resigned in protest at what he saw as the imposition of the changes by the High Representative.

Whilst Lajčák's reform was not designed to deliberately upset the ethnic consensus on which Bosnia's post-Dayton precarious stability arguably depends, he nevertheless was making a fundamental political point, namely that the Bonn powers still exist and as High Representative he has the right to use them if what are considered by the international community to be fundamental reforms are being blocked. On the brink of political crisis, a compromise agreement was reached between Lajčák and the Bosnian parliament on 30 November to streamline decision-making procedures in government and parliament, whilst preventing 'ethnic out-voting'.

But Lajčák's constitutional reform was not the only source of tension in relations with the EU. The issue of police reform had also caused a political crisis and stalled the progress of the SAA. The embroilment of police reform with the SAA and EU conditionality for BiH occurred as a consequence of one of Paddy Ashdown's most controversial acts before he finished his term as High Representative.

More than any other institution, Bosnia's policing system reflected the Dayton compromise and the ethnic division of the country. Whilst the RS had one unified police force, there were 11 different and largely independent forces in the ethnically fragmented Federation, all of which varied in size and exercised different legal authority. In effect there was thus no 'single security area within Bosnia' (Muehlmann 2007: 2). There was also a serious question of efficiency: in 2004 there were 16,000 serving officers. It has been estimated that, all things being equal and based on the norms across Western Europe, a country the size of BiH should have somewhere in the region of 11,000 police officers (ibid.: 2). Issues of over-staffing and excessive financial burden, in conjunction with lack of co-operation between forces plus the fact that police divisions reflected war-time boundaries, strengthened the case for police reform amongst the international community.

However, the momentum for reform was driven in large part by its political symbolism. A centralised police force delineated on technical rather than ethno-political lines would take away control of policing from the entities and in so doing stand as a trophy of the state-building efforts by the international community. Ashdown managed to convince Brussels to add police reform to its list of pre-conditions for Bosnia signing a Stability and Association

Agreement with the EU. But reaching a deal on police reform proved extremely difficult and nearly led to the worst crisis in Bosnia's post-Dayton history. Indeed, according to one BiH government official, the impasse over police reform has delayed Bosnia's progress with the SAA and EU accession by at least a year.[6]

For many commentators, police reform was simply a step too far for the Bosnian Serb leadership, for whom control over the police is seen as a critical component of their sovereignty and of the legitimacy of their state within a state. But the proposed reform also managed to upset the Bosniaks, who felt that by making formal reference to RS in the reform proposals, the HR (and by implication the EU) was acknowledging the legitimacy of the separate entities and therefore condoning genocide (or ethnicide). As already noted, police reform also stalled relations with the EU: although it had been accepted by the EU as a pre-condition, the Commission was not prepared to enforce it, on the basis that conditionality and enlargement are supposed to be voluntary processes (the Commission felt understandably uneasy about forcing police reform in order to then judge the Bosnians as having met objective criteria).

For critics of the police reform proposals, the attempt was overtly political and motivated by a desire on behalf of Ashdown to abolish the police force of the RS, against which allegations of politicisation and complicity with wartime agendas were rife. As a reform, irrespective of the political context, centralised policing is not particularly desirable, is uncommon across Europe, and, importantly, was not advocated in the expert report on the state of Bosnia's policing structure funded and commissioned by the EU itself. Indeed, had the police reform been implemented as proposed then it would arguably have been anomalous with other institutional networks within the state.

Not surprisingly the whole issue sparked a fierce and potentially corrosive debate about the role and mandate of international intervention within this fragile state. For critics, the intervention of Lajčák and his insistence that international intervention was justified in order to wrestle from Bosnia's elected politicians the perceived right to interfere with the constitution, captured the democratic deficit of Bosnian politics and the colonial overtones of the HR (Chandler 2007; MacDonald 2007). Indeed, aside from the harrowing prospect that, for the first time since 1995 and the Dayton peace accords, there was a real threat of renewed tensions, the crisis also resonated with deeper concerns regarding the very notion of the international community trying to build states and to manage post-conflict reconstruction. Ironically, Bosnia has until recently been held up as a model for Iraq and Afghanistan, not to mention Palestine and Sierra Leone (Caplan 2002).

The longer-term impact of the crisis on EU–Bosnian relations is less clear-cut and somewhat more difficult to measure. On one hand, despite bringing the country to the brink of fragmentation and its most profound crisis since 1995, ultimately compromise was reached on police reform and constitutional streamlining, thus paving the way for the SAA to be signed, and implying that despite the slow pace and the various hiccups along the way, EU conditionality is driving domestic reforms. On the other hand, the fact that the EU actually initialled the SAA in December amidst the crisis in a desperate attempt to bring Bosnia back from the brink of political disintegration without achieving agreement on either issue suggests a climb-down and sets a further precedent of EU weakness that will play into the hands of those in the region who see the EU as weak and indecisive. For Judy Batt, the crisis reflected the extent to which, despite opinion polls that suggest over 70 per cent of the public support EU integration, all of Bosnia's political leaders were prepared to gamble with EU conditionality and to sacrifice progress in signing the SAA in order to demonstrate their nationalist credentials (Batt 2007). Not only is this seen as a sign of Bosnia's political fragility, it also emphasises the limitations of the EU's 'soft power' and its strategy of tying domestic political reforms to integration.

Yet the significance of the fact that negotiation and dialogue, largely brokered and driven by Lajčák and the EU Enlargement Commissioner Olli Rehn, did take place must not be over-looked and too easily dismissed. The Bosnian parliament passed the police reform bill in April 2007 after lengthy negotiations; although the new legislation does not allow for the creation of a unified police force, despite this being 'the initial goal of the reform' (Vogel 2008), compromise between the composite ethnic elites has been achieved and the agreed framework stipulates that whilst the two entities will retain separate police forces, the expressed objective is to improve communication and co-operation. The main component of the legislation involves the setting up of seven central bodies to review complaints, the police budget, and to oversee training and forensics, although their authority over the entity police forces remains undefined.

But it is the political significance and symbolism of this that perhaps counts most. If compromise and negotiation, rather than a fundamental reconstruction of the Dayton architecture and its replacement with a 'normal' western-style state, are the way forward in terms of EU accession for Bosnia, then by facilitating compromise the EU has been able to set a positive and entirely useful precedent. The outcomes of both the police mission reform and the constitutional amendment concerning the Council of Ministers reform highlight the extent to which a decentralised Bosnia in which collective (ethnic) rights are in some contexts privileged over individual rights is perfectly congruent with EU norms and can form the basis of progress towards accession. Indeed, 'decision-making based on interethnic consensus' is far more consistent with the ethics and function of the EU than centralisation (Loza 2007: 3).

However, critics of what is perhaps a too optimistic conclusion rightly warn that the EU must equally acknowledge that

> (whilst) it is absolutely true that the country needs stronger and leaner central institutions . . . it will never get them if the EU falls for those often well-meaning views that portray Bosnia's inherent complexity as abnormal and arbitrarily describe its institutions as incompatible with the EU because they are based on the principle of ethnic consensus. (Loza 2007)

In other words, perhaps the most poignant lesson to be learnt from recent events is that there are limits to what EU leverage can, and indeed should try, to achieve. If the stakes and expectations are set too high, then there is a real danger that paralysis will prevail; unless demonstrable benefits in terms of progress towards accession accrue then leverage will be lost and, to quote the conclusions of the International Commission on the Balkans chaired by former Italian Prime Minister Giuliano Amato, 'the real choice facing the EU in the Balkans is enlargement or empire' (Batt 2007).

Donor assistance for civil society in BiH

As discussed in the second chapter of this book, donor intervention for civil society development across post-socialist Europe and the global South has been widely criticised within what now amounts to an extensive scholarly literature. Amid the case studies of particular countries and regions, a number of scholars have analysed and critiqued donor involvement in BiH (Belloni 2000; Deacon and Stubbs 1998; Fagan 2005; Kaldor 2003). Prior to discussing the specific impact of EU assistance for BiH, it is necessary to survey and acknowledge the criticisms that have been levelled more generally at western donor assistance for Bosnian NGOs, review the findings of earlier preliminary research on the impact of EU and international donor assistance, and to place the discussion of EU intervention in such a context.

Two fundamental points that need to be emphasised are, first, that despite scholars and commentators referring to 'the international community' providing assistance to BiH, as though the effort was a single, cohesive and strategic operation, the various aid agencies, bilateral and multilateral donors and philanthropic foundations that have operated in the country since the early 1990s are divided and the assistance provided is ad hoc, un-coordinated, with considerable duplication of initiatives. Second, the expectations regarding what NGOs and civil society can achieve – their transformatory capacity – are often exaggerated and somewhat unrealistic. Indeed, it seems as though all aspects of Bosnia's internationally led post-conflict transition hinge on civil society development (Belloni 2000). There is an implicit assumption that a vibrant sector of local advocacy networks can entrench democratic values, heal the wounds of ethnic conflict, facilitate economic growth, bring to an end the international administration and deliver EU accession (Chandler 1999).

Whilst not necessarily contradicting such findings, the more recent critique of western donor impact in BiH has tended to acknowledge that the professionalism and capacity of a core of domestic NGOs has been developed as a consequence of donor (usually EU) assistance, and that the role and function of NGOs has become well established. However, these studies also confirm that, nearly 15 years since large-scale donor intervention began, most projects and assistance still involve organisations providing services in lieu of, or in conjunction with, the state or the market, despite the rhetoric of building good governance and engaging NGOs in policy processes (Fagan 2008; McMahon 2007). Whilst in some sectors of NGO activity, such as women's organisations and economic development initiatives, the impact has been more sustainable and enabling, a significant proportion of aid has delivered no long-term benefit (McMahon 2007). Despite the emphasis placed on local ownership of projects and initiatives, much of what donors fund is generated exogenously and involves NGOs reacting to specific themed calls for projects (Delegation of the EC to BiH 2005: 75).

Whilst even the most cursory examination of NGO activity in Bosnia today reveals that most of the sector's activity, both at local and national levels, still involves providing services in the community, research carried out in 2004–5 by the author and other scholars illustrated a willingness of certain government authorities (municipal state and canton levels) to work with NGOs (Fagan 2006; McMahon 2007). It was argued that whilst politicians may be co-operating with NGOs under pressure from the international community, and though there remains significant variation between individual municipalities and cantons, this was undoubtedly a new and positive impetus. Whereas earlier research had recorded that NGOs operated entirely within the orbit of the international community, worked on projects proposed by donors, and paid little attention to the local administration (Sali-Terzic 2002: 175–94), a decade since Dayton there appeared to be at least an engagement between the sectors and the basis of some form of partnership.

The concern of earlier research was that there were few genuinely local NGOs operating in BiH in the initial post-war period, and the prominent organisations were basically engaged in humanitarian aid and reconstruction (Deacon and Stubbs 1998). NGOs were generally regarded by elites and the public with considerable suspicion – the term 'non-governmental' (*nevladina*) was interpreted as opposition to government and the issues that NGOs worked on were perceived as contentious and threatening. But by 2005 the situation had seemingly improved, with several examples of new linkages having been forged between networks of NGOs and government. For example, the Tuzla Reference Group, a coalition network of over 50 local Tuzla-based NGOs, had established good relations with the government and local mayor, and had entered into joint projects with regard to displaced persons and education.[7]

Reviewing the legacy of donor intervention in BiH from the perspective of 2005, although it was clear that progress had undoubtedly been made and there was evidence to suggest that initiatives to engage NGOs with ministries or state agencies were establishing new patterns of interaction and policy-making norms, the impact was very localised with much still depending on the particular canton, ministry or indeed locality. The most responsive municipalities were reportedly those, not surprisingly, in large urban areas such as Tuzla and Sarajevo, areas where NGO activity was most developed and established.[8] The ministries most likely to co-operate with NGOs were those engaged in aspects of policy-making where the EU has a particular interest or exerts particular pressure – human and minority rights, employment and poverty reduction.

Echoing the research findings of studies undertaken in other post-socialist locations, the existing research on Bosnia concludes that the greatest threats posed to the sustainability and the long-term impact of what amount to well-intentioned initiatives are the dependency of NGOs on a declining pool of donor revenue and the absence of alternative sources of funding, the consequence of which is the failure of recipient NGOs to engage with and represent indigenous civil society (Fagan 2006; McMahon 2007).

In essence, what the existing literature heralds is that a small core of professional NGOs will remain dependent on and wedded to the agendas of the EU, disengaged from grass roots civil society, and existing as adjuncts of certain state agencies and ministries, but without being granted full access (Fagan 2008). If the development strategy for Bosnian NGOs is to direct them towards state funding and closer engagement with government, without them having roots within civil society, the danger is, as Ruth Mandel has observed in her research on NGOs in Central Asia, that donor-funded organisations masquerading as civil society institutions will end up performing more of a civil service role – providing research and policy advice to the government on the development and implementation of its policies. They thus become GONGOs – government-organised NGOs – that are run and controlled by government, for government (Mandel 2002: 286). As cautioned in the earlier literature on civil society in BiH, this is a particular concern in the case of BiH, where the combination of the legacy of NGOs delivering humanitarian aid during the war and the ineffectiveness of the post-Dayton state to deliver basic social provision, alleviate poverty and deprivation and implement social policy, make the prospect of NGOs acting as para-state organisations a likely scenario (Deacon and Stubbs 1998). The danger is that such an NGO sector would not just substitute for the state, but would further weaken its remit by gradually siphoning off experts and officials with the offer of higher salaries and more favourable working conditions. It is in the context of such assertions and findings that analysis of the specific impact of EU assistance must be framed.

EU assistance for BiH

By the end of the 1990s the EU had become the largest single donor funding the reconstruction of BiH. With the introduction of the CARDS programme in 2000, and the confirmation of the EU's commitment to the Western Balkans at the Thessaloniki Summit of 2003, the focus of the Commission's assistance for BiH came to reflect much more the priorities identified in the SAp, namely, institution-building; strengthening infrastructure; justice and home affairs; economic development; cross-border co-operation; plus the promotion of social inclusion and integration.[9]

Drawing on its own experience of promoting democracy in CEE, and following the norm established by other international donors, the EU channelled a considerable proportion of its aid through civil society organisations, or at least what appeared to be the most tangible expression of civil society at this time, namely, NGOs. As noted elsewhere in this book, whilst CARDS funding, and subsequently IPA funding, for Bosnia has been channelled through state agencies and public bodies, a sizeable proportion of the available funds has benefited local NGOs. Developing civil society organisations has, since PHARE funding for CEE in the early 1990s, long been a key objective of the Commission and the EU can therefore plausibly justify funding civic and non-profit organisations to undertake various projects. Local organisations have also benefited from support provided through the European Initiative for Democracy and Human Rights (EIDHR), a global EU programme for the promotion of human rights and democracy.[10] As part of the SAp and the commitment to strengthening democracy and human rights in BiH, as well as helping the country to implement European standards and to gradually approximate its legislation and policies with the *acquis*, the Commission also funds NGOs to deliver a host of services and policy-related objectives. EU assistance channelled through NGOs is thus both structural and instrumental: it is an objective in its own right, but also a mechanism for achieving a plethora of political, economic and social objectives relating to the SAp, enlargement and regional stability. It is also the most tangible expression of the EU's commitment to developing good governance across various policy sectors, building environmental capacity, improving education, human and minority rights and encouraging economic reconstruction. In other words, the civil society development aspect is arguably somewhat incidental to the strategic goal and value of supporting NGOs as actors in the transformation of policy, knowledge and enforcement of European norms and processes (Fagan 2008).

The scale of EU funding for BiH is difficult to gauge, particularly as BiH is still only a potential candidate country whose progress in approximating EU standards and implementing various fundamental reforms has been slow and problematic, and, as a consequence remains ineligible for the extensive pre-accession funding awarded to acceding or candidate states. Added to this is the fact that Bosnia is a small country with a population of 3.5–4 million, with a relatively low absorption capacity for EU assistance. The overall amount spent by the EU on BiH since 1991 is in excess of €2.5 billion. In the first five years after the DPA the overall amount per annum allocated declined from €440 million in 1996 to €105 million in 2000. From 2000 to 2006 the main financial instrument under which Bosnia received EU assistance was the CARDS programme; the total allocation of CARDS funding for BiH in this period was €502 million.[11] By 2006 the annual allocation was down to €64 million, out of which the Commission spent €1 million supporting civil society organisations engaged in return and reintegration of refugees, plus a further €880,000 of EIDHR funding on micro projects with a similar focus. Similar amounts were spent in the two preceding years, but with a focus on the environment and human rights.[12]

Pre-accession financial assistance (IPA) for BiH for the period 2007–10 has been set at €332 million, with annual allocations set at €62.1 million (2007); €74.8 million (2008); €89.1 million (2009) and €106 million (2010) on the basis of the Multi-Annual Indicative Planning Document (MIPD) which was adopted in June 2007.[13] The main focus of aid in this period has been identified as 'the strengthening rule of law and public administration structures, economic and social development and democratic stabilisation, including support to civil society'.[14] The 2007 IPA programme also allocated €3 million during the period 2007–9 specifically for civil society development projects with a focus on 'strengthening local democracy and increasing the capacity of civil society to take part in political dialogue'.

Despite a considerable decline in the total amount of EU funding each year since the mid 1990s, the EU remains the largest single donor to the country, but not by a considerable margin: although the World Bank has reduced its commitment from $200 million (€130m) in 1997 to $40 million (€26m) in 2007, its assistance remains significant.[15]

What is also interesting to note is the amount of assistance received by the post-communist states that entered the EU as part of the fourth and fifth enlargements. During the 1990s, the Czech Republic was gaining funds of approximately €60–70 million per annum through PHARE. By 2000, the yearly average of allocated aid had increased to €100 million. In the two years prior to accession the allocation for the Czech Republic amounted to €103.8 million (2002) and €114.18 million (2003). In total the Czech Republic received in excess of €1.034 billion. Bulgaria, which entered the EU in January 2007, received about €400 million per year in the period 2004–6 and the amount of overall financial assistance increased by an average of 30 per cent, reaching 2 per cent of the country's GDP by the time of accession. Under its mid-2004 agreement with the EU, Bulgaria has received an additional €240 million on top of the previously announced funding of €4.4 billion for the 2007–9 period.[16]

No doubt in recognition that it had become the largest donor and provider of development aid, the Commission in Brussels engaged, in 1997, Dialogue Development, a Danish organisation, to develop a strategy for supporting civil society development in BiH. This subsequently became part of the 'EU/Bosnia and Herzegovina Consultative Task Force', established in 1998 as 'a joint vehicle for political dialogue and expert advice'. Although a strategic framework for civil society assistance was developed, a comprehensive civil society support programme was never agreed or finalised (Smillie and Todorovic 2001: 43–4). However, the importance of civil society as a developmental priority, and the framing of civil society assistance in terms of future accession, were established as, and have remained, core objectives of the Commission: 'a strong civil society in BiH is an EU priority: building democracy from grass roots level, to eradicate discrimination, reconcile ethnic tensions, and improve human and civil rights, is critical to fulfilling the Copenhagen political criteria for EU Membership.'[17]

The allocation of assistance in BiH: the local Delegation of the EC

Unlike the situation in Serbia or Kosovo, where the EAR is, or has until recently been, responsible for the distribution and management of EU assistance, it is the EC Delegation in Sarajevo that has responsibility for allocating and monitoring assistance, helping to define the focus of projects, and managing the allocation of project grants. The Delegation, which was established in July 1996, has been distributing and managing the Commission's assistance to NGOs in BiH since 2001, when CARDS funding became available for Bosnian organisations. The Delegation administers a declining amount of funds, allocated by Brussels and reviewed annually as part of the Multi-Annual Indicative Planning Document. The amount allocated for 2007 was €615,000 for CARDS and EIDHR projects, compared to €835,000 the previous year and the overall amount of funding available during the period 2007–13, as part of IPA, for civil society-related projects will be reduced and assistance will be geared towards two campaigns: improving local democracy, and strengthening civil society at the local level.

Intent on improving relations between the NGO sector and government, the Delegation undertook a mapping exercise to look into the areas of policy in which co-operation with NGOs was most appropriate, where it was not necessary, and which organisations to involve. The underlying aim was to standardise such interaction and to co-ordinate donor assistance to ensure that NGOs were given a greater role in the policy-making process. At the local level the EU exerted pressure on reluctant municipalities to open up to civil society organisations as the hallmark of good governance. If they refused they were heavily criticised and denied access to structural funds and other assistance. As a consequence the interaction between local officials and elites and the NGO community in Sarajevo, Tuzla and Banja Luka improved considerably, to the extent that projects have been co-funded, schemes and initiatives taken over by the state at the end of a funded project, and a greater degree of co-operation around strategic planning and poverty reduction strategies in particular.

Although the CARDS/EIDHR/IPA funding allocation to BiH are implemented by the EC Delegation in Sarajevo, the management of aid has yet to be fully delegated or decentralised. This means essentially that the Delegation is involved in the distribution process rather than in the setting of priorities, budgeting and the direct financial management of assistance. As the Commission noted in its 2007 progress report,

> preparations to implement the decentralised implementation system have been slow during the reporting period. The complex institutional and political environment in the country has adversely affected a number of projects

and implementation rates have recently declined somewhat, although they remain high.

In other words, the constitutional structure (the existence of two separate entities, plus the absence of state-level political institutions) has complicated the process of transferring financial management responsibility from Brussels to the Delegation.

Prior to the availability of CARDS and EIDHR funding the Delegation initially helped co-ordinate EC humanitarian assistance. The exponential growth in the number of NGOs operating in the country in the second half of the 1990s occurred largely in response to the existence of multilateral and bilateral donor organisations and their willingness to provide funding for 'civil society'. The number of NGOs competing for EU projects in the early years of this decade was high, with the criteria for allocation set significantly above the capacity of most local organisations. The application process for small EU project grants in BiH is, as in Serbia, the standard global template, which requires applicant organisation to have a basic knowledge of project psycho-management tools. Yet there was very little knowledge and capacity regarding the application process amongst local organisations when the CARDS money was first made available. Even today, the fact that applicant NGOs are required to submit a log frame, a logic matrix identifying how the overall objectives of the proposed project would further EU national objectives for BiH, to specify how the specific objectives of the project will enhance the sustainable development of the organisation, and to outline the methodology for measuring outcomes and identifying indicators of achievement, proves prohibitive for the vast majority of NGOs.

Not surprisingly perhaps, the Delegation initially found it extremely difficult to allocate CARDS funding designated for civil society organisations. The quality of the applications for the 2004 'civil society network-building' round was considered so poor that out of a potential €7 million, only €1.5 million could be allocated. The local Delegation concluded in 2005 that the serious absorption deficit in BiH was due to the process which was simply too complex for most local NGOs who lacked the basic capacity to even apply, let alone deliver, the kind of projects that the EU wished to support. Paolo Scialla, then the team co-ordinator for the Democratic Stabilisation Programme at the Delegation in Sarajevo, acknowledged that 'such complex management tools are not easy for people who have been using them for years'. It was recognised then, as it is today, that the reason funds repeatedly benefit a few larger NGOs, with whom the EU has worked over the past three to four years, rather than newer local organisations, is to do with the complexity of the process and the insistence that NGOs obtain match-funding.[18] Invariably this rules out smaller NGOs and benefits those that have already established contacts with USAID, the OSCE or some other large international donor. In other words, an NGO has to be pretty well established and connected to gain access to EU funds.

In 2004 most applicant and recipient organisations were based in Sarajevo, where the majority of donors including the EU are located. Beyond Sarajevo recipient organisations are located in major towns and cities across the Federation (Mostar, Tuzla) and, to a lesser extent, Republika Srpska. This reflects the proliferation of donor activity in the country more generally, and the failure of assistance to move much beyond the immediate post-war humanitarian aid domains of the international community. In 2005, about 50 per cent of applications came from organisations located outside of the main urban areas, but most were rejected because the organisations did not 'have the capacity to pass'.[19] In 2006 the proportion of applications received from out-side of the main urban centres remained at 50 per cent, but the proportion of these applications that was successful was 30 per cent. Despite the improve-ment, the over-concentration of funding amongst Sarajevo-based organisa-tions, or NGOs with their headquaters in Mostar, Banja Luka or Tuzla, remains a significant problem.

As is the case in Serbia, the number of EU-funded projects being imple-mented in rural areas or in small towns, often by locally registered organisa-tions, gives a false impression of the level of proliferation; wise to the objective of spreading resources and know-how beyond big cities, many of the larger NGOs work with partner organisations from regional locations to pursue projects. The main grant holder will invariably be the Sarajevo-based organisa-tion and the implementing partner will play a relatively minor role in the proj-ect. Whilst this does serve to extend the operation of projects and channel the assistance beyond urban locations, discernible hierarchies of power within the NGO community are, nevertheless, being enforced rather than challenged. The concentration of knowledge, expertise and capacity remaining within the hands of a narrow band of increasingly professionalised organisations, and the gap between this urban elite and smaller more enmeshed grass roots organisa-tions is augmented. The regional concentration of EU funding and assistance for NGOs is also a consequence of the deeper political realities of BiH: that there is little NGO activity in the eastern part of RS is due to a local political cli-mate that is hostile towards NGOs and their intervention in domestic politics; the absence of NGO activity in Herzegovina has more to do with the relative prosperity of the area and financial links with Croatia than with the failure of the EU to support local activities.

However, the reality of each project grant round is that despite receiving in the region of 100 applications for each call, only about 12–15 of these will be realistic projects worthy of detailed consideration. Indeed, the Delegation invariably works with the same NGOs in each round, referred to informally by the Delegation task managers as 'our clients', with very few new organisations emerging.[20] Indeed, between 2005 and 2007 the same core of six organisations – Bospo, Vesta, Mozaik, Fondacija lokalne demokratije, Red Cross Tuzla, Zdravo da ste – received funding in each project round, both for CARDS and EIDHR.[21]

In terms of the allocation process, the local Delegation can exercise very little leeway: the application form is a global template and the information required, the stages of the process, and any amendments are prescribed by the Commission in Brussels. Two important changes, agreed in Brussels and introduced locally in 2006, were the introduction of the concept note for macro projects (a summary of the project submitted first, if the proposal passes this first stage then more detailed documentation is submitted), and the requirement of stamped documentation to be submitted with the application was scrapped in 2006. Both procedural amendments streamlined the process of allocation and reduced the burden on NGOs to provide extensive documentation at the outset of the process. The only modification to the application process that the local Delegation was able to make was to allow NGOs to submit some of the additional documentation in the local language rather than pay for translations, and also that electronic copies of the additional material were not required.

The decision-making process regarding the allocation of project funding involved all proposals being assessed by a small group of local assessors, drawn from the NGO community and with some knowledge and experience of project management. Each proposal was sent to at least two assessors for their comments and grading and a short list of proposals was drawn up and considered by the group of assessors and the task managers from the Delegation. The advantages of using local assessors is that they will have a more tuned knowledge of local needs and priorities as well as the existence of other donor initiatives and projects already occurring. Such a perspective is particularly useful insofar as the problem of duplication between projects and donor initiatives is a significant constraint and a source of much criticism. The disadvantage is that they will inevitably know the organisations involved and the individuals proposing to undertake the project.

Once a decision had been taken to fund a particular project the monitoring and evaluation were undertaken by the two task managers from the Delegation. This involved site visits, the submission by the organisation of quarterly financial reports and a final detailed report of outputs to the Delegation. In contrast to the situation in Serbia the monitoring and evaluation were not sub-contracted but were undertaken by the Delegation staff.

On the basis of the fact that the Delegation did not check or monitor the outcomes of projects beyond the duration of the award, no assessment of the medium- or long-term impact or sustainability of funded projects could take place. The only informal assessment the Delegation made regarding sustainable impact was based on the increased capacity of certain NGOs to develop and manage subsequent projects. Indeed the research undertaken for this study would suggest that in the vast majority of cases the only long-term impact of most funded projects is the development of project management know-how for the individual organisation – most projects were not picked up and continued by the local municipality or an appropriate state agency.

Although the Commission carried out regular audits of the work of the Delegation, and could request evaluations of individual projects if it so wished, monitoring of the CARDS and IPA programmes in BiH was undertaken solely by the Delegation, and results were then fed back to the Commission to form part of the regular reports published by Brussels. However, the focus of such analysis is the administration of allocated assistance, with the Commission's judgements based on the reports and data submitted by the Delegation. Whilst this scenario is entirely consistent with the Commission's objective of gradually decentralising responsibility for the management of assistance to the local Delegation, the difficulty lies in the fact that in the interim decisions regarding the amount of funding, the focus of assistance, and the terms and conditions for allocating funds are still taken in Brussels and therefore the capacity of either the Commission or the local Delegation to modify objectives and change the focus of assistance in accordance with evaluations of project outputs is somewhat restricted and indirect.

When asked to comment on their interaction with the Delegation in the context both of the project application process and the monitoring stage, the majority of recipient NGOs reported that whilst communication and transparency were often unsatisfactory during the decision-making stage, once the project had been awarded organisations enjoyed close contact with the task managers and were able to access help and advice. However, the research revealed a high level of uncertainty amongst applicant and recipient organisations regarding the provision and availability of feedback. Although the

Delegation task managers were keen to emphasise that they were more than willing to provide detailed feedback on failed applications, this provision was not advertised and was offered on the basis that NGOs had to approach the Delegation. Consequently many organisations did not obtain feedback on their failed applications, and those that did tended to receive little more than generic comments ('your application has not achieved the minimum score required for relevance to the objectives'), offering little detail or guidance.

Indeed, several of the recipient organisations interviewed reported an apparent lack of clarity and transparency regarding the decision-making process. A view echoed several times was that 'we never know when they will sit and discuss our projects, when they will decide; we can wait for half a year or one year for results'.[22]

An additional criticism to be levelled at the process of application concerns the type of training offered by the Delegation to prospective applicant organisations. The Delegation held two open sessions per year, one for each call for projects. The training offered at these sessions was basic, focusing on technical aspects such as how to complete the application process and some further clarification regarding the focus of the project call and financial aspects. The sessions, which were conducted in the local language rather than in English (the language of the process), lasted for about two hours.[23] Whilst this was useful for organisations that had little or no experience of applying for funding, organisations that had been awarded a number of project grants required more sophisticated training to enable them to develop larger macro projects, or to develop proposals for extending existing micro projects. The absence of comprehensive training, particularly for more experienced organisations with a track record and existing project-management capacity, had actually prompted a couple of the larger NGOs to offer specific training in EU project grant writing either separately from or in conjunction with the Delegation.[24] Several organisations reported that they found it difficult to understand certain questions and to ascertain what information was being asked for. The Delegation in Sarajevo has refused to translate the forms into local languages; however, the Centre for Civil Society Promotion has provided a translation and placed this on its website.[25]

The challenge for the EU is clearly to develop further the capacities of the successful NGOs with whom it works. Whilst a few NGOs had graduated from micro projects to applying directly to Brussels for large macro projects,[26] most of the organisations with whom the Delegation worked were engaged in small 12-month projects, moving from theme to theme rather than developing large programmes and building specific specialisations. The Delegation was also criticised by certain NGOs for failing to clarify how particular project calls fitted into the EU's broader objectives for BiH.

However, perhaps the most complicated criticism for the Delegation to address was the claim that the project application process actually masked considerable weakness and a lack of capacity on the part of applicants. This was particularly the case where municipalities applied for EU funds in conjunction with a local NGO. Despite declaring itself the lead applicant, the municipality was often significantly weaker in terms of knowledge of the process and understanding of the proposed project than the NGO. However, municipalities had greater resources to commit to the process of completing the application form. In other words, the ability to complete the form and to mobilise the resources necessary to put together an application was not a true measure of the capacities of applicants.

Scope, focus and impact of EU-funded projects

According to the Delegation task manager responsible for the allocation and monitoring of CARDS and EIDHR project funding, the ideal projects, worthy of EU assistance, were those 'that have three key components: working with the government on legislative aspects; then to work in the field and to prepare activities, and to be able to implement these activities'. The sort of projects that were particularly favoured are those that involved 'a narrow action' – not too ambitious in terms of what they intended to deliver, but were able to influence legislation, prepare activities and deliver the programme in conjunction with the municipality or other relevant state agencies.[27]

Although the broad themes under which projects were supported was reasonably clear-cut – environment, support for returnees and victims of torture, promotion of local democracy, human and minority rights, sustainable economic development – the actual range of projects and the scope of the activities funded through EU micro grants as part of CARDS or EIDHR were wide and outputs varied considerably.

For similar amounts of funding (between €60,000 and €80,000) projects delivered strikingly different outcomes in terms of policy input, quality of service provision and the extent to which there was a creation of knowledge. For instance, the organisation Fondeko received €61,000 to conduct a survey into the attitudes of 3,000 students towards the environment, hold a series of small workshops, and to produce and distribute an environmental handbook to college students in Tuzla, Doboj and Zenica and another booklet for teachers and educators.[28] The publications were factual and not directly related to any particular policy development or environmental agenda; they were not available as an electronic resource.

The Delegation provided a similar amount of money (€56,000) to the organisation Fondacija Lokalne Demokratije to undertake a project in 2006 that involved compiling a detailed report based on testimonials from women victims of rape and torture during the war. The project provided, with the help of legal experts, specialist analysis of which laws needed to be changed in order to protect women and to grant them legal status on a par with victims in Republika Srpska.[29] The report, which was presented to the Federal Assembly as part of a wider campaign, was compiled on the basis of meetings held in each canton. The Assembly accepted all the recommendations included in the report, and a new law was presented for ratification in September 2006.[30] Of all the EU-funded projects analysed in BiH, FLD was the only organisation apparently directly engaged in policy deliberation and advocacy. Yet the politicisation of their project and the impact they were able to exert on the Federal Assembly has to be placed in context: the issue of victims of rape and torture committed during the war gained high-profile status after the release of the Bosnian film *Grbavica*. The internationally acclaimed film by Jasmila Zbanic, which tells the harrowing story of a Sarajevan victim of rape, was nominated for numerous awards and was internationally acclaimed and was released just as FLD's project was drawing to a close. The organisation was able to exploit the fact that several international organisations, including the Council of Europe, latched on to the issue and exerted pressure on the Bosnian government to take action to protect victims of rape and torture.

Other projects run by the organisation were orientated towards service provision and training, and were thus more typical of EU-funded projects in BiH generally. They included managing and establishing networks of NGOs across the country to provide assistance for victims of violence; training school teachers in Sarajevo canton to recognise victims of domestic violence; and a campaign to remove the names of indicted war criminals from schools.[31]

An EU-funded project undertaken by the same organisation in the late 1990s involved establishing two shelters in the Sarajevo canton for women victims of domestic violence. This project saw the EU initially provide 70 per cent of funding and the cantonal ministry of social affairs providing the remaining 30 per cent over a two-year period. In the only case of its kind, the ministry ultimately assumed 70 per cent financial responsibility for the shelters after the EU project ended therefore maximising the sustainable outcome of this particular EU initiative and building the sort of cross-sectoral partnership that is extremely rare in BiH. Indeed, the vast majority of EU projects were not continued beyond the duration of the project, nor did they usually lead to longer-term partnerships between the non-governmental and governmental sectors. Hitherto, all the projects undertaken by FLD have involved either the compilation of data and policy-related information appertaining to re-integration and dealing with the legacies of war. However, in response to a call for proposals from Brussels in 2007 for macro projects on the theme of eco-tourism, the organisation proposed a scheme to reconstruct a village outside Sarajevo. The decision to apply for larger funds and to engage in this kind of activity stems from a realisation that small one-year grants from the EU do not provide the organisation with long-term sustainability; they need to employ more staff, obtain bigger premises and to generally expand the organisation even if this involves engaging in different types of activities and projects.

Several of the projects funded by the Delegation resulted in the provision of important services and training, particularly in the field of education. What was striking about such projects was the amount achieved for relatively small amounts of funding. Examples of two such 'good value' projects involved edu-cational multicultural and inclusive training for schoolteachers (Step-by-Step) and a project to improve the provision of special educational needs within pri-mary education within Sarajevo (Duga). In the case of the latter, the organisa-tion received two small EU grants for 12-month projects to provide, in the first instance, support and training for teachers working with children with SEN in six communities across the Sarajevo canton, and in the second project, to pro-vide advocacy training for parents of children with special needs in six schools within the Sarajevo canton. The aim of this latter project was to enable parents to obtain better resources and provision from their local school and munici-pality. The impact and outputs of both projects were, considering the small size of the grants and the short time-frame, impressive: over 300 teachers received support as part of the first project, which also saw the publication of a lengthy teachers' guide; the second project supported 120 children and their families, ran 28 workshops for parents, school managers and municipal education officials.[32]

Although ostensibly the projects involved low-level interaction between the NGO and government or state agencies – Duga obtained written permission from the cantonal ministry of education to work within the schools selected for the projects – the actual governance impact was slightly greater: participation in the workshops and training sessions enabled parents, teachers and govern-ment officials to interact, to discuss and plan provision, and fostered a raised awareness on all parts concerning the needs of children and their families with learning difficulties. What Duga also pushed for as part of the discussions was a change in the curriculum at canton level to take account of special needs, but also for the entity ministry to address inclusive education principles and ideas. The aim here was to build up the advocacy skills of parents and communities so that they, rather than the NGO, will ultimately push for change and engage with ministry officials and education policy makers.

However, it has to be acknowledged that whilst Duga's project was apparently successful in providing training to over 300 teachers in six communities, involving parents, social workers and community leaders and building their advocacy skills, the involvement of the municipality and the education authorities was minimal. In the end the only contact with government involved obtaining written permission from the Sarajevo canton education ministry to organise the project and to work in schools, and the participation of a junior minister at a roundtable discussion at the start of the project.[33]

What is noteworthy about the organisation Step-by-Step is that they have a very clearly defined focus and strategic plan and that, in contrast to other Bosnian NGOs, have only responded to EU project calls with a specific education focus. The organisation, which was established in the mid 1990s as part of the Soros Foundation in BiH, is not dependent on EU funding, receives money from a wide array of international donors, and is also established as a local foundation.

Step-by-Step has run two EU-funded projects: the first, a 12-month micro project awarded in 2005, was entitled 'Parenting with Confidence' and involved the provision of pre-school activities for children and parenting skills workshops for parents in three communities with a high proportion of marginalised groups (particularly Roma families). The organisation managed to obtain additional donor funding from CIDA (Canadian International Development Agency) to extend the initiative into three further communities. Although, as is the case with most EU short-term projects, the initiative ended once the grant ran out, there was a sustainable element and longer-term governance aspect to this project: the organisation managed to convince each ministry of education in BiH (there are 13 in total, plus seven pedagogical institutes, including cantons, the two entities and Brcko) to appoint a co-ordinator within the ministry to work with Step-by-Step to promote child-focused learning and the principles of the Parenting with Confidence programme. This marked an important development insofar as it brought a vestige of co-ordination to the provision of education in BiH, particularly in the absence of a state-level education ministry. The co-ordinators, who were trained by Step-by-Step but were employed by the ministries, were responsible for appointing trainers in local schools, organising in-service training as well as helping teachers and schools plan for the needs of SEN pupils. The programme co-ordinator of Step-by-Step summarised the objective of the project thus: 'we do not want ownership of this (training reforms) . . . we want child-centred methodology (practiced) across BiH.'[34]

In terms of understanding why this particular EU-funded initiative involving a local NGO was successful in engendering co-operation across the state/governmental and non-state/non-governmental sectors, much perhaps had to do with the fact that the issues being promoted by Step-by-Step were very much in tune with the focus of education reform in BiH since 2002. In other words, there was an incentive on the part of the ministries and officials to work with the NGO to deliver shared objectives. But the fact that Step-by-Step is a relatively long-established (1995) professional organisation with international links, a highly professional and trained staff, and considerable project management and training know-how undoubtedly goes a long way to explain the successfulness of the projects. In this case the EU successfully supported an existing initiative, providing capacity assistance and resources for a well-established organisation with clear strategic goals.

Typical of several EU-funded initiatives in the country, a project entitled 'Enhancing Good Governance and the Promotion and Protection of Human Rights in BiH' and run by the organisation AEOBiH set out to provide assistance and training in community development in three rural municipalities (Derventa, Stolac and Maglaj). The aim of the project was to involve the local community in strategic planning, to augment their advocacy skills and capacity to contribute to decision-making, and to prepare and improve the quality of project proposals to be considered by the local municipality. For example, to help residents apply to the municipality for road repair and improvements, but also for ecological changes and development of schools and other public facilities.

In the case of Derventa municipality, for example, the project targeted the serious issue of electricity supply in the area. The local municipality did not have responsibility for the supply and maintenance of power and the outcome of the project was that municipal officials and representatives from the local community jointly, and successfully, lobbied the entity-level electricity company. Many of the other schemes proposed and developed as a consequence of the project also came into fruition: subways were cleaned for children to use, roads were resurfaced, community centres re-built for returnees. Most often the project resources benefited the community organisations – *mesna zajednica* – that had existed under the socialist period, but where these were not in place, for example in Stolac, they were established as part of the initiative.

Although the EU-funded project was successful and delivered tangible out-comes in the three areas, the case also highlighted the impact of EU funding on NGOs and how engagement with the process of applying for small short-term grants can transform organisations quite significantly. AEOBiH is a long-standing Bosnian NGO that has over 1,100 members from across the country. Its members include former OSCE staff, judges and members of the political and judicial establishment, whose interests lie in elections, electoral reform and monitoring, and the education of voters. All other projects and activities involved election-related activities and in this sense the EU project was a diver-sion from the organisation's long-term goals. The decision to apply for EU funding – the organisation has made seven applications in total, out of which only one has been successful thus far – was born out of the recognition that the EU has become the most significant donor in the country and that other sources have declined. Senior staff within the organisation acknowledged that, whilst their future sustainability depended on cultivating a relationship with the Delegation and acquiring a funding track record, the impact of such a strategy was likely to be a change in the type of projects and activities on which the organisation works.[35]

AEOBiH staff found the process of applying for EU funding 'a big com-mitment . . . (taking two members of staff) 15 full working days'. This was par-ticularly noteworthy in an organisation with considerable existing capacity compared to other Bosnian NGOs; the programme co-ordinator of AEOBiH trained other NGOs in project proposal writing and has excellent English language skills.

The vast majority of projects surveyed involved, as already noted, the provi-sion of a community or public service, sometimes, though not always, engag-ing state agencies or ministries in the process. Typical of such initiatives was a project run by the Sarajevo-based environmental organisation Ekotim, which received an EU grant in 2006 to help the local municipality in the town of Kresovo, 35 km from Sarajevo, to construct an environmental action plan. The €88,000 project, obtained in conjunction with a larger separate organisation, involved Ekotim undertaking research and liaising with local businesses, local utility companies and the public in order to prepare a plan for reducing waste, which was then adopted by the municipality.[36] However this was just one aspect of the EU-funded project; the main focus was to engage school children in recycling activities in the town with the aim, through an education campaign, of reducing the use of plastic bags. This component engaged government only insofar as reducing waste was a priority within the Kresovo municipality's strategic development plan.

A somewhat different project, jointly funded by the EU and USAID, began in 2005 with the direct aim of building co-operation between the NGO sector and government. This initiative, run by the organisation Civil Society Promotion Centre, provided the only example of a project involving the direct construction of governance interaction. The project involved the organisation working closely with the Council of Ministers (the state-level government) with the aim of creating new regional networks within the NGO sector and also establishing a code of practice governing relations between organisations and government.[37] The two outcomes of the project were an agreed code signed in May 2007, and the creation of a network of 300 NGOs committed to the terms of the agreement and ready to engage with government ministries and state agencies. The most tangible outcome of the agreement (and the project) was more formal and effective interaction between NGOs and local government in the 142 municipalities across the country, plus the establishment of a government office at state level for co-operation with NGOs. No such formal national-level co-ordination previously existed and the hope is that this will greatly improve the co-ordination of interaction as well as the quality of the policy partnerships. Interviewed in May 2007, towards the end of the project, the organisation also hoped to establish an NGO council within parliament as a means for more frequent and improved communication, and to encourage greater transparency in the funding of NGOs by municipalities.[38]

The organisation also received EU funding for various other projects involving what might be termed governance interaction between the sectors. For instance, a project started in December 2006 aimed to engage NGOs and the ombudsmen of both entities in the monitoring of human rights in 30 municipalities across the country.[39] The focus of the project was to gather information and data on rights violations and to monitor the way municipalities dealt, or failed to deal, with cases of abuse. This data was then used as the basis to involve the ombudsmen as well as local organisations and experts and to push for legislative change where necessary.[40]

Conclusion

What is immediately evident from the qualitative data on recipient NGOs in Bosnia is that EU assistance delivered some considerable benefit, particularly with regard to service provision. However, the impact varied considerably across projects and initiatives: in some cases €70,000 resulted in a project that had clearly transformed the lives of target communities, had provided life-improving skills, or engaged government or state agencies in the process of legislative review or the enactment of new regulatory frameworks. In other cases the outcomes were far less impressive and delivered no observable sustainable benefit beyond the terms of the project. Whilst all the issues funded, with very few exceptions, addressed critical issues that were worthy of donor assistance, it was not always immediately evident what the focus of a particular initiative might be in terms of the SAp goals or the wider enlargement agenda.

What the research data on EU assistance in BiH illustrated was the extent to which impact is determined as much by institutional and political realities as by the existing capacities of recipient organisations. The constitutional set-up in Bosnia, which comprises state weakness and political fragmentation, somewhat paradoxically both weakens and strengthens the role of NGOs: the EU funds organisations to take on roles that would otherwise be undertaken by government or the market, but ultimately the power of the NGO sector to form sustainable partnerships with the state and to ensure a long-term advocacy role in policy deliberation and enforcement is limited by the incapacity of government agencies.

4
The EU in Serbia

Introduction

The primary aim of this second empirical chapter is to provide an exposition of the empirical data and analysis of EU assistance to Serbia delivered in the context of the SAp and under the remit of CARDS assistance. The data presented and the core argument of this chapter are derived from extensive qualitative and quantitative research of the projects funded by the European Commission through the European Agency for Reconstruction (EAR) and, to a lesser extent, the local Delegation of the Commission in Belgrade during the period 2004–7. The research focused specifically on the focus and outcomes of the assistance, the process of allocation and monitoring, as well as consideration of the various constraints on the effectiveness and sustainability of the projects from the perspective of recipients, but also from that of the EAR and the officials within the Delegation.

The chapter will begin by briefly sketching the political context in Serbia and the basis on which the EU has become involved in the provision of assistance. Much of the assistance is delivered through NGOs, as providers of services and as representations of civil society. But the highly contested nature of the concept of civil society in Serbia, the bitter disagreement regarding what constitutes civil society, its remit and the parameters of its power, reflects the deep-seated rifts that characterise the country's contemporary politics. Some discussion of the politics of civil society is thus deemed necessary in order to highlight the contentious aspect of EU assistance and the controversy surrounding NGOs. The remaining sections of the chapter provide detailed analysis of the projects funded, their outcomes and an analysis of the various constraints on effectiveness and the sustainability of outcomes.

Serbian politics after Milošević

The so-called 'democratic revolution' of 5 October 2000, the peaceful transfer of power that removed Slobodan Milošević from office, generated great enthusiasm and high expectations both nationally and internationally regarding the prospects for genuine regime change in Serbia. However, the absence of high-profile 'roundtable' negotiations, such a familiar emblem and intrinsic feature of the revolutions of Central and Eastern Europe at the end of the 1980s, or indeed any significant resistance on the part of the old elite, suggests, with hindsight, that Serbia's 'transition' was different and in some way flawed.

Although the process of regime change in Serbia appeared to resemble what Share (1987) refers to as a 'transition through transaction', the former elite was not displaced from the judiciary, business and the security services. Indeed, the transaction, inasmuch as there was one, involved the leaders of the Democratic Opposition of Serbia (DOS), the anti-Milošević coalition, making a compromise deal with the old elite in order to form an interim government and hold early parliamentary elections in Serbia. Since the powers of the Yugoslav President were fairly limited, the opposition needed to gain control of the republican parliament to rule effectively.[1] Although the socialists had no interests or obligations to yield early elections, they did so in exchange for guarantees that the new government 'would not take supra-legal revenge on them or their assets' (Krnjevic-Miskovic 2001). The deal also ensured that the old elite, now convinced that Milošević could not survive and defend their interests, managed to retain a privileged position, exercising control over the pace of reform and shaping the process of 'regime change' in early October 2000 (Vasic 2005). Indeed, both the army and the state security services (JSO) remained largely unreformed, certainly until the assassination of the Serbian prime minister, Zoran Djindjic, in 2003.

The governing DOS coalition, which was composed of 18 parties, all claiming a share of executive power, was plagued with difficulties from the outset. So much so, that the process of decision-making was increasingly transferred from state institutions to the DOS presidency, where small parties had a disproportionate weight.

Not surprisingly, the main bone of contention within the coalition concerned the pace and nature of reforms. Divisions were particularly pronounced between Prime Minister Djindjic, who was a proponent of radical and speedy reforms, and President Koštunica, who insisted that existing (socialist-era) institutional procedures were upheld, thus slowing the pace of reform quite considerably. The conflict between the two sides was exacerbated by the issue of co-operation with the ICTY and the extradition of Milošević in particular. Co-operation with The Hague was a condition for the disbursement of financial aid by the West; Koštunica's opposition to co-operating with the extradition demands therefore led to a political stalemate culminating in Koštunica's Serbian Democratic Party (DSS) pulling out of the DOS and joining the opposition in June 2001.

Though the retreat of the DSS did not undermine the DOS government as such, it did put an end to the unity of the so-called 'democratic bloc' and led to the re-emergence of the same political divisions that had characterised the opposition during the Milošević era. It also contributed to the disillusionment of the vast majority of voters, who increasingly disengaged from politics, as illustrated by the massive boycott of the elections for the president of Serbia during 2002. The political schism generated additional constraints to the implementation of the reforms being promoted by Djindjic, who was increasingly forced to rely on extra-governmental institutions and decrees in order to bypass the parliament.[2] Electoral competition amongst the democratic coalition prevented the new authorities from carrying out institutional reforms necessary for the consolidation of democracy (Lazic 2005: 132). Indeed, the new authorities were unable to introduce a new constitution and to substantially reform the judiciary, security and media sectors.

The political paralysis combined with the absence of economic and fiscal reforms (such as the controversial 'tax on extra profit' which was meant to penalise those that had profited and become wealthy by corruption and collaboration with Milošević) suggested a stifling continuity with the Milošević era, with the business elite continuing to play an important role in political life, providing financial support for different parties, and receiving concessions, lucrative contracts and political favours in exchange. Moreover, during this period the power and prestige of politicians on both sides of the political divide was heavily dependent on their respective relationships with the security sector, whether it be the Yugoslav army in the case of Koštunica, or ties with the Serbian state security services in the case of Djindjic (Edmunds 2008: 33–4).

The overriding feature of Serbian politics during this period was relationships of mutual dependence between politicians and security actors, which provided the latter with a high degree of autonomy and influence particularly with regard to the issue of co-operation with the ICTY. Despite JSO interference and the emerging split between Koštunica and Djindjic over co-operation with the tribunal, increasing foreign pressure meant that the government had little option but to co-operate and tackle organised crime.

The government responded to the assassination of Prime Minister Djindjic in March 2003 by introducing a state of emergency and measures to purge rogue elements of the old regime. If this period was characterised by the gradual corrosion and collapse of the DOS coalition, it also witnessed a renewed political mobilisation of citizens. Allegations of corruption and continuous scandals involving members of the governing coalition fuelled a growing sense of political apathy and disengagement.[3] This prompted a rebirth of mass mobilisation and protest, which was orchestrated by the opposition with the intention of bringing down the DOS coalition.

The early parliamentary elections held in December 2003 brought important changes to the Serbian political scene. From then onwards, the right-wing SRS, whose leader is indicted for war crimes by the ICTY, established itself as the most important single party in the country. Koštunica's DSS emerged in second place, and thus gained a leading position amongst the 'democratic' bloc. The DOS coalition dissolved prior to the elections, and several of the constituent small parties failed to win enough votes to enter parliament.

No longer President of the now defunct rump Yugoslavia (which had been reconstituted as the State Union of Serbia and Montenegro on 4 February 2003), Koštunica aspired to be prime minister and set about constructing a minority government with a number of small parties (SPO, NS and G17) that had emerged from the ruins of the DOS. Most controversially, the government also relied on the support of Milošević's Socialist Party of Serbia (SPS). Bereft of its assassinated leader, the most liberal and pro-western of all Serbia's parties, the Democratic Party (DS) was forced into opposition having failed to reach an agreement with the DSS. The party did, however, partially recover political influence in June 2004, when its new leader, Boris Tadić, won the presidential elections in a close run-off with the SRS candidate, Tomislav Nikolić, a victory repeated in 2008.

While the new government pursued important economic reforms, there was considerable doubt as to whether the Koštunica government would carry out the liberal reforms proposed by the DOS coalition. Indeed the DSS-led government was accused by both domestic and international critics of turning Serbia into an illiberal democracy, 'rehabilitating Milošević-era personnel and policies' reinforcing nationalism and failing to make a clear 'break with the past'.[4] Notwithstanding the slow pace of economic and domestic political reforms, it was the government's approach to co-operation with the ICTY, consisting of providing material and legal support for those indictees who voluntarily surrender to the tribunal, which sparked the most controversy. Although initially this policy proved relatively successful in getting war crimes suspects in the dock, it irritated foreign governments and human rights activists who considered it half-hearted.[5] Co-operation with the ICTY eventually came to a standstill as the authorities refused to arrest and extradite those war criminals that did not surrender. This issue was increasingly jeopardising Serbia's relationships with the European Union and in May 2006 the EU suspended negotiations over the Stabilisation and Accession Agreement (SAA) in response to the government's failure to hand over the former Bosnian Serb general Ratko Mladić.

Serbia and the EU:
political context and recent developments

Serbia's relationship with the EU in the post-Milošević era has been inextricably bound with the status of Kosovo, compliance with the ICTY, human rights and the process of democratisation. Indeed, EU accession, influence and assistance strike at the heart of debates concerning nationalism and identity, the influence of the Orthodox Church versus liberal (western) rights and freedoms, human and minority rights versus ethno-nationalism and the ethnic state, and the status of civil society, all of which have characterised the country's political life and discourse since the early 1990s and the disintegration of Yugoslavia.

But it is undoubtedly the issue of Kosovo that has, and to an extent continues, to over-shadow and shape Serbia's relationship with Brussels. Prior to February 2008 and the Assembly of Kosovo's declaration of independence, the polarisation between EU accession on one hand and Kosovo's independence from Serbia on the other seemed a stark and intractable obstacle to progress. The dichotomy was underscored by a fundamental tension between Serbia cultivating closer relations with Western Europe and the EU, and its political proximity to Russia, the major source of opposition to Kosovo independence within the UN Security Council. During 2006, amid stalemate in negotiations with Brussels, commentators viewed the Kosovo issue as the key independent variable that determined foreign policy and dictated political and social attitudes (anti-European, anti-Western, anti-liberal) in contemporary Serbia.

Assessing Serbia's political development from the perspective of early 2009, in light of recent developments – the arrest by the Serbian security forces of Radovan Karadžić in July 2008, the re-election of President Boris Tadić and a pro-EU DS-led government, and the signing of the SAA – one is forced to concede, however tentatively, the dawn of a new political era, characterised by closer ties with the EU and predicted progress towards accession. Years of recalcitrant nationalism and anti-EU posturing under Koštunica have been replaced by a new pro-EU consensus. This has been brought about in large part by the declaration itself, which immediately ended the uncertainty and sense of brinkmanship that had stalled relations with the international community. But it is also a consequence of the outcome of the presidential and parliamentary elections and the timing of the EU's decision to sign the SAA.

Despite bitter recriminations against the EU by DSS politicians, and attempts made to link EU accession with Kosovo's independence by former Prime Minister Koštunica, the signing of the agreement in April 2008, during a parliamentary election campaign being fought squarely in terms of Kosovo versus the EU, undoubtedly helped shift the political consensus by giving a clear sign to Serbian voters that EU accession was now, after months of stalemate and wrangling, a serious prospect and that the Commission took Serbia's membership seriously. The signing of the SAA also helped solidify support for the DS-led 'For a European Serbia' parliamentary group. Following much wrangling after the May elections, the formation in July 2008 of a DS-led coalition (comprising the DS, G17, SPO, LSV and SDP) under the premiership of Mirko Cvetkovic, confirmed the pro-EU shift that had occurred with the re-election of Boris Tadić as president at the start of the year. If there were still lingering doubts regarding the extent to which change had occurred, the arrest in July 2008 and subsequent extradition to The Hague of Radovan Karadžić, the indicted war criminal accused of orchestrating the 1995 mass killings of Bosniaks in Srebrenica, confirmed the shift towards co-operation with the demands of the EU and the international community.

Perhaps the key to understanding the subsequent pace of progress – which has been remarkable and undoubtedly very rapid – is change within the powerful security services. The nationalist and close ally of Koštunica, Rade Bulatović, was replaced as head of the security services by Saša Vukadinović, a respected career investigator with a track record in smashing Belgrade mafia networks, just prior to the arrest of Karadžić.

The EU response has been enthusiastic but still appropriately quite guarded. Commission officials and foreign ministers from member states have called for Serbia to be placed on a fast-track to EU membership, which essentially means allowing for the ratification and application of the SAA and thus the prospect of candidacy status. However, although Olli Rehn, the European Commissioner for enlargement, has readily acknowledged that the arrest of Karadžić represents a 'milestone' in Serbia's relations with the EU and demonstrates that the new government is 'very serious' about co-operation with the ICTY,[6] he acknowledges that significant obstacles remain, not least the requirement of the EU for Serbia to recognise the independence of Kosovo. Though the new pro-western government has clearly prioritised EU membership over Kosovo – Vuk Jeremić, the foreign minister of the new government, commented after the arrest of Karadžić that 'European integration is the utmost priority of this government' – the DS-led coalition government remains resolutely opposed to recognising the sovereignty of the disputed territory and has engaged the International Court of Justice (ICJ) in its legal challenge.[7] There is also the issue of the arrest of the other fugitive, Ratko Mladić.

What events during 2008 suggest is that the Kosovo issue was ultimately less intractable than broadly generally assumed, and that despite talk of a deadlock and divided loyalties, Serbia's relationship with Russia is less important than the prospect of EU membership. In addition, Russia's surprising acquiescence on the issue may well prove ultimately to be the most significant variable. Indeed, even prior to the parliamentary election, during the previous Koštunica-led government, a political fault-line seemed to have opened up between those, such as Vuk Jeremić, the foreign minister, who were keen to emphasise that Serbia's key foreign policy priority was EU entry, and those DSS members loyal to Prime Minister Vojislav Koštunica, who continue to affirm that there could be no negotiation on Kosovo's independence.

In terms of EU accession, the tasks that lie ahead are considerable. Whilst the fact that nearly a decade since Milošević's defeat Serbia has failed to become 'a decentralised, modern country adjusted to European standards'[8] requires the enactment of fundamental laws, it also requires affirmative action to deal with corruption and illiberal factions amongst the elites. As Edmunds has recently argued, it is hard to contest the claim that Serbia is a democracy that has successfully undergone a process of democratisation (Edmunds 2008). Where the transition has been most deficient and where Serbia still seems poised between Russia and the West is with regard to the entrenchment of liberal norms and the capacity of the state to enforce and uphold such values. Rather than there being a significant outright resistance to democratisation, there has occurred in the post-Milošević period what Edmunds describes as 'a co-option of the practices and procedures of democratic politics through the emergence or persistence of informal institutions of governance' that has culminated in a situation whereby 'the process of democratisation has actually facilitated the consolidation of illiberal interests in Serbian politics and society' (Edmunds 2008: 4). The basic argument here is that practices such as the so-called 'reserved domains', whereby certain interests and organisations in society are impenetrable and are beyond the control of democratically elected elites, or control of the media, or the power and influence of the security forces and the military, have been able to continue and co-exist alongside democratic institutions. Indeed, for critics the façade of democracy and the over-arching processes of democratic elections merely provide a cover for illiberal practices to flourish.

Significant progress has been made since 2000 in removing corrupt elites from political life, establishing a new formal institutional framework in which day-to-day politics takes place, as well as enacting a swathe of new laws designed to approximate EU standards and to formalise and institutionalise democratic politics. Yet the informal networks of the socialist period have proved not only hard to penetrate, but have actually gained a new momentum in the context of economic liberalisation, globalisation and the ubiquitous emphasis on governance (Kostovicova 2006). These networks, which are both a fusion of economic and political linkages extending beyond Serbia's new borders and encompassing ethnic networks and allegiances, have been able to exploit the fragmentation of formal politics, the instability of coalitions and the overall dominance and patronage of certain personalities (Edmunds 2008: 7).

Such a reality immediately places Serbia closer to Russia and other so-called illiberal democracies (Krastev 2006). Serbian politics in the post-Milošević and post-Yugoslav period has been characterised by the power of informal governance networks encompassing transnational networks of corruption, unregulated economic activity, trafficking and a host of other illegal global linkages that appear to wield far greater power and legitimacy than the formal democratic institutions and processes (Kostovicova 2006). This then poses the question of how successfully, through its twin-track approach of assistance and conditionality, the EU has managed to penetrate such networks and construct new modes of governance that engage formal and informal, state and non-state actors (Börzel et al. 2008). The danger is that rather than foster transparent and non-hierarchic networks, assistance will simply instrumentalise and institutionalise existing networks and corrupt linkages. In other words, will the process of building governance, engaging NGOs, moving decision-making and service provision beyond formal suppliers and policy makers actually strengthen the transnational networks in Serbia that are weakening state capacity and threatening the consolidation and penetration of democratic processes?

If progress towards Europeanisation is to be found anywhere, it is in the realm of the economy and meeting EU criteria with regard to economic liberalisation and trade. But even here long-awaited and fundamental reforms, such as the creation of a legal and regulatory framework to entice foreign investors

and combat endemic corruption, have yet to be fully enacted and implemented. A recent OECD report on Serbia noted that 'corruption is an obstacle
to doing business . . . and undermines investment and economic growth'.[9]

Nevertheless, the political reality seems to suggest an overriding momentum and consensus regarding co-operation and compliance with EU requi-
sites. Public opinion surveys during 2007 suggested widespread support for
EU membership amongst the population at large.[10] However, whilst most
commentators agree that there has undoubtedly been a shift in favour of the
EU and away from support for hard-line nationalism, what enthusiasm there is
rests on limited knowledge regarding what the process will involve. Thus far
the pace of progress has been haltingly slow, with the prospect of membership
remaining distant. In order to harness the positive momentum and to thwart a
political backlash tangible progress needs to be made towards candidate status
and ultimately full membership.

This will involve facing some significant difficulties, including the arrest of
Mladić and other remaining indicted war criminals, and issues relating to
respect for human and minority rights, not to mention recognition of Kosovo.
In their annual publications for 2005 and 2006, the Helsinki Committee for
Human Rights in Serbia have documented a swathe of human and minority
rights abuses committed by the Serbian state without any reprimand from the
previous Koštunica government (2004–6).[11] Critics contend that tacit support
for the EU means nothing more than the government making certain legal,
institutional and procedural changes to accommodate and gain access to EU
aid and assistance, without even attempting the necessary fundamental shift in
political values, practices and norms ultimately required for full entry.

Civil society: the ideological battleground

The role and function of civil society, the status and influence of non-governmental organisations, and the attitude of the government towards including
civil society in political life represents the political and ideological battleground
in contemporary Serbia. Since the early 1990s it has stood at the frontier
between reform and stagnation, between a descent into semi-authoritarianism
and genuine regime change. Risking severe repression, civil society organisations – in particular the 150 NGOs that formed IZLAZ (exit) 2000 – played a
critical role in the downfall of the old regime by campaigning for free and fair
presidential elections and helping to mobilise voters, particularly the young
(Minic and Dereta 2005: 79). Civil society thus came to represent the liberal
democratic conscience of Serbia and, not surprisingly, the political inclusion

and legal status of civil society organisations has subsequently stood as a powerful measure of regime change, providing a lens on political liberalisation, westernisation, and the upholding of human and minority rights (Biserko 2006).

NGOs in Serbia:
antipathy or accommodation?

Critics of the Koštunica government's attitude towards civil society have either tended to focus on the absence of a coherent and enabling legal and fiscal infrastructure from within which NGOs and civil society organisations can maximise their role and influence, or have sought to highlight the political animosity and deliberate condemnation of organisations deemed by the regime to be political opponents. The two issues are, of course, connected. The previous Koštunica government lacked the political will to strengthen civil society and this explains why the draft law on NGOs was not enacted. Indeed, the law was originally drafted in 2001 and was about to be presented to parliament for ratification by the reformist government of Zoran Djindjic. His assassination and the collapse of his government delayed the passage of the legislation. The law was about to be presented to parliament again towards the end of 2006, just prior to the collapse of the Koštunica government. It is almost certain that the law will be enacted during this parliament; the current coalition government is broadly in favour of enacting this basic piece of legislation. The Council of Europe and, rather belatedly, the EU have also exerted pressure on the new government to enact the law.[12] However, once passed the law will simply offer NGOs legal status; their capacity to raise funds, to gain tax exemption and to exist financially as charitable organisations will have to be enshrined in subsequent legislation. Nevertheless, granting NGOs legal status effectively gives them recognition in Serbia as legitimate entities. Such is the animosity that has been directed towards NGOs in recent years, this is seen as an important first stage.

The other civil society: pariahs of the state

In stark contrast with the 'institutionalised' NGOs, several of which receive EU project grants and are engaged in low-level policy deliberation, the major domestic human rights advocacy groups (HRG) continue to experience a difficult relationship with the Serbian authorities. The widely unpopular and politicised nature of their activities, essentially centred around issues of war crimes and transitional justice, makes them a prime target of nationalist attacks and an uneasy partner for reformist elites.

Essentially composed of Belgrade-based intellectuals, most of these organisations were established in the beginning of the 1990s as anti-war movements. During Milošević's rule, they represented an alternative voice to the domestic nationalist discourse, and became internationally prominent by exposing the war crimes and human rights abuses perpetrated by the Serbian authorities. Like most independent organisations, the HRGs were the targets of continuous repression by a semi-authoritarian regime, which tolerated critics only to the extent that they did not endanger its hold on power.

In spite of the political changes initiated in October 2000, the activities of human rights organisations remained highly contentious and unwelcome by the authorities. The new government clearly had no intention of addressing the human rights violations and atrocities perpetrated by the former regime in the neighbouring countries and at home. This became increasingly evident as cooperation with The Hague Tribunal was met by vocal opposition within the ranks of the new political elite. The failure of the Yugoslav Commission for Truth and Reconciliation further corroborated this state of affairs. The irreconcilable ideological divisions and conflicting interests within the ruling elite became increasingly prevalent. On the one hand, civil society activists and liberal factions in government promoted the idea of creating a truth commission in order to establish a record of human rights violations perpetrated by the former regime and redress the victims. On the other hand, the conservative circles represented by Koštunica, who established the Commission through a presidential decree, saw it as an opportunity to consolidate the nationalist narrative and appease the pressure of the International Criminal Tribunal for the former Yugoslavia (ICTY). In those circumstances, this initiative proved unworkable from the start.

The transitional justice agenda was thus taken on by domestic HRGs, which were already fully integrated in regional and international human rights networks as a result of their activism during the 1990s. These organisations constituted an important source of local support for the war crimes trials at the ICTY. They assisted the prosecutor's office in putting together evidence and providing legal expertise, as well as offering practical and psychological support for victims at the local level. Local organisations, such as the Humanitarian Law Centre, also participated in the dissemination of the court's findings in partnership with the ICTY's outreach office in Belgrade. In addition, the HRGs have played a major role in supporting and monitoring domestic war crimes trials since the War Crimes Chamber was established at the Belgrade District Court in 2003.

In terms of advocacy work, human rights organisations have focused their activities on sensitising public opinion over the devastating legacy of nationalism and war – a project commonly labelled 'facing the past'. This primarily consists of promoting public acknowledgement of past atrocities and exerting pressure on the authorities in order to generate political accountability. The campaign reached a peak in the summer of 2005, as the tenth anniversary of the Srebrenica massacre was approaching.[13] It was marked by the broadcasting of a video footage featuring the execution of six Bosniak teenagers from Srebrenica by members of the Serb paramilitary unit 'Škorpioni'. This video, which was made public by the HLC, instantly sparked off the debate over the Srebrenica massacre and led to the organisation of public actions, such as the provocative display of billboards reminding the residents of Belgrade about Srebrenica. Eight NGOs came together to draft a declaration condemning the massacre in Srebrenica for the Serbian parliament to adopt. Whilst the initiative was eventually turned down due to opposition from the far-right Radical Party, Milošević's Serbian Socialist party, and the Serbian Democratic Party of Prime Minister Koštunica, it nevertheless succeeded in bringing the issue of war crimes into the realm of domestic politics and the public domain. It also led President Tadić to symbolically attend the commemoration of the tenth anniversary of the Srebrenica massacre.

The HRGs were overtly critical towards the supposed new 'regime' embodied by Vojislav Koštunica, which they blamed for perpetuating public denial of atrocities committed in the name of the Serbian nation and reinforcing the political culture of ethno-nationalism.[14] Despite the change of government in May 2008, members of this group continue to perceive and portray the new authorities as an extension of the nationalist rule established in the 1990s. But political contestation comes at a high cost. The major human rights organisation activists – Natasa Kandić, Sonja Biserko, and Biljana Kovačević-Vučo – have been subjected to a fierce campaign of intimidation and harassment orchestrated by the most conservative elements in society. The onslaught against what amounts to less than ten organisations is predominantly personal and extremely vindictive. The prominent women who run several of these organisations have been the target of verbal attacks and harassment perpetrated by politicians and leading media commentators. As well as their sanity and loyalty to the state being put to question, they are accused of being part of the communist elite, or not being truly Serb.[15] Questions have also been raised regarding the financing of these organisations, with the suggestion that they are the recipients of illegal funding, or are on the payroll of various international mafias. In April 2007, a prominent journalist who extensively covered the issue of war crimes was the target of a bomb attack in the centre of Belgrade.[16]

Besides being in open conflict with the nationalist elites, the HRG are also highly critical towards those factions of civil society that co-operate with, or have become partners of, the government. The split within what used to constitute a common opposition front against the regime of Milošević is manifested by the divorce between organisations seeking to establish a pragmatic dialogue with the new authorities, and those radical human rights groups challenging the foundations of the new order. The divergent views were publicly expressed through a lengthy polemic between members of civil society that took place in the weekly newspaper *Vreme* in 2002.[17] On the one hand, the human rights activists blamed the independent media, especially *B92* and *Vreme*, for collaborating with the elites in concealing and mitigating the war crimes and failing to mention the responsibility of Serbian society. In their view, public disregard for war crimes trials was the intended result of inadequate media coverage of these issues in Serbia. On the other hand, these charges were refuted by representatives of the media sector who attributed the failure of Serbian society to address the legacy of war crimes to the incapacity of the ICTY and local human rights organisations to generate sufficient public engagement with Serbia's recent past. Indeed, the human rights NGOs are subject to severe criticism from their former comrades for being excessively politicised and for having adopted an aggressive strategy of 'confronting' the public with the past, which has not produced the desired effects on society.

Although co-operation with The Hague tribunal is an intrinsic component of the EU conditionality towards the Western Balkans, EU assistance for civil society in Serbia has largely bypassed those organisations dealing with war crimes and transitional justice. Indeed, EU policy with regard to war crimes in the Western Balkans essentially consists of pressuring the governments from the region to co-operate with the ICTY (Rangelov 2006). It does not involve any support for local human rights advocacy groups, which do not have access to EIDHR funding. This policy can be explained by the reluctance of EU institutions to get involved in any kind of partisan politics at the domestic level. As mentioned earlier, war crimes issues are extremely sensitive and highly politicised. This is illustrated by the frequent clashes between HRGs and right-wing organisations that promote nationalist values and glorify the suspected war criminals. While most of these right-wing organisations are affiliated to the Serbian Radical Party, several representatives of the most prominent HRGs sit on the political council of the Liberal-Democratic Party. In those circumstances, any support for HRGs from the EU would be interpreted as involvement in domestic politics and open hostility towards the nationalist elites.

On the other hand, the EU approach to developing civil society has reinforced the divergence between human-rights organisations and what may be termed the 'institutionalised' civil society of NGOs. Such divisions intensified in April 2007, when several human rights NGOs appealed to the EU not to sign the SAA with Serbia before it had handed over all suspected war criminals to The Hague.[18] In addition, several organisations have suggested the EU adopt a new kind of dialogue that would include 'civil society, youth, small entrepreneurs and pro-European parties'.[19] The 'institutionalised' NGOs, led by the European Movement, immediately reacted by expressing their disagreement with these appeals.[20]

In spite of these divergences, the different factions within civil society have shown that they are willing to overcome their differences when their common interests are imperilled. This is best illustrated by their common appeals calling upon the EU to sign the SAA with Serbia as soon as possible, and their joint condemnation of anti-European discourses in the wake of the presidential elections in January 2008. Indeed, it would seem that, contrary to the negative media portrayal, the default stance of the HRGs is actually to rally to the cause of accelerating Serbia's rapprochement with the EU in order to prevent 'non- and quasi-democratic forces from once again isolating the country'.[21]

EU assistance to Serbia

EU assistance to Serbia has, since 2000 and the fall of Milošević, largely focused on institution-building, the strengthening of the country's infrastructure, justice and home affairs, economic development and cross-border co-operation. Although re-building the economy and developing the infrastructure in order to attract foreign investment have been overriding priorities, this has been combined with measures to strengthen democratic governance and political processes. Indeed, one of the first initiatives launched in 1999 during the last days of the Milošević period was support for municipalities in the form of a programme called 'Energy for Democracy'. This essentially involved the EU providing energy to those towns that had held democratic elections and were being denied oil by the embattled Milošević regime. Though the fuel was provided by the EU as part of humanitarian relief for the country, it essentially established the two cornerstones of EU assistance: support for democratic forces at the local level, and the provision of resources as part of the re-building of the country. The Energy for Democracy programme initially supported seven towns (including Pirot and Nis), but was extended to the whole of Serbia after October 2000 and the demise of Milošević.

Support designated directly for civil society – not as part of a reconstruction or infrastructure project – is a more recent focus and has only become a designated aid objective in the context of IPA. Indeed, during the 1990s it was American donors such as the Soros and Rockerfeller foundations that provided support to the civil society organisations battling against the Milošević regime, with the EU dealing directly with the government rather than with NGOs. After October 2000 and the change of leadership, more emphasis was placed on working with civil society and building partnerships around emergency relief and infrastructural development. The Zagreb Summit of 2000 and the start of the Stability and Association process with what was then still the Federal Republic of Yugoslavia was in a sense a turning point, enabling local NGOs to gain access to resources through the CARDS programme and various EIDHR initiatives designed to build state capacity, improve administrative know-how, or develop the provision of social services.[22]

The European Agency for Reconstruction

The European Agency for Reconstruction (EAR) represents the main arm of EU assistance in Serbia. The agency began its operations in Serbia in 1999, providing emergency relief, particularly the provision of energy, in Kosovo immediately after the ending of hostilities between NATO and the Milošević government.[23] Although NGOs are engaged as implementing partners, or are granted service contracts and tenures, most EAR funding is channelled through the Government of Serbia in the form of large infrastructure projects, which are signed directly with the state. The Agency's most recent project, which is to reconstruct and repair district-heating systems in five towns – Valjevo, Čačak, Užice, Subotica and Pančevo – across the country, is typical of the sort of assistance projects the EAR has overseen since the end of the 1990s.[24] It is no exaggeration to say that 'there is barely an aspect of Serbian life that the EAR has not touched'.[25] Today, most EU aid and assistance for Serbia, as part of CARDS, is administered by the EAR, which, via its regional office in Belgrade, implements the Commission's Annual Action Programmes for the country. The Agency essentially implements schemes and projects agreed by the Commission and the Serbian government. Indeed, EAR funds arise from the financial agreement signed between the government and the Commission.

The EAR's mandate in Serbia, which was extended twice, came to an end in December 2008 when the Local Delegation assumed responsibility for administering the Commission's priorities and funds for Serbia in the context of the IPA framework. Critics of this decision emphasised that the EAR had proved to be an efficient aid agency, which enjoyed significant authority and devolved and decentralised power, and that such flexibility and capacity may well be lost when funding is administered by the Delegation. Up until its closure in 2008 the funding priorities for the EAR were essentially a combination of those highlighted in the European Commission's 2002–6 Country Strategy Paper, the associated three-year Multi-annual Indicative Programme (MIPs), the recommendations arising as part of the Stabilisation and Association process (SAp), which started again in June 2007, and the European Partnership priorities.

Economic and infrastructural development: the EAR's main focus

The Agency had specific responsibility for administering and implementing the economic assistance aspects of the SAp, hence its heavy involvement in infrastructural and energy related projects. In addition to economic and social development, the MIP for 2005–6 also identified democratic stabilisation, good governance and institution-building as developmental priorities. Though the EAR did not specifically involve itself with democratic development, there was obviously overlap, particularly with regard to supporting civil society organisations. In practice the agency's mandate to build economic capacity was broadly interpreted and included significant assistance for the development of public administration. For example, during 2006 the EAR funded a Human Resource Management Service for training civil servants, and the development of a pay strategy for the public sector in general.[26] The Agency was involved in long-term support projects for municipalities and the development of local government. Such initiatives tended to involve the building of administrative and communication capacity in, for example, areas such as the Sandzak region of south west Serbia where there is a large Bosniak community.

However, the bulk of the agency's work was administering and implementing large-scale infrastructure projects, often as part of larger initiatives for which Serbia has obtained development loans. Examples of recent projects include a €5 million air filter project for the Kostolac power station in eastern Serbia (EAR Annual Report 2006: 15), part of a €400 million investment in the power sector alone.[27] Other significant projects included assistance to improve border crossing facilities and improved transport routes at Batrovci border with Croatia, or the development of a National Blood Transfusion Strategy, including a Blood Transfusion Centre in Nis, which is part of a €200 million loan to the Serbian government from the European Investment Bank.

EAR support for civil society

As was the case with nearly all EU initiatives and assistance examined for this research, EAR projects tended to involve local NGOs in some way, either as implementing partners or as direct beneficiaries of projects. In all its various schemes the agency placed emphasis on partnerships between NGOs and government. For example, as part of the agency's €6 million scheme to provide specialised equipment to vocational education and training centres as part of a larger project to modernise such training across the country, local NGOs were involved in delivering various aspects of the reform and in providing training.

Of the €1.28 billion of aid committed to the country between 2002 and 2008, the EU has, initially through the agency and subsequently through the Delegation, provided €11.5 million specifically for the support of civil society.[28] In 2006–7 the EAR ran seven grant programmes designed specifically for civil society development, which benefited local NGOs in 50 municipalities in central and western Serbia. These programmes tended to benefit organisations operating in socially deprived areas, working on issues and in areas where the EAR was already active; namely, environment, education, EU compliance and promotion, and regional integration. The administration and monitoring of these small grant projects was out-sourced to various implementing partners, such as the European Movement, a local NGO network.

The overriding aim of civil society assistance, whether administered under the auspices of the EAR or the local Delegation, has been to engage local NGOs in joint projects, to build their managerial and administrative capacity to manage projects, and to enable organisations to apply for further funding. Generally much of the agency's aid for NGOs focused on strengthening the capacity of civil society organisations to participate in policy development and the implementation of poverty reduction measures. Local NGOs have also been supported to deliver various social services in conjunction with local authorities. In particular, the aid has been targeted towards supporting civil society organisations and encouraging them to participate in the preparation of the Poverty Reduction Strategy Paper through the setting up of the Civil Society Advisory Committee, a forum of local NGOs, the aim here being to augment the input of NGOs within consultation processes around local poverty reduction strategies.

EU funds were also used to establish a Social Innovation Fund (SIF), which, in conjunction with the Ministry of Social Affairs (now the Ministry of Labour, Employment and Social Policy), provided resources for joint projects between government and non-governmental sectors with particular regard to economic regeneration and development, employment and social service provision. In addition, a separate fund (Fund to Support Civil Society), designed to support projects concerned with improving the legislative and fiscal context in which NGOs operate, was established. This fund has also helped to strengthen the input of NGOs within planning and implementing community development programmes.[29]

What appear to be a myriad of EAR initiatives, all seeking to support civil society in some way or other, had at their core the objective of building NGO capacity for project management, and to develop the agency of NGOs within various broader policy initiatives. The Agency's commitment to working closely with NGOs and to providing what it described as 'on the job training' (budget psycho-management, record-keeping, accounting, as well as tutelage on EU norms and practices) reflects the underlying emphasis on supporting and professionalising civil society organisations as a means of realising broader development objectives – economic regeneration, policy compliance and bureaucratic efficiency. In terms of improving the project management capacity of the NGO sector, EAR officials believed the agency was reasonably successful: over 60 per cent of applications used to fail the first stage of the process because the log-frame or other aspects of the form had not been completed correctly. In 2006–7 this was reduced to only 30 per cent, which does suggest an improvement in the quality of applications and know-how within the NGO sector. This improvement was aided by the existence of independent experts in Serbia who provided NGOs with training and assistance.[30]

EAR Assistance at the local level – the Regional Development Agencies (RDAs)

In the context of working with local NGOs around poverty reduction strategies, the agency also worked closely with local mayors to encourage their engagement with local NGO networks. It was acknowledged that success was limited, with some mayors 'more inclined than others to hold open forums with NGOs and to adopt a more interactive approach'.[31] Perhaps in recognition of the limitations of working with local mayors and the slow pace of administrative reform, the EAR helped establish Regional Development Agencies (RDAs). Serbia still does not currently have regional administrative units (any such reform is extremely politically sensitive and has been inextricably tied to the status of Kosovo), with the only decentralised administrative strata being 167 municipalities. Across member states, particularly new member states, the EU relies heavily on regional administrative tiers as conduits for the transmission of aid – the *acquis* specifies that adequate structures must be in place to manage funds – and thus the RDAs were established across Serbia for this purpose.

However, the long-term impact of these institutions is less certain. The RDAs are, after all, regional development agencies in name only; they are not part of the formal administrative structure in Serbia, and have actually been established as private companies, largely through partnerships between for-ward-looking municipalities keen to access EU funds, and local businesses. Mayors can select board members, but ultimately the RDAs operate entirely separately from the local authority. As the RDAs are not administrative units and have no devolved political or administrative power their role is simply con-sultative and advisory, typically providing information to municipalities, busi-nesses and the EAR on, for example, the number of unemployed in a particular locality, training needs. RDAs also work closely with local NGOs, several of whom are likely to be involved in EU-funded projects. In essence, therefore, they have acted as the EAR or the local Delegation's partners 'in the field', helping to co-ordinate projects, bringing together expertise and sectors of the community.

The overriding objective of the EAR was to administer funds and devise projects for infrastructural development, with the emphasis placed firmly on stimulating economic growth as a core objective. This obviously was a far-reaching and overlapping remit that resulted in the agency during its tenure becoming engaged in aspects of democratic development, administrative reform, civil society and community development. With regard to judging EU support for political reform, it is important to remember that the EAR was pri-marily a development agency with considerable authority and executive power, seeking efficiency. The Agency was keen to engage NGOs at all levels of its work and prior to its closure suggested to the Commission that the IPA frame-work should make large-scale regional and socio-economic development pro-gramme aid available to NGOs rather than just to government and state agencies, so that NGOs could apply directly for development funds. But this was primarily born out of frustration with the inefficiency and slow pace of state agency reform, rather than a commitment to developing NGOs and civil society. Reflecting on its legacies, the agency acknowledges a fundamental con-straint with regard to developmental assistance based on trying to build inter-action and partnership between NGOs and government: most initiatives and the interaction between local actors is invariably donor-driven, with the threat that once the project ends the communication will also end. However, positive legacies and sustainable outcomes did occur; an EAR field manager with responsibility for local projects observed:

> In Versac [in the north east of Serbia], they [women's NGO] were talking to the mayors because we were there ... because of the project. But when I went back 12 months later, the municipality had provided a fund for NGOs.[32]

The Local Delegation of the European Commission to Serbia

Since January 2009, on closure of the EAR, the European Commission's Delegation to the Republic of Serbia ('the Delegation') assumed responsibility for administering and co-ordinating EU assistance to the country. The Delegation administers EIDHR micro projects, which have only recently been made available to Serbia and are awarded to local NGOs. For the first call for proposal in July 2006, the themes were 'fostering a culture of human rights' and 'advancing equality, tolerance and peace', which are typical initiatives promoted by the EIDHR.[33] The number of applications received for this call from NGOs was 108, out of which 21 project awards were made. The project grants allocated were relatively small, delivering between €20,000 and €80,000 to recipient organisations, mostly for self-contained, year-long projects. Although most of the funded projects involved the lead NGOs working across the country in collaboration with local partners, the majority of recipients were Belgrade-based NGOs with an established reputation for managing projects. In other words, projects tended to be broad in terms of their geographic reach, but the successful NGOs were based in the capital and had a proven track record of project management.

The Delegation also undertakes certain administrative responsibilities for macro grants awarded by Brussels to Serbian organisations as part of the EIDHR global programme. Though the contracts for macro projects are signed with Brussels, the Delegation undertakes field visits to the Serbian partner organisations within a large project, and performs other monitoring duties. The Delegation generally deals with political development, civil society, human and minority rights, whereas economic development projects as part of CARDS were previously the responsibility of the EAR.

In terms of monitoring and evaluation, the Delegation is required by the Commission to submit an annual report about the projects, to undertake field visits and engage in regular dialogue with recipient NGOs and to participate in their events. The reports compiled by NGOs and submitted to the Delegation form the basis of the Summary Report sent to Brussels. Compared to the EAR, or to the Bosnian Delegation, the capacity of the Serbian Delegation is as yet extremely limited. There are just two employees responsible for evaluations of project proposals and the monitoring of successful projects, as well as over-seeing all of the operational and financial aspects of micro awards.[34]

EU-funded projects in Serbia: focus, impact and outcomes

The remainder of this chapter will provide an overview and assessment of EU-funded projects in Serbia between 2004 and 2008. As already noted, project grants comprise a key element of assistance and are the most tangible expres-sion of EU intervention. It is also important to note the extent to which the EU is becoming the main donor for NGOs and civil society organisations. Whilst several of the European and American donors have withdrawn or scaled down their involvement, the EU is setting the agenda for those that remain, both with regard to the focus of assistance (emphasis on the objectives of the Stabilisation and Association process agenda) and in terms of organisational management and delivery expectations. In other words, the EU is a critical player and through its micro and macro grants is defining the operational and organisational norms of recipient NGOs.[35]

The majority of projects funded by the EU in Serbia involved some kind of partnership, however nominal, between NGOs and government. Indeed, the bulk of EU funding (administered by the EAR) actually benefited the Serbian government, either directly as contracts and tenures for specific infrastructure development, or indirectly through project grants involving NGOs. Whilst the latter mostly involved NGOs offering a social or public service that was not otherwise being provided, the EU, via the EAR and later through the Delegation, encouraged the government to stimulate NGO activity and co-operate with the non-governmental sector. In other words, in channelling its aid through organisations the EU attempts to engage and target the govern-ment. This was reflected in the nature and focus of funded projects, which either tended to involve NGOs co-operating with the state in the provision of social or medical services to sections of the community – for example, psy-chosocial support for victims of torture and the rehabilitation of concentration camp victims,[36] or contained an education, training or employment skills com-ponent, usually targeting a specific marginalised community, or working specifically with internally displaced persons (IDPs) in a particular area.[37] Several projects provided training for key workers such as prison guards, teachers or social workers.[38] There were also several examples of projects that focused on some form of human rights education for high school students or younger children and their parents. For example, in 2005 the Belgrade Centre for Human Rights was awarded €50,000 by the EAR, under the CARDS category of 'promotion of human and minority rights and gender equality', for a project to promote knowledge of human rights in 15 secondary schools across the country through a series of lectures and workshops. The project, which involved between 500 and 600 students and resulted in the organisation producing a publication and a competition for students, did not, however, engage the ministry of education or local authorities other than asking the assistant minister for schools to judge the competition. In a subsequent project with a similar focus – workshops and training with 16–18 year olds on different religions – and also funded by the EU, there was some contact between the organisation and the Ministry of Education, but only to gain permission for trainers or educators to work in schools, which is a legal requirement in Serbia. Neither project involved policy interaction or service provision. However, in terms of the sustainability of outcomes, the initiative continued beyond the 12-month project and the end of the EU grant, but was funded by the Soros Foundation.[39]

The *Belgrade Centre for Human Rights*, which was successful in two out of the three applications it made to the EAR, is typical of the sort of Serbian NGO that received EU project grants. It is relatively long established (1995) and employs more than ten full-time staff, the majority of whom are professionals recruited for their specific expertise. The organisation has international links (they are the Serbian branch of the International Association of Human Rights Institutes), and the director is an academic who has significant experience in applying for and managing project grants. The organisation had little apparent difficulty in securing the 20 per cent match funding from another donor that the EU requires. Additional donors included various embassies, foreign development agencies and multilateral donors.[40]

But not all skills training programmes funded by the EU delivered sustainable outcomes. The aim of a €67,000 project run by the NGO Srpski demokratski forum (Serbian Democratic Forum) from March 2006 for 12 months and funded by the EAR was to enhance the employability of young refugees and IDPs in the vicinity of Belgrade.[41] This involved organising English-language and computer classes and providing assistance in searching for jobs and further training. The project entailed co-operation between the NGO and the National Employment Service (Nacionalna sluzba za zaposljavanje) in Belgrade, but only in terms of the state agency providing a list of local citizens registered with the service and referring people for the project. For its duration, the project provided a service, however small-scale, which was not otherwise offered, either by the national employment service or the private sector.

Unless a state agency or local municipality took over the running of the provision, or provided funding for the NGO to continue with the project, the sustainable long-term benefit of such skills and training projects was extremely limited. Under EU rules, it is not possible for the organisation to apply for additional revenue from the Delegation to extend the project. The only option for an NGO is to apply for a different project on a broadly similar theme, but this depends on whether the theme of the latest call for projects is relevant. In the case of the SDF project, the organisation applied for EU funding for similar programmes focusing on legal support for IDPs, but for the communities within Belgrade who benefited from the project there was no sustainable long-term impact other than improved skills for 100 or so 18–35 year olds. The local municipality did not take over responsibility for the training, or engage SDF in providing services elsewhere in the municipality.

Recent calls for proposals as part of both CARDS and EIDHR have focused on aspects of minority and human rights. Not surprisingly, several funded projects therefore contained a rights dimension, usually focusing on providing support to marginalised groups within civil society, either in the context of helping them exercise their legal rights or in terms of enabling them to access economic, social and political resources.

Unless the outcome of such projects was direct advocacy around a new piece of human or minority rights legislation emanating from an international treaty or agreement that Serbia has signed, or resulted in more effective implementation of an existing law, the sustainability of the project outcomes surveyed for this research was questionable. The dilemma faced by recipient organisations was that a short-term project of between €50,000 and €100,000 enabled them to help only a fraction of those affected by the particular issue. For example, the organisation Pomoc deci received several EU project grants to work on strengthening the capacity of Roma organisations and communities, and assisting Roma communities with the process of birth registration. However, due to EU rules and procedures, it was not possible to extend any of the projects into neighbouring communities, or to widen the scope of the provision beyond the terms of the award. The difficult task faced by the organisation was how to frame their activities in terms of the latest EU call for proposals so as to secure additional funds for on-going projects, whilst at the same time ensuring a consistent strategic development focus for the organisation. Whilst the organisation was in fact quite successful at obtaining a succession of projects, enabling them to continue supporting Roma communities and exerting some influence at municipal level, the shifting focus of EU projects nevertheless meant that certain initiatives, such as helping Roma people to gain registration or to provide employment training, were not continued despite their merits and small-scale effectiveness. For instance, in 2007 the organisation shifted from working on a project to improve the school attendance of Roma children to focusing on Roma organisations developing environmental programmes and services in response to the 2006 call for proposals which focused on environmental protection and awareness.[42]

A large proportion of the projects funded by the EAR and the Delegation aimed primarily to provide services in communities, either in lieu of the state or the market, to supplement existing state provision, or to expand a service already provided by the recipient organisation. However, although it was not immediately obvious what was the governance or policy dimension to such projects, qualitative interview data revealed that partnerships with the state were nevertheless formed, and recipients were assuming an advocacy role as projects progressed. For example, the organisation Victimology Society of Serbia received €22,000 of EU funding in 2005 for a project to provide support for victims of crime. The grant covered a range of activities for victims of burglary and muggings in and around Belgrade, the promotion of advice and counselling services offered by the organisation, and the production of a booklet listing the various services available to crime victims. Though the organisation, which at the time relied on the EU for 85 per cent of its overall revenue, initially obtained grants to extend its community support services, through subsequent projects it begun to advocate on behalf of crime victims, witnesses, victims of trafficking and sexual assault. This occurred in the particular context of revisions to the Family Code in Serbia during 2005.[43] As with several of the other NGOs regularly receiving EU assistance, the Victimology Society has international connections – it is a member of the European Forum for Victim Services, which as an organisation has close links with the European Commission.

Where the interaction between state agencies and recipient NGOs was perhaps greatest and most effective was in the context of projects relating to Poverty Reduction Strategy Papers (PRSP), or other international initiatives, whereby NGOs received EU funding to assist local municipalities or the state in the constructing of action plans and strategies, collecting data and delivering outcomes, or were engaged in monitoring the impact and implementation of such initiatives. Indeed, the research revealed that the more successful organisations that had managed several projects, and where there was some interaction between the sectors, tended to engage with government as implementing partners or facilitators. There were numerous examples of such interaction: during 2006 the organisation Srpski demokratski forum worked with municipalities and the government to facilitate the re-admission of people coming back to Serbia as part of the re-admission agreements negotiated with neighbouring states.[44] The organisation Srpski savet za izbeghce (Serbian Refugee Council), a relatively new (2004) but particularly successful and effective organisation, ran an EU-funded project providing assistance and training for practitioners working with returnees, such as tutelage in international and domestic frameworks for refugee re-admission, recommended good practice, and advice on how to deal with returnees sensitively. The grant also funded the creation of a virtual support network connecting professionals working with returnees in Serbia with their counterparts across Western Europe.[45] Such projects engaged professionals and highly skilled individuals within the NGO sector in the implementation of social and political obligations relating to a high-profile EU initiative; in such instances the NGO trained and built the capacity of experts to provide specialist services in the community. These were in many respects the most tangible outcomes of EU assistance.

The partnership between EU-funded NGOs and the Serbian government functioned most effectively in the context of the PRSP and the implementation of strategy goals. This is, of course, due in large measure to the fact that as the core state plan for poverty reduction, the PRSP is of great importance not just to the World Bank, IFIs and the Serbian government, but also to the EU itself, whose Stabilisation and Association criteria coalesce with PRSP objectives. In terms of the sustainability of project outcomes, it appeared that NGO initiatives focusing on PRSP that are initially funded by the EU were more likely to attract state funding once the project has ended. A good example of such interaction between PRSP objectives and EU-funded projects was the initiative 'Local Coalition for Poverty Reduction of Vulnerable Youth' run by the Belgrade organisation Grupa 484.[46] The aim of this 12-month €87,000 project, which finished in May 2007, was to monitor the implementation at the local government level of PRSP objectives regarding vulnerable youths in five localities. The project aimed to build the capacity of local organisations to monitor progress of measures to, for example, reduce youth unemployment and infant mortality, and to generally build knowledge of strategies and objectives within the local community. Due to the fact that levels of knowledge of PRSP amongst citizens, local NGOs, local government officials and employees proved to be extremely low or non-existent (despite the fact that the plan had been agreed in 2003), prior to conducting any monitoring or evaluations, the project involved a series of seminars in the five areas providing basic

information about PRSP. As part of the project Grupa 484 gathered quantitative data on unemployment and poverty, but also monitored the development
of initiatives such as the formation of local unemployment councils and
audited the capacity of officials to evaluate implementation. As the project progressed the NGO took on an advocacy role at the local levels, pushing for co-
ordination between local offices of the Social Protection Agency and the
National Employment Service, and for a change in approach regarding the registration of unemployed young people.

A further example of positive interaction between EU-funded NGOs and
state agencies around a specific international initiative to which Serbia is a sig-
natory was the 2005–6 EU initiative 'The Roma Decade'. In 2006 the Belgrade-
based NGO Pomoc deci received funding directly from Brussels (as part of
EIDHR) to help the government produce an action plan to improve the housing, education and employment opportunities of the large Roma minority. The
initiative stipulated that local municipalities had to draw up individual action
plans. To this end the EU funded Pomoc deci to establish links between Roma
organisations and local authorities in seven municipalities, to run joint training
sessions and establish concrete development projects that would lead to better
integration of the Roma community within the municipality. What emerged
from the project was a host of survey documents outlining the needs of the
communities (skills shortages, housing needs, lack of education, etc.), which
were then used as the basis for the municipalities' development plans. In terms
of building longer-term intra-sectoral partnerships, the interaction established
between Pomoc Deci, municipalities and government agencies was sustained:
the organisation had an official partnership agreement with the ministry of
education to implement the UN Millennium Development Goals which
involved helping to recruit and train Roma teaching assistants for local schools.
Such co-operation and partnership with the ministry of education delivered a
dividend to the NGO insofar as it makes it far easier to obtain EU project
grants, which stipulate intra-sectoral partnership as a key criterion.

It has been illustrated above that interaction between NGOs and state agencies in Serbia proved most effective in the context of international initiatives,
or particular policy frameworks, where the government needs and depends
upon the assistance of organisations to fulfil its obligations and to implement
programmes. The partnership is even more effective when the initiative is a
core EU priority, or if the government is favourably inclined rather than indif-
ferent or opposed to the outcome.

A project, already referred to above, undertaken in 2007 by the Serbian
Refugee Council (Srpski savet za izbeghce) and focusing on Roma refugees

from Kosovo and Serbia returning from Western Europe, offered a very good illustration of how and in what context effective partnerships between NGOs and the state can emerge. The project involved the organisation providing training for local civil servants and, in particular, the Centre for Social Work in Belgrade in order to improve the absorption of the returnees. It also included the production of a compendium for government officials to use and refer to in their dealings with all aspects of refugee return, combining best practice with a practical guide and overview of relevant legal frameworks. In addition to the compendium, the sustainable legacy of this project is the existence of trained officials within local municipalities able to process and assist returnees. In other words, the project led to an increase in state capacity, or at least raised the functional capacity of certain state agencies. The most important point to emphasise about this project is that the theme – refugee return – was, and remains, a key priority for both the EU and the Serbian government: the latter is positively inclined towards helping refugees who fled Serbian territories during the wars of Yugoslavia's succession to return to the country today; for the EU, refugee return is a vital component of stabilising the region. The organisation also had significant capacity prior to the project. It has a small but highly skilled workforce with experience of applying for and managing external project grants. The bulk of their income at the time came from the Danish Ministry of Foreign Affairs in the form of a three-year institutional grant. This provided them with a degree of stability not available to other NGOs; it meant that they were not as reliant on short-term grants and were able to generate the 20 per cent match funding for the EU-funded project from internal resources. The fact that they also worked in tandem with other NGOs and have established a network of organisations working on refugee-related issues also won them favour with the EU and, to a lesser extent, the government.

Insofar as the vast majority of EU-funded projects involved NGOs providing training or other services, policy advice and data, or acting as implementing partners for EU or other international initiatives to which the Serbian government is committed, EU funding did not ostensibly engage local NGOs in political or contentious activities. Indeed, the only context in which EU-funded projects did engage NGOs politically, and where the political objectives were more overt, was with regard to the promotion of European integration. The EAR, via a specific initiative called the European Integration Fund, provided funding for NGOs to work on promoting aspects of European integration in communities across the country.

The Centre for Democracy Foundation, a Belgrade-based NGO, ran a typical project of this kind during 2005–6. The project, entitled 'European Policies and Strategies in Local Communities', was awarded €45,000 to develop and spread knowledge about the EU and the accession process amongst local members of parliament in the Zlatibor region of western Serbia. The project involved training sessions and workshops on European ideas and values, the benefits of membership and the criteria for membership, and practical advice for political elites on how to mobilise and motivate pro-European citizens. The project resulted in the publication of a handbook, written by academics, and involved 75 local politicians and political party activists. The Centre has also received EIDHR funding for similar projects, in particular, a €573,000 grant awarded directly from Brussels to run three training schools for parliamentarians and university students studying political science and other humanities subjects. The aim of the project, which ran from 2002 to 2005, was to improve the quality of political leadership in the context of European norms and values and to train the current and next generations of political leaders.[47]

The Centre for Democracy Foundation, which undertook both projects and tenders for specific service contracts, was heavily dependent on EU funding; in 2005 this constituted 71 per cent of the organisation's total revenue. Whether as small project grant or service tender, the EU-funded activities involved either the promotion of Europeanisation, or some aspect of socio-economic reform with a distinctly EU policy dimension. For example, a project entitled 'Women Return to Labour' and funded by the EAR engaged the NGO in the provision of educational programmes in Belgrade to help women back to work. The Centre employed trainers to run intensive workshops for 180 women aged between 35 and 50. Though the overall aim was to build their capacity to obtain employment generally and to become more active in finding work outside of the home, particular emphasis was placed on employment opportunities within the tourist and hospitality industries.

Other projects have included 'Government and Business in Practising Social and Economic Rights'. This 18-month €80,000 initiative, which began in March 2007, aimed to develop knowledge amongst 500 small companies about social and economic rights, EU norms and the European Social Charter in particular. This project was perhaps one of the best examples of intra-sectoral partnership insofar as it involved a coalition of local NGOs from nine locations across Serbia, meeting with officials from the ministries of health, employment and legal affairs as well as with businesses. But the project also involved providing forums for workers to talk about violations of their rights and to open up dialogue with employees. As Svetlana Vukomanović, the Director of the organisation observed, this aspect of the project was particularly important insofar as 'the idea of being fired in socialist Yugoslavia was as unknown as having to understand your rights as a worker'.[48] The project also involved an advocacy component, with the aim being to lobby both for the ratification of the European Social Charter, and for the better implementation and enforcement of existing laws regarding workers' rights.

According to the EAR and the Delegation, the overwhelming majority of funded projects were completed and the objectives and outputs realised. Trainings and workshops happened, at which public sector workers, the unemployed, students, political leaders attended and gained knowledge and skills; NGOs drafted reports and compiled data that was then submitted to relevant ministries or agencies. However, the case of a particular failed project provided considerable insight into the potential difficulties in using short-term projects as a vehicle for building partnerships between NGOs and state agencies. It also highlighted the tension that can arise when NGOs become service providers and seek to engage state agencies in the process of delivering training and assistance in communities. In 2005 the organisation Centre for Civic Initiatives (CCI) signed a contract with the EAR for a project to deliver skills training for a specific group of unemployed people living in Belgrade. The organisation was informed by the EAR that their partner in the project was the National Employment Agency, who would supply the names and details of the target group and facilitate the training by supplying expertise and materials. The NEA refused to provide the necessary data on the basis that it was unconstitutional to do so. After some discussion between CCI and the NEA it was revealed that the agency wanted to be paid to do the training, sought financial benefit from the project, and was withholding vital employment data on this basis. CCI was told that they should attempt to obtain the data by positioning themselves in social security offices and approaching people directly. The legal situation was complex: as state employees working for a government agency, staff at the NEA were not permitted to be paid in addition to their salaries for work undertaken during their working hours. Whilst the project was to be carried out during normal hours, the initiative constituted additional work for NEA employees. Ultimately CCI pulled out of the project on the basis that they could not co-operate effectively with the NEA and were reprimanded by the EAR for doing so.[49]

Constraints on impact: the legal and fiscal context

There has clearly emerged within Serbia a small group of recipient organisations that have significant capacity to apply for EU grants, manage projects, and fulfil the various legal and fiscal obligations required of them. These organisations have become adept at completing the logic framework and are able to deploy internal resources towards completing the application form and mobilising the required information, such as bank details and legal documents. However, interviews with recipient NGOs and research into the experience and consequences of various EU-funded projects revealed the extent to which the impact of assistance channelled through NGOs was constrained by a host of procedural, institutional and fiscal factors, emanating from the realities of Serbian law and process, but also from the rules and procedures of the EU itself.

The most immediate difficulties faced by recipient organisations stemmed from the unreformed fiscal and legal framework within Serbia. Indeed, most of the NGOs interviewed for this research complained about the procedural difficulties they encountered in managing the financial aspects of a project grant. The regulatory framework governing the non-profit sector in Serbia today is based on two legal frameworks from the socialist era: 'The law on public and social organisations and citizens associations' from 1982 (amended in 1989), and 'The law on the affiliation of citizens in associations, public organisations and political organisations that are established on the territory of the Socialist Federative Republic of Yugoslavia' from 1990. Whilst NGOs have some legal status, and the process of registration is relatively straightforward, the fiscal position governing NGOs and non-profit organisations is far less clear.

Serbian law states that non-profit organisations are exempt from taxes on income up to RSD 300,000 (around €4,000). However, since 2004 all additional income is levied at the standard rate of 10 per cent.[50] The reality is therefore that generally NGOs are treated the same as for-profit companies.[51] Since July 2005 EU-funded project grants have been classified for tax purposes as 'gifts' and are therefore levied at the lower rate of 5 per cent. This also pertains to donations from foreign sources, except for 'gifts' that 'exclusively serve the purpose for which the organisation was created'.[52] This is immediately problematic for NGOs in receipt of projects to work on issues around which the organisation was founded. It also represents a legal anomaly insofar as if the grants are indeed 'gifts' then it seems inappropriate that the recipient organisation should have to report to the government on how the money is spent.

Salaries paid by an NGO, and the cost of renting premises, are taxed at the normal rate. Goods and services purchased as part of a grant from a foreign organisation based in a country which has signed a bilateral agreement with the Serbian government, or a grant awarded by the EU, are exempt from VAT. For donations from bilateral donors from countries, such as Holland, that have not signed an agreement with Serbia, there is no such exemption and the full rate of VAT is applied. For example, the organisation Pomoc deci was in receipt of a grant from the Dutch government; all expenditure emanating from this grant was subject to the normal rate of VAT on the basis that the Dutch government had not signed an agreement with Serbia.[53] Since 2005, certain scientific, cultural, and religious organisations, plus humanitarian or development aid have been exempt from VAT.

However, even when applicable, the process of obtaining the exemption is complicated and acts as a considerable constraint. All items of expenditure for the project have to be certified, which involves getting a stamped certificate from the tax office outside Belgrade; there is no single document or certificate granting a blanket exemption that could be shown to suppliers. Instead, every invoice has to be stamped separately. This is particularly problematic for NGOs operating away from Belgrade, in small towns or rural areas, where local suppliers are unfamiliar with the process of granting tax exemption even if the documentation is presented to them. For such organisations the cost of obtaining the exemption – travelling to the tax office, obtaining invoices etc. – is often higher than the value of the exemption itself.[54]

Indeed, the research revealed several examples of organisations experiencing considerable difficulties in obtaining tax exemptions. The experience of the European Movement in Serbia, which needed to purchase a car as part of an EAR-funded project, illustrated the extent to which the constraints of domestic fiscal realities are exacerbated by EU rules relating to project management. The organisation was required, according to EU Regulations, to buy a new car that had been built within the EU rather than a second-hand locally produced vehicle that would have been considerably cheaper. However, it took over a year for the European Movement to obtain the requisite tax exemption certificate for the Peugeot car they were intending to buy, and it proved almost impossible to obtain a customs exemption certificate. As the project was well underway and the value of the funds for the car had, as a consequence of changes in the exchange rate, dropped quite considerably, the organisation was forced in the end to buy a locally produced Zastava car.[55]

EU rules governing project allocation and monitoring

The first criticism to be levelled at EU processes is one that is not necessarily specific to Serbia: decision-making and the allocation of resources is seen by recipients to be a slow process. For example, the Belgrade Centre for Human Rights submitted an application to the EAR for a micro project in August 2006; they received a request for further information in November, were informed that they were successful in December, but the project was not signed until

April 2007. The delay is in large part due to the need to carry out various checks, particularly for projects involving several 'in the field' partner organisations. Nevertheless, the difficulty imposed on NGOs is that the required co-funding arrangements and the involvement of other organisations or agencies often cannot be stalled for eight or nine months. For example, if a project involves employing psychologists or educators, the individuals lined up may no longer be available once the project is finally ready to start. Moreover, small donors that have agreed to provide match funding for the project may no longer be prepared to offer the requisite amount, particularly if the rates of inflation or exchange have fluctuated so that the amount of money required is now significantly greater than when initially agreed.

Organisations that received one or more project grants and had experience in dealing with the EAR and the Delegation voiced concerns regarding the EU's apparent insensitivity to the fiscal situation in Serbia and the local context, the inflexibility of procedures, and the Commission's failure to put pressure on the government to establish an appropriate and enabling institutional framework for NGOs. Indeed, despite over a decade of assistance to Serbia, a significant proportion of which has been channelled through NGOs, the EU has placed no overt pressure on the government to improve the fiscal situation, or to simplify the process for tax exemptions. Moreover, whilst the rules and regulations for funding local organisations and the procedures that govern auditing and financial management of projects are the same as those that apply in existing member states, the fiscal situation in which Serbian organisations operate is entirely different. For example, without continuous funding or demonstrable assets, national banks will not offer the guarantee required by the EU to establish a project grant with an NGO. Certain organisations manage to obtain the requisite guarantees, but this is usually due to them having personal connections with a particular bank and the concession is made as a favour. The situation is further complicated by the fact that not only does the EU insist that all financial reporting occurs in euros, it also stipulates that grants must not be transferred into local currency. Serbian law does not actually permit organisations to hold revenue in a foreign currency and stipulates that deposits must be converted to RSD within one week. However, as with many aspects of fiscal law, a deposit in foreign currencies is not actually prohibited: there is a missing clause in the law stipulating that this is possible which means that most national banks are reluctant to allow the deposit of euros and recipients are forced to find a bank that will exercise a degree of latitude. That the EU only pays 80 per cent of an award at the start of a project is also a problem insofar as fluctuations in exchange rates can significantly diminish the value of the award by the end of the project. This can result in an organisation discovering that half way through a project it has insufficient revenue to pay salaries or to hire premises because the actual value of the award has diminished.[56]

A further complication for recipient NGOs is the EU rule, which applies to the provision of EU development projects globally, that only four-fifths of the total cost of a project proposal will be funded by the Commission and that the remaining 20 per cent of revenue must be sourced either from another donor or from an organisation's own funds. However, in both Serbia and Bosnia-Herzegovina, and no doubt in many other post-socialist or developing states, this rule is highly contentious. It serves to narrow the scope of funding and locate project grants solely in the hands of a narrow band of organisations that are financially better endowed. It also ensures that the same Belgrade-based core of relatively large and financially successful organisations dominate each round of project grants. The problem is essentially that organisations have to prove to the EAR that they have secured 20 per cent match funding or have sufficient internal assets in order to be considered for a project grant. Smaller organisations, located in local communities or rural areas outside of Belgrade, will invariably have limited access to bilateral foreign donors, all of whom are based in the capital or in large urban areas. Considering the average salary in Serbia is €150 per month, it is unrealistic to expect an NGO to have assets in the bank of €15–20,000 corresponding to 20 per cent of a typical EU micro grant. Only an elite of relatively developed and well-resourced NGOs are likely to have sufficient capital assets to mobilise the additional 20 per cent of revenue; the vast majority of local NGOs, regardless of the quality of their project proposals or their capacity to run a successful project, are effectively disqualified from applying for or obtaining an EU grant. The consequence of this, as noted above, was that capacity assistance and project management know-how were funnelled into a narrow band of organisations. Newly established, local organisations, such as Education Centre of Roma, based in Sabotica, near Vojvodina and the Hungarian border, that were involved in projects as partner 'in the field' organisations and therefore had the capacity to operate and run good projects, stood little chance of obtaining a project grant because they lacked the necessary financial resources.[57]

Conclusion

From the outset the focus of EU assistance in Serbia, delivered through the EAR, was infrastructure reconstruction and energy sector modernisation in particular. The focus on democracy promotion, human rights, or civil society development came later and they have only recently become priorities, largely as a consequence of the SAp and pre-accession considerations. If the EU accession process does gain momentum and the pace of reforms initiated by the DS-led government increases, then the focus of EU assistance and the impact of project grants will become even more critical. Whilst policy development and approximation with EU norms will obviously be a prime focus, so too must the emphasis on human and minority rights, the development of political and social pluralism, and the expansion and liberalisation of civil society. Both sets of objectives hinge on the development of governance and the interaction between state and non-state actors.

Thus far the most tangible legacy of EU assistance in Serbia would appear to be the existence of a tier of professional NGOs with significantly developed capacity to apply for and manage small and medium-sized grants. However, there is little evidence of the diffusion of expertise and know-how to small local organisations, whose absorption capacity for assistance remains low. There is also little sign of the larger recipient organisations being able to take on larger projects. In other words, even amongst the organisations that are most successful at dealing with the EU, their capacity to manage projects seems to have stalled and the developmental impact of assistance seems low.

The most important finding of the research undertaken in Serbia is that the interaction between recipient NGOs and government or state agencies occurs at a low level and invariably involves little more than the granting of licences or the provision of data. If NGOs do gain access to policy forums as a consequence of EU projects, it is in the context of collating data and producing reports. Most of the activities generated by CARDS funding involved NGOs providing services in communities either in lieu of or in conjunction with the state and the market.

In part this reality can be explained in terms of the legal and fiscal context in which NGOs operate. However, the requirements of the application process, the management of projects and the monitoring requirements, plus the ever-changing focus of project grants, the short-term nature of the awards, and the stipulations regarding match funding in conjunction have produced and maintained a hierarchy of distinctive organisations that are increasingly dedicated to obtaining and managing EU project grants, irrespective of the focus or theme. The scope of funding, the impact of EU project grants, and the capacity of recipients to build on successful projects are constrained as much by the absorption capacity of the non-governmental sector and by the process of grant allocation as they are by political contexts and legacies in Serbia.

5

Quantitative analysis of EU assistance to Bosnia-Herzegovina and Serbia

Introduction

The aim of this third empirical chapter is to provide an exposition of the quantitative analysis undertaken for this research in order to offer some additional analysis relating to the impact of project grants on recipient organisations, their attitudes towards the EU and the process of application, the number of projects they have managed and their success rate, as well as providing basic data on the size and capacities of the NGOs with whom the EU Delegations and the EAR engages in both locations. Whilst the information in the last two chapters was drawn predominantly from qualitative interviews with recipient NGOs, the analysis included here is drawn almost entirely from quantitative (and some qualitative) analysis of an electronic questionnaire[1] completed by 69 recipient organisations in both locations.

Hypotheses as to the institutionalisation of social movement organisations

To evaluate the governance impact of such assistance, and to examine the interaction between EU-funded NGOs and government/state agencies, four hypotheses are constructed. These are derived largely from the theoretical literature on the institutionalisation of social movement organisations, and the work of Van der Heijden (1997) in particular.

Whilst the focus of the research was not specifically to measure the institutionalisation of NGOs, the interaction between state agencies and the organisations funded by the EU – the degree of co-operation, proximity and shared objectives between the actors – is a measure of governance and the distribution of power between state and non-state actors. The literature on the institutionalisation of social movements thus offers an entirely relevant theoretical framework for hypothesising the interaction. Indeed, Meyer and Tarrow's description of institutionalisation as 'the routinization of conflict and the adherence to conventional and legitimised rules of engagement by movement actors' (1998: 19) reflects the concern of scholars of collective action to explain and theorise the increasing proximity between once-radical anti-systemic social movements, and the evident interdependence of government and non-governmental civil society actors. In an attempt both to examine the transformation within social movements organisations that facilitate such proximity with the state, and to characterise the nature of the interaction, Van der Heijden distinguishes between *internal* and *external* institutionalisation.

Internal institutionalisation is defined in terms of professionalism and centralisation. In essence, to be part of governance networks, non-governmental organisations and social movement organisations have to become more professional and develop their internal management capacity to meet the challenge of co-operation within policy networks. Measures of internal institutionalisation would therefore be the extent to which an organisation develops its bureaucratic structures, its internal management structures, and the professionalism of its operations. The centralisation aspect refers to the emergence of a core office or centre of operations emerging with managerial and bureaucratic capacity. The more professional an organisation becomes the greater the role played by career professionals, and particularly those with specific skills and knowledge, such as management and financial expertise. There will be less reliance on volunteers, campaigners and casual staff. A critical component of internal institutionalisation, according to Van der Heijden, is an increased capacity to mobilise resources. Thus, if EU aid is strengthening the capacity of NGOs to interact with the state, then we would expect recipient organisations to be developing their internal organisational capacity and professionalising their operations as a consequence of the assistance they receive. We would anticipate evidence of increased organisational sustainability, which in effect means a developed capacity to raise revenue.

The key feature of *external institutionalisation* is an increasingly important role played by non-governmental actors within governance networks and within policy arenas (Rootes 2003: 3) and that this should correspond to 'those working in organisations . . . come increasingly to speak the same language as government and business (with) . . . informal contact between specialists in the civil service and those with similar expertise in organisations . . . based on shared technical and professional norms' (Doherty 2002: 134).

Drawing on the conceptual framework of institutionalisation, the research questionnaire was designed to test four hypotheses:

1. EU assistance channelled through NGOs in BiH and Serbia helps to pro-
    fessionalise the organisation (developing the capacities of their central
    offices and increasing the number of professional paid staff with specific
    expertise);
2. EU micro and macro projects engage recipient organisations in policy and
    governance networks;
3. EU assistance channelled through NGOs serves to strengthen govern-
    mental capacity by enabling state agencies to develop skills and to facilitate
    the provision of services separately, or in conjunction with, NGOs beyond
    the tenure of the specific project;
4. EU assistance helps foster and strengthen the long-term sustainability of
    recipient organisations.

Professionalisation and sustainability of recipient NGOs (Hypotheses 1 and 4)

With regard to the first hypothesis, a series of observations can be drawn from
the data relating to the development of professionalism amongst recipient
organisations. Those NGOs receiving EU grants in Serbia and BiH were more
long-established than might have been assumed: only 2.9 per cent were established 'less than 6 months ago', and the vast majority, 78.3 per cent, were established 'more than 5 years ago' (Table 5.2).

   However, whilst recipient organisations were quite long established, they
were small operations with little evidence of internal expansion and particularly developed capacity. The number of staff they employed (Table 5.1) was
relatively small, with 40 per cent of organisations employing less than five full-
time members of staff, with only 11 per cent (eight respondents) having a staff
of more than ten. During semi-structured interviews with a sample of organisations from both states (40 in total) respondents were asked whether the size

Table 5.1 Human resources

How many people work for the organisation full-time and part-time?		*Per cent*
F/T	0	4.3
employees	less than 5	40.6
	between 5 and 10	33.3
	more than 10	11.6
	more than 20	10.1
P/T	less than 5	33.3
employees	between 5 and 10	47.0
	more than 10	19.7

Table 5.2 Organisation established

When was your organisation established?	Frequency	Per cent	Cumulative per cent
Less than 6 months	2	2.9	2.9
More than 12 months	2	2.9	5.8
Within the last 5 years	11	15.9	21.7
More than 5 years ago	54	78.3	100.0
Total	69	100.0	

of their organisation had altered over the past four year. In 86 per cent of cases the number of employees in 2007 was similar to or the same as in 2003.

However, the data gathered as part of the semi-structured interviews revealed that in a majority of organisations that had successfully managed at least one EU project, staff were employed and recruited specifically for their professional or specialised expertise, which was usually the ability to complete project applications, knowledge of logic frameworks and financial management and competent English language skills. For example, the Bosnian organisation, Mozaik, which was the recipient of four CARDS/EIDHR-funded project grants since 2004, had a team of three designated staff members working on project applications and the organisation recruited staff with financial management and accounting expertise. The low number of full-time or part-time employees did not necessarily reflect the capacity and size of the organisation; several of the organisations interviewed claimed that they were able to quickly recruit professional staff to work on funded projects and thus temporarily expand the size of their organisations. For example, whilst the Sarajevo-based organisation CTV Most, which managed EU-funded projects providing psycho-social therapy and support for victims of torture and violence, had less than five full-time members of staff, the grant funding enabled them to employ various health professionals on a part-time contractual basis.[2]

The funding situation within an organisation is obviously a critical indicator of its development, professionalism and long-term sustainability. As illustrated in Table 5.4, the vast majority (85.5 per cent) of NGOs in receipt of EU assistance also obtained grants from other donors. The EU only ever provides a maximum of 80 per cent funding for successful project applications; the remaining 20 per cent, which has to be secured prior to the start of the project, must be obtained either from another international or local donor, from the state, or from internal resources of the organisation.

It is this requirement of the application process that precludes less well-established organisations from obtaining project grants. In the projects analysed for this research match funding was obtained in the vast majority of cases from other international donors (usually small European or American bilateral donors) or, in a small number of cases, from the organisation's existing resources.

The data suggests that there was a high level of dependency on foreign donor revenue amongst recipients of EU assistance, and that the availability of state funds for civil society was limited in both locations.[3] It also suggests that recipients of micro grants were generally those with existing capacity to raise donor revenue, had experience of managing project grants, and were relatively speaking more sustainable than other NGOs. However, it needs to be recognised that dependency on smaller foreign donors is not necessarily a sustainable source of income; evidence from the Central and East European states that joined the EU in 2004 and 2007 suggests that as EU assistance increases and progress towards accession occurs, small bilateral and multilateral donors withdraw their support quite rapidly (Carmin and Vandeveer 2006). There was already evidence to suggest that this was occurring in both Serbia and BiH.[4] The findings also confirm the view that there was a narrow dissemination of EU assistance and that project grants were being located amongst a narrow elite of organisations that had already crossed a development threshold.

Growth in the number of passive fee-paying members of an organisation is widely recognised as being indicative of a shift towards institutionalisation and increased professionalisation, and as a sustainable strategy for reducing dependency on transient donor funding (van der Heijden 1997). Of the 69 organisations surveyed as part of this research, only 10 per cent (six organisations) had a registered membership of more than 200 people; in 80 per cent of cases (55 organisations) the number of registered members was less than 50. Overall there was not a single organisation that generated more than 10 per cent of its income from membership fees. Of the 40 organisations interviewed, none reported that it invested resources (including staff time) in the development of fee-paying membership, whereas in all cases significant resources were directed towards obtaining foreign donor (predominantly EU) income. In practically all cases (38 organisations of the 40 interviewed) the percentage of overall revenue from foreign donors had remained more or less constant since 2004; in all cases there was a reported increase in EU-derived revenue as a proportion of overall income, and a prediction of greater dependency on EU funding in the future.

Table 5.3 Duration of the project

Duration of project	Frequency	Per cent	Cumulative per cent
Less than 12 months	18	26.1	26.1
12 months	36	52.2	78.3
18 months	9	13.0	91.3
24 months	5	7.2	98.6
36 months	1	1.4	100.0
Total	69	100.0	

In light of the growing dependency of organisations in both locations on EU project grants, a relevant indicator of sustainability is therefore the length of these projects – how secure and long-term the funding is on which organisations are increasingly coming to rely.

The majority of organisations (52.2 per cent) had received, or were in receipt of, projects lasting for 12 months (Table 5.3); the vast majority (91.3 per cent) of projects ran for no more than 18 months; and only a fraction (less than 10 per cent) were tenable for two years or more. The majority of projects (78.2 per cent) received grants of up to €100, 000 (Table 5.5). This usually corresponded to a maximum of 80 per cent of the total cost of the project (all recipients are, under EU rules, required to obtain match funding of 20 per cent as a condition of the award). Only 10 per cent of Bosnian or Serbian organisations that had received EU project grants were awarded funds in excess of €250,000; the vast majority of awards were for what the Commission defines as micro projects (€50–100,000).

Table 5.4 Funding from other donors

Are you currently receiving funding from other international donors?	Frequency	Per cent
Yes	59	85.5
No	10	14.5

Table 5.5 Size of grants

Size of grant	Frequency	Per cent	Cumulative per cent
Less than €10k	2	2.9	2.9
€10–50k	15	21.7	24.6
€50–100k	37	53.6	78.2
€100–250k	8	11.7	89.9
More than €250k	7	10.1	100.0
Total	69	100.0	

Professionalism and a focus on policy

The objective of becoming a professional organisation rather than a campaigning or community group, and a greater emphasis placed by an organisation on influencing government policy, is seen as tangible evidence of the external institutionalisation of recipient organisations. Whilst it is acknowledged here that many successful organisations in western liberal democracies combine such a focus with radical activism (e.g. Greenpeace, Amnesty International), the importance attached to influencing elites is used in this study as a measure of institutionalisation and the potential construction of governance networks.

Recipient organisations were asked as part of the questionnaire: *How would you describe the aims of your organisation?* They were given the following choices, which they were instructed to rank in order of importance:

- We want to be a professional organisation.
- We want to influence government policy.
- We want to change public opinion.
- We want to defend our community.
- We want to influence decision-making in the EU.

The percentage of organisations ranking first the objective 'be a professional organisation' was 40 per cent, with 30 per cent (20 respondents) ranking it either 4th or 5th. Over half (54 per cent) of organisations ranked 'influence government policy' either 1st or 2nd. Nearly a quarter (24 per cent) of respondents ranked 'defend our community' as 1st or 2nd. This suggests that an overwhelming majority (94 per cent – 65 respondents) specified either becoming a professional organisation, or influencing government policy as a key priority (1st or 2nd).

Respondents were also asked as part of the questionnaire: *How would you describe the impact that EU funding has had on your organisation?* The vast majority of recipients across both states (95 per cent – 62 respondents) acknowledged that 'EU funding has strengthened our organisation'. As a measure of their dependency on EU project funding and thus their overall weakness as an organisation, recipients were also asked to agree or disagree with the statement 'We would not exist without EU funding'; only 7.7 per cent (five respondents) confirmed this statement to be accurate and not a single recipient organisation felt that engagement with the EU had 'weakened their organisation'.

Qualitative analysis of the interview data gathered from recipient organisations and from the Delegation in Sarajevo and the EAR in Belgrade suggested that the same few organisations tend to receive project grants in each bi-annual project round, and that when partnerships with local or regional organisations were established for the purpose of the project grant application, in 90 per cent of cases this involved the larger city-based NGO as the dominant partner.[5] Interview data also revealed that in all cases in which such partnerships were formed, the local partner organisations is not a local chapter of the dominant organisation, or formally part of the larger organisation's internal structure. There was also no evidence of amalgamations occurring; rather, evidence gained from interviews suggested that co-operation between city-based and local (weaker) NGOs is simply for the purposes of the former obtaining EU project grants (partnerships with smaller local organisations is identified as a desirable criteria by the Commission). The narrow focus and dissemination of aid was also reinforced by the fact that in 2006 both CARDS and EIDHR project grants were allocated by the Local Delegation in Sarajevo to the same five organisations,[6] referred to by the Delegation as 'our clients'.[7] This suggests that the EU's aim to diffuse capacity-building know-how widely amongst non-governmental organisations and other civil society organisations is proving unsuccessful.

Analysis of the quantitative data confirmed many such findings: nearly two-thirds (60.9 per cent – 42 respondents) of organisations in receipt of a project grant during the research period had previously been awarded EU funding (Table 5.6). Furthermore, 75 per cent (51 respondents) of recipient organisations were based in large cities (Mostar, Tuzla, Banja Luka, Novi Sad), with 47 per cent (32 respondents) based in the capital cities of Sarajevo and Belgrade (Table 5.8)

However, the data also revealed that a significant number (33.3 per cent) of successful grantees were new organisations being awarded project grants for the first time. Whilst in both countries a core of established NGOs do appear to dominate each grant round, the data also suggests that organisations have rarely been awarded more than three project grants (Table 5.7).

Table 5.6 First application to the EU?

	Frequency	Per cent
No	42	60.9
Yes	23	33.3
Subtotal	65	94.2
Missing	4	5.8
Total	69	100.0

Table 5.7 How many applications made to the EU by your organisation have been successful?

	Frequency	*Per cent*	*Cumulative per cent*
0	5	7.2	8.3
1	13	18.8	30.0
2	16	23.2	56.7
3	9	13.0	71.7
4	7	10.1	83.3
5	5	7.2	91.7
6	4	5.8	98.3
7	1	1.4	100.0
Subtotal	60	87.0	
Missing	9	13.0	
Total	69	100.0	

Table 5.8 Location of organisation

	Frequency	*Per cent*	*Cumulative per cent*
Sarajevo or Belgrade	32	46.4	47.1
Mostar, Tuzla or Banja Luka	19	27.5	75.0
Other	17	24.6	100.0
Subtotal	68	98.5	
Missing	1	1.4	
Total	69	100.0	

Engagement in governance networks (Hypotheses 2 and 3)

The focus of EU assistance for BiH and Serbia as potential candidate countries, delivered through the framework of the CARDS programme, has been to strengthen each country's capacity to meet the Copenhagen political criteria, 'enhance administrative and judicial capacity and encourage some alignment with the *Acquis*.[8] This immediately orientates assistance to the democratisation of political elites and the process of government, administrative reform of state bureaucracies, judicial and market reform.

It is not surprising therefore that in its calls for proposals, however large or small, the Commission (via the local Delegation in BiH or the EAR in Serbia) places overt emphasis on building good governance, inter-sectoral partnerships between government and non-governmental organisations, some aspect of service provision, and a contribution of the project to policy development as tangible desired outcomes. From analysis of the questionnaire data it appeared as though the second hypothesis ('EU micro and macro projects engage

Table 5.9 Does the project involve you working with state/government?

	Frequency	Per cent
No	11	15.9
Yes	52	75.4
Subtotal	63	91.3
Missing	6	8.7
Total	69	100.0

recipient organisations in policy and governance networks') would be proven partially correct. The extent of NGO-government interaction (either at national, regional or local level) was initially tested by asking the organisation whether the EU-funded project required them to work with government or state agencies (Table 5.9), to which 75.4 per cent of respondents replied that their projects did involve interaction with government. The data also suggested that the majority of projects involved NGOs working with other organisations and thus contributing to the strengthening of networks and the general infrastructure of the non-governmental sector (Table 5.10).

However, as discussed at some length in the two previous chapters of this book, the issue of interaction with government and state actors was followed up during semi-structured interviews. Each respondent interviewed as part of the sample survey was asked detailed questions regarding the nature of this reported interaction. It was revealed that in the vast majority of cases this did not actually involve NGOs playing an active role in policy development or deliberation, but typically involved them having gained a letter of support from relevant state agencies or government ministries as part of the application process for the project, gaining some kind of data relevant to the project (e.g. lists of schools, prisons, unemployed persons), or being granted permission to undertake the project in public institutions. Interviews with 5 out of the 11 organisations that had claimed their project did *not* involve them working with government or state agencies revealed that in all but two cases, the project

Table 5.10 Does the project involve you working with other organisations?

	Frequency	Per cent
No	14	20.3
Yes	50	72.5
Subtotal	64	92.8
Missing	5	7.2
Total	69	100.0

involved the same level or type of interaction with government ministries or state offices as projects being undertaken by organisations that had claimed there was interaction with government.

Impact of EU assistance and attitudes of recipients

Thus far analysis of the survey questionnaire data has measured the growth and capacities of recipient organisations, their interaction with government and state agencies, and attributed various development trends to the existence of EU assistance. An alternative measure of impact is to look at the attitudes and opinions of recipient organisations regarding EU funding and their perceptions of the impact such aid has had.

The questionnaire data revealed (Table 5.11) that the vast majority of organisations (90 per cent) felt that EU funding received through project grants had strengthened their organisation; nearly half of all respondents (43 per cent) felt

Table 5.11 Impact of EU funding[a]

How would you describe the impact that EU funding has had on your organisation?	Agree
'EU funding has strengthened our organisation'	90%
'Applying for EU funding has been a distraction from our work'	6%
'EU funding has helped us connect with similar organisations'	43%
'EU funding has helped us connect with the local community'	45%
'EU funding has prevented us from working in the community'	2%
'EU funding has had no impact on our organisation'	1%
'We would not exist without EU funding'	5%
'EU funding has helped us connect with similar organisations in neighbouring countries'	19%
'EU funding has changed the issues we work on'	10%
'EU funding has weakened our organisation'	0%

Notes

a Respondents were asked to tick statements with which they agreed and were instructed that they could tick more than one box.

Table 5.12 Question: 'Do you think the process (of applying for an EU project) next time would be . . .'

	Frequency	Per cent
As difficult	21	30.4
Easier	45	65.2
More difficult	3	4.4
Total	69	100.0

that EU assistance had enabled them to connect with similar organisations, whilst still enabling them to connect with the local community (45 per cent). Whilst the qualitative analysis of the interview data suggested that recipient NGOs were becoming increasingly dependent on the EU as the main source of revenue, the survey data revealed that only 5 per cent felt that they would not exist without EU funding. This suggests that whilst the EU represents a critical source of income, recipient organisations are perhaps somewhat stronger than imagined, have greater capacities, and are more sustainable than initially assumed.

A further positive finding is that whilst a third of recipients (28 per cent) found the application process 'difficult' or 'very difficult' (Table 5.14), the majority (70 per cent) found the process 'manageable', while two-thirds believed that the process of application to the EU would be 'easier next time' (Table 5.12), and practically all recipients (98.5 per cent) intended to apply again to the Delegation (Table 5.13). This is a significant finding insofar as one of the major concerns of the EU, the EAR and the local Delegations has been the low absorption capacity of the non-governmental sectors in both countries.

Table 5.13 Question: 'Would you apply for an EU grant again?'

	Frequency	*Per cent*
Yes	67	98.5
No	2	1.5
Total	69	100.0

Table 5.14 Question: 'How did your organisation find the process of applying for EU funding?'

	Frequency	*Per cent*	*Cumulative per cent*
Very difficult	8	11.8	11.8
Difficult	11	16.2	27.9
Manageable	48	70.6	98.5
Easy	1	1.5	100.0

Analysis and discussion

EU assistance channelled through NGOs, regardless of the specific project focus, prioritises the building of good governance. In terms of the Stabilisation and Association process (SAp), this essentially means fostering partnerships between the state and the non-governmental sector in the context of policy development, implementation and service provision. For the Commission, it would seem that 'good governance' is code for all aspects of regime change: economic liberalisation, building institutional capacity, the formation of new laws and policy, compliance and implementation, as well as public service provision. In essence, governance is conceptualised as *purposive* activity with the aim of transforming norms, values and behaviours (Rosenau 1995).

This book seeks to examine the extent to which CARDS and EIDHR assistance for BiH and Serbia has contributed to the development of governance by successfully engaging state and non-state actors in the context of project grants. From the perspective of quantitative questionnaire data from recipient NGOs, the aim of this chapter was to evaluate the degree to which organisational capacities are being augmented, to consider the types of skills and knowledge being obtained as a consequence of EU assistance, and the impact of assistance on the internal management and resource deployment of the recipient organisation. In addition, the intention was to examine, as an indicator of governance, whether partnerships are being built between state agencies and the non-governmental sector, and the exact nature of such interactions.

The research revealed that a narrow core of NGOs *has* become more professional and gained project management know-how; these organisations are undoubtedly wedded to EU development aims and processes. However, in terms of how many organisations benefit and whether the assistance extends across both countries, the impact of CARDS and EIDHR grants is limited: most recipients (75 per cent) are located either in capital cities or large urban areas and although the actual projects take place across both countries, the spread of know-how is narrowly focused. Indeed, the most discernible and tangible outcome of assistance is an increased capacity of between 10 and 15 organisations in Serbia and BiH to manage small project grants. These organisations dominate each call for proposals and work closely with either the EU Delegations or the EAR. Whilst there has clearly been a transfer of knowledge and expertise from the EU to recipient organisations, the size of organisations has not generally altered. In sum, the knowledge transfer is limited and the assistance has helped augment quite specific capacities. For example, there is little or no evidence of the ability of recipient organisations, as a consequence of EU assistance, to mobilise political resources, to extend campaigns within civil society, or to raise additional revenue.

In terms of building closer policy interaction between state and non-state actors the research revealed virtually no evidence that this was occurring as a consequence of EU assistance. State agencies co-operated with NGOs within the confines of specific short-term projects, but at the most basic and often arbitrary level (granting a permit, providing a letter of approval, supplying data). Where there was interaction between the sectors around policy or service provision, this tended to involve the state agency effectively sub-contracting research or development tasks to an NGO. The short-term nature of the EU-funded projects, and the lack of provision for extending initiatives into other localities, widening the focus or remit, or renewing the contract at the end of the grant period is of particular concern as it has obvious implications for the building of sustainable governance. Initiatives to develop employment skills in marginalised communities, or the provision of training for school teachers simply stopped once the project came to an end, along with the co-operation or interaction between the NGO and the particular state agency. Apart from a local municipality taking over partial responsibility for the running of a safe house established initially by an NGO,[9] there was no instance revealed whereby engagement with an NGO as part of an EU project resulted in a sustainable partnership being established. The overriding sense is that government offices and state agencies were prepared to co-operate with NGOs as part of small discrete projects where there was some mutual benefit (the provision of a service or a training scheme), but only within the confines of the project and at a low level of interaction.

Conclusion

Such findings would appear to partially explain why, despite nearly a decade of EU intervention, state weakness remains a critical development issue in both countries. However, the continued weakness of the Bosnian and Serbian states is symptomatic of a far more deep-seated structural reality, which cannot be explained simply in terms of the limited impact of EU intervention assistance. Efforts to build good governance are thwarted by the persistence of what Kostovicova and Bojičić-Dželilović (2006) refer to as 'trans-national networks' that thrive upon and reinforce weak state capacity. According to the authors, these networks are hard to define and are the product of a combination of legacies: the informal distribution and parallel economy networks of the socialist period, the wars of Yugoslav succession during the 1990s and the (contested) reconfiguration of state borders, international intervention and liberal economic reforms. These opaque networks prosper in the unregulated economic and political spaces and thrive on state weakness and bureaucratic inertia; they comprise a mix of nationalist elites and state bureaucrats, 'criminal gangs, diasporas and ordinary trades people' (2006: 232). Whilst their contemporary efficacy is in a sense the product of globalisation – these transnational networks prosper in the confusion surrounding national versus international, formal versus informal, state versus non-state – the forces of globalisation have merely intensified and enabled processes deeply embedded within the recent history of Yugoslavia and the successor states. International assistance both during and since the wars has been incapable of dislodging the power of these networks; the EU, now the dominant source of development aid, has, it would seem, also failed to penetrate and bring forth a decline in their influence and their control over both the state and the economy. Instead, as suggested by this research, assistance serves to reinforce, or at least not challenge, the status quo; development aid channelled through local NGOs compensates for failings in state provision and low levels of market penetration. Whilst project grants do enable citizens to access services that would otherwise not be provided, this inadvertently legitimises and at times empowers the transnational networks and corrupt elites intent on sustaining state weakness and a pervasive climate of poor regulation and compliance. There is little prospect that the good governance initiatives of the EU, reduced as they are to building low-level interaction between state agencies and a handful of NGOs, will challenge structural realities and usurp the entrenched power of elites.

6

EU assistance and intervention in Kosovo: lessons learnt?

Introduction: the EU in Kosovo

Kosovo's unilateral declaration of independence in February 2008, after a period of eight years under direct UN administration on the basis of Security Council Resolution 1244/1999, presented the international community with a serious political and legal challenge. For the European Union, which has, since 1999 and the Kosovo war, been closely involved in almost all aspects of governance in the province, and has repeatedly confirmed its commitment to offering all the so-called Western Balkan states full membership, the declaration of sovereignty by a politically and economically weak territory poses particular difficulties. Though the EU's presence in the region is well-established – the United Nations Mission in Kosovo (UNMIK) was essentially a coalition between the UN, the EU and the Organisation for Security and Co-operation in Europe (OSCE) – and its role more generally in international politics is greater and more clearly conceptualised (Bretherton and Vogler 2006; Risse-Kappen 1996), the Commission's intervention in Kosovo is nevertheless unchartered and not without contention. Despite the continued political presence of other international agencies, the EU is the main actor and donor in post-independence Kosovo. Yet, as Papadimitriou notes, 'on the eve of . . . independence in February 2008, the record of the UN administration – of which the EU has been an integral part – in Kosovo was mixed and highly contested' (2009: 10). Part of the problem for the EU has been that its record is hard to disentangle from that of the overall impact of international intervention.

However, the image of the EU has also suffered as a consequence of the failure of Kosovo's economy, for which the Commission was given responsibility as part of the UNMIK coalition. According to the Commission's own statistics, 37 per cent of the population live in poverty and in 2005 GDP per capita was the lowest in the region despite the EU's efforts to stimulate growth and investment (EC 2006: 38). Whilst it is certainly the case that economic recovery is the key to Kosovo's stability and ultimately its sovereignty, criticism of the EU's role has to be placed in context: any improvement in the economy is hampered by the weakness of the Provisional Institutions of Self-Government (PISG), the indigenous state or governmental structure set up in 2002 but which now, de jure, governs Kosovo. It barely needs stating that the weakness of the PISG was in turn a consequence of the unresolved status of the province until 2008 and thus the responsibility for economic failure cannot be laid entirely at the door of the EU. Nevertheless, the perception of the EU's legacy, reiterated by several of the recipients of aid within the NGO sector interviewed for this research, is at best one of rather haphazard and inefficient distribution of aid, and at worst total failure to deliver economic recovery.

Such criticisms and dilemmas notwithstanding, it has to be acknowledged that the provision of assistance to Kosovo has been the most extensive and ambitious foreign policy and external relations mission for the EU to date. The main focus of the Commission's post-independence intervention is building the judicial capacity of the new state. In practice this involves a hugely resource-intensive process of professionals from EU member states shadowing local judges and law enforcement agencies and officers. The most discernible contrast with other interventions in the Western Balkans and post-socialist Europe is that mention of democratisation and democracy promotion is scant and has been subordinated to an overriding emphasis placed on the rule of law, state capacity and efficiency, and (most importantly perhaps) local ownership. Overall, the Commission is now the territory's largest single provider of aid by a wide margin, having committed €2 billion from 1999 to 2007 with an additional €60 million invested in 2008 as part of the IPA annual programme for vital infrastructure projects. Despite the extensive resource commitment the final cost of which has not been estimated and obvious uncertainty surrounding Kosovo's capacity to meet the terms of EU conditionality, the Commission remains steadfastly committed to Kosovo's European perspective. The EU has financed a comprehensive scheme of capacity assistance for Kosovo's initially hybrid (i.e. the Provisional Institutions of Self-Government – PISG) and, now, official government. All in all, the EU has, since 1999, gradually assumed the task of state-building for a state that has only just come into existence, but the sovereignty of which still remains disputed. The Commission's responsibilities are extensive: it has assumed full financial as well as administrative responsibility for the implementation of the civilian aspects of the UN's concept of supervised independence for the disputed territory, is in charge of the custom services, manages the somewhat embryonic privatisation process, and oversees regulatory control of the economy and the banking and financial sectors (Papadimitriou et al. 2007). Although it was widely assumed, both before and after the declaration of sovereignty, that the UN would hand over all power and responsibility to the Commission, a year hence the EU still shares its responsibilities with UNMIK (the UN Mission in Kosovo). Nevertheless, in contrast to pre-February 2008, the Commission is today the dominant partner able to assume a leading role, particularly with regard to the rule of law.

More than any other candidate or potential candidate country in the Western Balkans, Kosovo will be guided and assisted towards membership by the Commission itself. Whilst this in no sense guarantees early entrance or extenuation with regard to meeting the strict criteria, it does mean that state-building, governance and the rule of law are inextricably bound to EU accession in a way not witnessed elsewhere in the region: ultimately it is only membership for Kosovo that will undoubtedly signal the success of EU assistance and intervention. The EU's relationship with Kosovo is thus somewhat hegemonic insofar as it combines corrective powers a reformulation of the role of the international community – with the rigidities of conditionality. Whilst the Commission's commitment to Kosovo appears unshakeable and the resource endowment substantial, a number of serious constraints on progress towards the European perspective are at play: the main obstacle is the extent to which Kosovo can meet the strict Copenhagen criteria, not to mention the various other political, economic and social obligations and conditions. The case of Kosovo undoubtedly raises questions regarding the effectiveness of conditionality and the potential serious gulf between formal compliance and 'on the ground' change. Whilst such concerns are pertinent to all potential candidate countries in the region, they take on a new dimension in the context of Kosovo due to the particularly weak state of the economy and an embryonic and nebulous state infrastructure. In such a situation talk of democratisation and good governance is somewhat overshadowed by concerns regarding the rule of law, sovereignty and the functional capacity of the state. While it is not specifically the focus of this study, it is nevertheless essential to recognise the extent to which Kosovo presents the EU with distinct and long-term challenges: as the EC Progress Report of 2008 notes, 'the living conditions of the most vulnerable communities have not improved . . . [t]he proper implementation of legislation and its monitoring are not ensured [nor is there a] strategy for reconciliation and inter-community dialogue'.

During the period since 1999 the EU has attempted to deliver its objectives on the ground through a complex network of formal and ad hoc institutions, agencies and policy instruments. Devising an effective and appropriate institutional infrastructure was difficult for the Commission, partly because its role in Kosovo was, as noted above, initially as a constituent part of UNMIK. As the terms of the EU's engagement altered during the period (particularly after the riots of March 2004 which destabilised the security situation) to embrace the impetus of engaging local municipal elites within the process of governance, but also to take on a larger role in security, new institutions and mechanisms became necessary. The diffusion of responsibilities across six different institutions – the European Agency for Reconstruction (EAR); the European Union Monitoring Mission (EUMM); Common Foreign and Security Policy (CFSP) field office; the EU Liaison office, EULEX (police and justice) and a European Union Planning Team (EUPT) – has aroused a great deal of criticism from scholars who question the effectiveness or 'actorness' of the EU (Papadimitriou et al. 2007). The overlapping remits, perceived duplication of roles, and a general sense of a mosaic of different actors and institutions has been compounded by the fact that the UN, the Council of Europe as well as NATO were also present in Kosovo during this period. The most visible expression of EU involvement and assistance was, up until its closure in 2008, the EAR, which, as a development agency, has proved itself to be efficient and effective elsewhere in the region. However, the difficulty for the Commission during the period 1999–2008 was that whilst its institutional presence reflected a development agenda based on humanitarian aid and economic redevelopment, its actual role and objectives were increasingly moving towards a political and governance role. The reason for this apparent disjuncture is that the Commission had no independent presence in Kosovo during this time largely because Kosovo was (and still is) not an internationally recognised state; in essence, the EU entered in one capacity but rapidly found itself with responsibility for a different set of objectives and cast in a somewhat different role.

In delivering its assistance for Kosovo via the IPA and EIDHR frameworks the Commission has followed what appears to be an established process based on the SAp/European Partnership framework. As is the case elsewhere in the Western Balkans, the Commission's leverage to ensure compliance and the realisation of the new conditionalities for Kosovo is based on the promise of future accession. If indeed the overall approach does differ from intervention in BiH or elsewhere it does so largely in terms of degree and an augmented focus on law reform and policing. For critics, despite the EU's now dominant role, there is little that is new or indeed bespoke about the post-independence approach: it is seemingly a continuation of the 'standards before status' policy pursued by the UN Security Council in the early years of this decade, which aimed to build the functional capacity of the state administration as a foundation on which to develop future sovereignty (Weller 2008). Indeed for some commentators there is a stifling continuity between strategies designed by the international community to deliver 'supervised sovereignty' after 1999, and the current EU approach based on extensive measures across various sectors designed to deliver improvements in governance and the delivery of services (Pond 2008: 102).

Today, the main manifestation of the EU's presence in Kosovo is EULEX, the European Union Rule of Law Mission in Kosovo. Described by the Commission as 'the largest civilian mission ever launched under the European Security and Defence Policy (ESDP)', the role of EULEX is not to govern Kosovo – it is not an EU version of the Office of the High Representative in BiH – but 'to assist and support the Kosovo authorities in the rule of law… specifically (with regard to reform of) police, judiciary and customs', to establish sustainable and accountable law enforcement agencies within the new state, and create a 'multi-ethnic police and customs service, ensuring that these institutions are free from political interference and adhere to internationally recognised standards and European best practices'. In the provision of its assistance and monitoring for judicial authorities and law enforcement agencies, EULEX comprises three components: police, justice and customs. However, whilst the purpose of the Mission is primarily to provide technical assistance and advice for all aspects of the legal service and authorities, it also 'retain(s) a number of limited executive powers'.

The discussion above has sought to provide a context and overview of the EU's engagement in the territory since 1999 with the aim of highlighting the significant constraints on effectiveness and successful impact, but also illustrating the nature of the challenge. What cannot be over-emphasised within a discussion of the EU and Kosovo is the extent to which the success of EU intervention and the pursuit of Kosovo's European perspective is dependent on a renewed momentum for enlargement for the Western Balkans, and is contingent upon the political and economic progress of Kosovo's neighbours, particularly Serbia. It also has to be acknowledged that attitudes towards the EU in the country will continue to be determined by the performance of the EU 'on the ground'. The EU is in many respects trapped in a vicious circle: some commentators have been keen to emphasise a somewhat dichotomous relationship between attitudes towards the EU and an overriding pro-Americanism. If economic progress remains slow and the prevailing view of the EU agencies is one of poor performance, then a positive engagement with the enlargement conditions is likely to stall, feeding an already manifest albeit latent scepticism towards the whole EU project; this in turn will further weaken the capacity of the EU to use conditionality to drive change and build the efficiency of the fledgling state and the economy.

However, it is perhaps all too easy to focus exclusively on the limitations of external involvement without fully acknowledging indigenous structural constraints that exert a profound impact on the success of assistance in the region generally and specifically in Kosovo. In terms of the specific form of assistance examined in this study – engaging local NGOs and civil society organisations in the delivery of capacity assistance and state-building – a significant constraint is the small size of the professional middle class. As Pond observes in a recent article, 'Serbia, despite the hemorrhage of Belgrade's middle class in the past two decades . . . has outstanding lawyers, prosecutors, judges and human rights watchdogs. Kosovo, by contrast, does not . . .' (2008: 107–8). We begin with an in-depth analysis of the state of civil society in Kosovo, its evolution and current capacities.

Civil society and the non-state sector in Kosovo – the challenge for EU assistance

The period since 2000, and the arrival in Kosovo of numerous foreign donors, prompted a significant increase in NGO activity. However, any attempt to analyse the strengths and capacities of civil society in Kosovo, map the civil society landscape, or to examine the difficulties in strengthening the non-state sector, must begin by distinguishing between the relatively small sector of registered NGOs, established in large part since 2000, beneficiaries of donor aid, that appear to represent a new form of civil society activism, and the much more opaque informal and ethnicised networks rooted in local communities and originating from the pre-1999 era. The number of registered organisations, the majority of which are likely to be newly established NGOs, has increased from around 130 in 2001, when registration first began, to over 3,000 today. However, numerous studies of civil society development across post-socialist Europe have emphasised the extent to which registration is generally a poor reflection of capacity, activities or political engagement and provides little insight into the number of NGOs with any significant capacity (Carmin 2010; Fagan and Sircar 2010). Indeed, the only comprehensive and reliable study of civil society undertaken by the Kosovo Civil Society Foundation (KCSF) in 2005 concluded that:

[M]any, if not most, registered CSOs are either moribund or dormant, or lacking sufficient capacity to carry out meaningful activities. Civil society's voice is incoherent, its actions uncoordinated, and as a sector it has been unable to attract serious attention from either the fledgling local government or the UN administration (UNMIK). Public understanding of the aims and values of civil society in Kosovo is confused and CSOs have so far failed to command significant public support or participation.

The research undertaken for this study during 2008 did not discover any evidence that the situation had changed in any way. The experience of NGO development elsewhere in the region and across post-socialist Europe in general would suggest that the newly established organisations are likely to be more involved in service provision than in political or policy advocacy (Fagan 2008).

Whilst the EU and other foreign donors have long since framed their democracy promotion and post-conflict reconstruction aid in terms of support for civil society, civil society's role seems particularly critical in the case of Kosovo: aside from helping to construct EU-compliant policy frameworks (good governance), efficacious CSOs and NGOs could play a critical role in promoting democracy within a society with no experience of liberal democratic politics, particularly with regard to respect for and the articulation of minority and human rights. The role of NGOs in bringing forth change in social policy, in stimulating economic activity, and mobilising citizen participation in local development is significant and should not be under-estimated.

Not surprisingly, the development of civil society in Kosovo is constrained by a similar set of factors that have determined the democratic impact and institutionalisation of associational activity elsewhere in the Western Balkans, and indeed across post-socialist Europe more generally. NGO activity is largely confined to urban centres; a small corps of organisations have become flexible and adaptable in terms of the issues on which they work, but have failed to significantly develop their institutional capacities, their links with communities or their political linkage. Kosovan NGOs, like their Bosnian, Serbian or indeed Bulgarian counterparts, have become semi-professionalised conduits of overseas development aid. The few successful NGOs are not necessarily those that work on the most pressing and pertinent issues, or have the best connections with community networks, but are the ones that are most adept at running projects, have the greatest flexibility to adapt to changing issues and funding patterns, and can switch from donor to donor. The prevalence of informal and personal networks is one of the key constraints identified in the literature that is particularly pertinent to the development of institutionalised civil society in southern Europe and the Balkans (Howard 2003; Sampson 2002). In Kosovo the disconnect between new, western-funded NGOs – 'formal' civil society – and indigenous civil associations and community networks is a particular difficulty and one that takes on additional dimensions in the fragile states or where the legitimacy of the state remains contested (Fagan 2006, 2008). However, in the case of Kosovo, the situation is particularly complex: whilst there has been a growth in NGOs and new CSOs as a consequence of the availability of foreign donor revenue, both the more recently established NGOs that have received donor support, as well as the more enmeshed civil society networks are wedded to the parallel governance experience of the 1990s. In contrast to CEE, where foreign donors supported new stratum of NGOs in the 1990s as part of pro-regime support after transition, donors have assisted NGOs in Kosovo in the context of the delivery of emergency aid, or in their support for independence from the Serbian state and the pro-Belgrade political parties that dominated the formal sphere of Kosovo politics. The defining characteristic of Kosovo's NGOs and CSOs, whether fledgling local associations or more professional NGOs, is therefore opposition to the state and parallel existence. During the 1990s, civil society activity where it existed amongst the ethnic Albanian population was indivisible from political party development and the emergence of clandestine political institutions. The challenge for the EU and other donors is therefore to coax such embryonic manifestations of civil society into engaging with the state and the international community, to separate civil society from political parties and elites, and to connect the new sector of NGOs with community-based networks and with the governing institutions.

Decentralisation, minority rights and the weak state: the challenge for civil society

In theory at least, the easiest way to trigger such engagement is through subsidiarity and the decentralisation of decision-making; civil society development is arguably facilitated where there is a level of decentralisation of decision-making, bringing autonomy closer to citizens and communities in order to facilitate engagement. However, in Kosovo the notion of decentralisation is inextricably bound to the contentious issues of refugee return and minority rights. Bureaucratic decentralisation has become politicised to such an extent that any suggestion of transferring decision-making to municipalities is immediately framed in terms of the status issue and viewed as an attempt to promote specific political interests against the sovereignty of the PISG and the Kosovan state. Pilot projects to decentralise decision-making with regard to, for example, environmental management and strengthening the capacity of local government have met with fierce opposition and have been promptly abandoned. Although the situation for minorities in the territory has improved somewhat since the riots of March 2004 – outbreaks of inter-ethnic violence are now extremely rare – the issue of minority return remains a serious constraint not just on decentralisation, but also on any attempt to coax communities into engaging with the state institutions and the legitimation of municipal and state authorities. Whilst the fact that the Serbian minority in the north continues to boycott the new institutions of governance and refuses to participate in political processes is the most obvious and high-profile constraint, Kosovo's other minority communities – Bosniak, Roma, Egyptian, Ashkali – are equally disenfranchised and non-integrated.

It is impossible to construct any worthy evaluation of civil society or the non-state sector in Kosovo without referring to the weak state of democratic governance. Whilst it is easy to be rather sanguine about the potential prospect of EU intervention generating the development of governance almost from scratch and without the obvious complexities of post-Dayton Bosnia, the fact that Kosovo remains governed through a complicated and opaque system with two separate structures contradicts any notion that Kosovo presents the Commission with a *tabula rasa* for constructing good governance. The rather stifling reality that any attempt to build good governance and civil society must confront is that, more than a year since the declaration of independence, the international status of Kosovo as a universally recognised sovereign state remains in dispute. From this reality stems the fact that the authority of UNMIK and the balance of power between the UN and the EU remains unclear, and the institutions of self-government (formally the PISG) weak. The difficulty for NGOs has been that whilst the PISG proved itself to be fairly open to consultation, decision-making within the much more monolithic UNMIK was remote and largely impenetrable for local NGOs with limited capacities and experience. Indeed, key policy decisions during the 1999–2007 period were either taken outside of Kosovo's borders, or were done so in the context of security and stability and were therefore not conducted in a framework of open deliberation. Whilst the gradual involvement of domestic elites in the governance of the province from 2002 onwards did provide, in theory at least, an opportunity for civil society to engage in governance, the dual system of government, with shared competencies and complex division of responsibilities, has nevertheless undermined the ability of citizens and NGOs to affect decision-making by obfuscating power and accountability. Not only were the powers of the various governing institutions deemed to be opaque, the reporting of decisions in the various local media was scant.

The conclusions reached in the KCSF report of 2005 regarding the weaknesses of civil society and NGOs and the challenges faced in terms of strengthening the non-state sector remain entirely relevant five years later: the sector needs a much clearer definition and understanding of its goals, objectives and roles; organisations running projects and operating in the orbit of donors need to become more connected and rooted in communities and within the issue networks they claim to represent; organisations need to forge strong and sustainable relations with other actors and sectors; the sector must seek to strengthen not just project management capacity, but develop knowledge, expertise and resources in order to engage effectively in governance interaction.

EU assistance: the process of allocation

The programming and delivery of EU assistance for Kosovo, as with BiH and other PCCs, is done in the context of 'centralised de-concentrated management'. This basically means that because the Kosovo government does not yet have the capacity to manage and administer EU assistance, the Commission is much more directly involved in the distribution and allocation of aid than is the case in candidate countries such as Croatia or Macedonia. In terms of identifying priorities or assistance, the Commission relies heavily on the Agency for Co-ordination of Development and European Integration in Pristina. In practice, the agency, which operates in a not dissimilar way to the Directorate of European Integration in Sarajevo, is part of the prime minister's office and thus has, in theory at least, critical executive functions. The agency plays a critical role in co-ordinating as well as helping to devise the focus of assistance. In line with the broad objectives outlined in the European Partnership for Kosovo (2008) the agency works with all government ministries and state agencies to identify development priorities for EU funding and viable project proposals. Agreed proposals are submitted to the Commission in Brussels for checking and evaluation. The Commission will contact all relevant DGs to see whether the proposals fit in with the overall development agenda for Kosovo, as well as seeking the opinions of EU member states regarding whether there is investment interest or opportunities for sharing information. There is also consultation with the World Bank and the UN as well as other development agencies operating in Kosovo.[1]

Once potential funding proposals have been agreed, a Financial Agreement, signed between the Commission and the Government of Kosovo, commits various financial envelopes and an overall amount of funding for specific development areas. The implementing phase then starts, with 'terms of reference' being drawn up and calls for projects and tenders advertised. This aspect of the process is undertaken not by the government, but by the European Commission Liaison Office (ECLO), which is now responsible for the entire allocation and evaluation process.

The ECLO distributes EIDHR and IPA funding through bi-annual calls for proposals, in much the same way as the EC Delegations in Sarajevo and Belgrade. Despite the specific circumstances of Kosovo, much is determined by the rules of the Commission; the operational procedures are the standard global ones that govern EU external relations and there is no flexibility with regard to the requirement, for example, that NGOs provide 20 per cent of an EIDHR-funded project themselves either through match funding or their own resources. However, where there is room for flexibility – the IPA guidelines do permit field offices to determine the percentage of match funding – the ECLO tailors their procedures to meet local conditions.

The most significant contrast between the provision of assistance by the ECLO in Kosovo and the situation in BiH and Serbia concerns the emphasis placed on the provision of training for potential applicant NGOs. Whereas in the other two locations perspective applicants are offered a rather general half-day training workshop at the Delegation in Belgrade or Sarajevo prior to the submission deadline, during 2008 the ECLO provided far more extensive capacity training for local NGOs in six locations across the country. Such bespoke provision represents a recognition of the fact that the local NGOs likely to apply for IPA funding lack basic capacity and have significant training needs. As far as the ECLO is concerned, the core areas of weakness are: reporting and transparency; auditing and financial management; and recruitment and project management.[2]

EU assistance in practice: the European Agency for Reconstruction (EAR)

It is important to recognise when assessing the delivery of EU development aid channelled through civil society and NGOs, that under UNMIK jurisdiction democratisation and institution-building were led by the OSCE rather than the EU or the UN. This is not to suggest that the EU did not provide support for civil society and democracy promotion during the 1999–2008 period, as indeed it did, but it was not an EU priority as such. In fact the Commission was responsible for a vast array of reforms and competencies under the broad umbrella of 'economic reconstruction'. Where the EU did provide support for and engage NGOs was in the context of EIDHR and CARDS funding which was, until June 2008, the responsibility of the European Agency for Reconstruction (EAR) field office in Pristina. With the EAR office now closed, the role has been transferred to the European Liaison Office (ELO).

In the last months of its operation in Kosovo, just prior to the hand-over of EU assistance programmes to the ELO, the EAR was able to complete a number of development projects and initiatives that reflect its overall focus and involvement in Kosovo. Civil society organisations and NGOs were funded by the EAR in the period up until 2008 in the context of these broader development initiatives.

Throughout the region the agency places considerable emphasis on economic development and building skills and capacity for growth and employment. The EAR office in Pristina targeted resources towards the sustainable return of displaced persons and in 2008 completed a project facilitating the return of 27 Roma, Ashkali and Egyptian (RAE) families to their previous villages and to rebuilt houses within the Klinë/Klina Municipality. The agency also ran a large Stabilisation of Communities (SSC) project, with the aim of providing funds for a grants programme to support community development, to be administered by local NGOs. In total the initiative supported 225 financed projects, with 74 new awards being made during 2007–8. The EAR is keen to emphasise that in addition to providing recipients with training on financial management and marketing, the assistance has also led to the creation of over 400 jobs.[3]

During its lengthy tenure, the agency has also provided match grants and technical assistance for private businesses as part of its commitment to enterprise development and job creation in the impoverished and more rural Northern Kosovo region. Several awards have been made to NGOs and businesses in rural areas as part of the Fund for Agro-processing and Industrial Revitalisation (FAIR) programme.

Drawing on the EU's over-arching focus on the rule of law and justice, the agency has also run projects providing support to the Ministry of Justice and other key justice institutions. For example, a recent project (2007–8) focused on building the capacities of the institutions involved in security and justice to realise EU standards and compliance. In terms of institutional support, the EAR has instigated a number of projects. It has provided support for the development of the parliamentary assembly in Kosovo with the intention of aligning practices and procedures with the norms of EU member states. In particular, there has been training offered to develop parliamentary oversight, transparency, accountability and effectiveness. A separate institution-building initiative has seen the provision of support for the Ministry of Economy and Finance (MEF). The agency also completed a project during 2008 to assist the Ministry of Agriculture, Forestry and Rural Development (MAFRD) on agricultural land utilisation issues. Among other results, the project helped to tighten control over misuse of agricultural land for building and industrial development purposes, to introduce land taxation, and to enhance environmental protection. With regard to support for agriculture, the agency has also provided institutional support to MAFRD in order to provide training for ministry staff on collection and analysis of data in accordance with the standards of the EU Farm Accountancy Data Network (FADN).

A particular focus of aid to Kosovo, and to the Western Balkan region as a whole, has been to develop better understanding of the EU as well as to support compliance. One such initiative under this remit saw the EAR team up with the United Nations Development Program (UNDP) office in Kosovo to run the Capacity Building for European Integration (CBEI) project. As the EAR report for 2008 notes, 'the project deployed 35 advisors in EU affairs to respond to specific requests from public institutions, achieving substantial progress in fields such as donor coordination, gender equality, anti-corruption policies, construction legislation and intellectual property rights'.

The EAR acts most effectively as a construction agency and has arguably enjoyed considerable success in infrastructure redevelopment in Kosovo and across the region. Although EAR-funded municipal development projects and social infrastructure development projects in the north have been interrupted since the declaration of independence and the more precarious security situation around the Serbian stronghold of Mitrovica, much has been achieved in terms of road-building schemes, sanitation, and energy sector development in particular. With regard to the latter, the agency has funded studies to evaluate the commercial, technical and environmental benefits involved in switching to renewable energy sources in Kosovo (solar, wind, geothermal, wood and other biomass).

Specific initiatives for supporting civil society and NGOs

In the period from 2001 to 2008 the EAR field office in Pristina targeted EU aid specifically towards strengthening the capacities of key local NGOs that were deemed to have a sufficient initial capacity and potential to manage the allocation of EU assistance, run training and capacity-building workshops for

smaller and weaker organisations, as well as manage larger development projects. One such organisation was the Kosovo Civil Society Foundation (KCSF),
which received EAR grants in this period to build its own internal capacity to
run training seminars and to become an indigenous grantee. The EAR was evi-
dently concerned about the absence of what might be termed intermediary
organisations and foundations able to act as conduits for international donor
revenue and capable of selecting and monitoring recipients. By 2005 KCSF
was, as a consequence of capacity assistance training from the EAR, able to
allocate EU funds on behalf of the agency to local organisations for micro projects in five key priority areas of reconciliation, minority rights, gender equality,
youth and culture.

The first call for projects and funding round administered by the ELO was
for an EIDHR initiative focusing on human rights and promoting civil society
in 2008. The funds available for allocation were €873,000 of which €800,000
was successfully allocated. The call generated 30 applications in total, of which
nine received funding. Compared with other countries in the region, this represents a good proportion of successful applications. Of the nine grantees, at
least two had managed an EU grant before, either as part of a regional programme or as part of an EAR scheme, and the remaining seven had never
received EU funding. The ELO was particularly pleased that it was able to allocate grants to organisations that had never previously had EU funding.[4]

The first IPA call for project proposals in Kosovo occurred in January 2009
and at the time of writing no allocation decisions have been made. The focus of
the call is four-fold: (1) environment; (2) equal opportunities; (3) children's fes-
tival; (4) provision of assistance for children with special educational needs.
The emphasis on education, environment and rights is immediately consistent
with the themes identified in Serbia and BiH and congruent with the overall
aims of the Commission for Kosovo It is also likely that, as in the other
locations, such a focus will encourage and result in the funding of projects
that provide services in communities, offer training and skills workshops and
cultural/social events.

Case studies of EU support: Care Netherlands (Pristina)[5]

The local Pristina-based chapter of the international NGO, Care Netherlands,
received CARDS funding of just under €1m in 2006 from the EAR as part
of the 'community stabilisation programme' initiative. It must be emphasised
that although the Kosovo branch of Care acts as a local NGO, it has the
advantage of being able to access significant resources and expertise from the

international organisation. This has proved extremely important in applying for and managing the EU project grant. The 20-month project was to support the integration of Roma, Ashkeli and Egyptian (RAE) communities across Kosovo. This project is particularly noteworthy because it focused attention on the small minority communities that are often overlooked in the context of discussions about minorities. The EAR provided funds of up to €3 million for three separate programmes within Kosovo focusing on minority community support; the other two initiatives focused on the Serbian minority in the north.

There were three broad objectives for the project: helping RAE communities to engage in society, community development and support for RAE NGOs. The project funded work in four regions, 21 areas where members of the three communities live. In practice the project delivered support and training for teachers working in the communities, building the capacities of teachers and support staff, local NGOs and providing support for health and education initiatives. The aim was to transfer skills and to build knowledge that could then be deployed in the communities and thus deliver sustainable long-term outcomes. Some of the activities engaged the NGO and its partner organisations directly with state agencies: for example, Care organised a health awareness campaign specifically targeting minorities in the four target regions in conjunction with the National Institute for Public Health in Pristina; another aspect of the project involved working in conjunction with the Ministry of Education to deal with illiteracy and school drop-out rates within RAE communities. Co-operation between the NGO and the ministry was 'very good' and resulted in the ministry providing accreditation for the training sessions and courses run by Care, as well as facilitating interaction between project workers and school principals and directors.

There was also a strong economic component to the project, with Care distributing 90 small grants to community initiatives as part of the overall objective of 'supporting the economic development of RAE communities'. These grants have been used to support traditional crafts, but also agricultural development, tailoring and SMEs that can potential offer economic sustainability and development and facilitate employment in what amount to extremely poor communities. The initiative also involved Care working with both local businesses and municipalities in an attempt to encourage them to employ members of the RAE communities. Care have used the project resources to also encourage members of the RAE communities to register as job seekers, to participate in training schemes and to raise awareness of employment rights and social benefits that are typically not accessed by members of minority communities.

In terms of supporting civil society development, which was a key overall focus of the project, Care organised basic capacity-training for community organisations as well as helping to set up groups from scratch. Insofar as there are high levels of illiteracy in RAE communities, and practically no experience of organisational activity let alone NGO management, the Care team provided very basic support – helping members of the communities to set up meetings, to establish women's, men's and youth groups and assisting them with drawing up community action plans to present to the municipalities. The project's aim of helping to build the advocacy skills of community organisations and spokespersons so that they could represent issues and campaign for community projects and needs at municipality level was vital in terms of building democratic civil society, but it was also significant in terms of engaging communities with state institutions and politics.

Despite the clear goals and objectives of the project, results were rather mixed. The Care executive in Pristina was disappointed to discover that out of the 13 organisations that had been trained and supported as part of the initial stage of the project, only seven were subsequently able to submit further project applications and these required significant revisions and re-drafting. Whilst the project had helped to establish RAE NGOs with formal premises and established boards and other trappings of professionalism, it was recognised that this was only an elementary stage in the process of building organisational management capacity. Ultimately the survival of local community and grass roots organisations depends upon the capacity to secure future and sustainable external funding. High levels of illiteracy and limited knowledge of English and the absence of project management know-how and financial management services within local communities does not bode well for the development of such structures beyond the terms of Care's engagement. Where there was most success was in terms of mobilising community groups and encouraging them to voice collective concerns and to identify strategic development plans. As the director of Care observed, the difficulty remains that

> [W]hilst there are ... lots of good activists, who are fired up and keen to become involved, they have no idea how to manage or apply for projects ... EU assistance is based on the assumption that NGOs will continue to apply for projects, work on different issues and develop their capacity through projects.

Such a rationale appertains both to large organisations such as Care, with the capacity to administer and distribute seed-corn civil society aid in Kosovo, as well as to the recipients that it trains and helps launch.

Federation of Independent Trade Unions (BSPK)[6]

BSPK was established as an independent trade union in 1990, but it also defines itself as an NGO on the basis that it is literally 'non-governmental'. It also claims to be 'one of the largest NGOs in Kosovo' on the basis of membership numbers. Notwithstanding the fact that the organisation receives no state funding (the majority of revenue comes from membership fees), BSPK is, according to the organisation's president, Haxhi Arifi, still viewed by citizens as a governmental rather than non-governmental institution. Whilst the organisation has some interaction with the Pristina-based Chamber of Commerce and the Ministry of Labour, this is not in the context of policy development. Indeed, BSPK does not currently engage in any advocacy work because 'there is no government interest in employment issues at the moment'. Whilst this may well change – a new Council for Economic Affairs was established in late 2008 and changes in labour laws are very likely as a consequence of EU influence – as it stands there is currently no provision or protection for workers and the unemployed in Kosovo. The organisation operates as an advice and resource centre and is thus inundated with requests for help which it lacks the resources to deal with; this is the key issue they face as an organisation.

BSPK is a member of the International Trade Union Confederation and receives funds from international trade unions and labour organisations. BSPK has received two EU grants, both of which were for projects lasting 12 months, as well as grants from other international donors. BSPK was awarded the two project grants from the EAR as part of a general call in 2006 entitled 'civil society development'. The aim and focus of the projects was to develop community participation in economic development.

Although the organisation anticipates continuing interaction with the ECLO, the impact of EU funding on BSPK and the experience of managing two small EU projects was not deemed to have been particularly positive for the organisation. The application process proved difficult largely because BSPK lacked staff with sufficient competency in English to complete the process quickly and efficiently. Indeed, making the application was only possible at all because of the help provided by a Danish expert, who was working in Pristina for an international agency at the time and provided free advice and guidance. Although BSPK did access assistance from the EAR, the support provided was too basic and they derived most support and help from the various international partner organisations with which they have links.

Once the project began the monitoring and financial reporting requirements were not so difficult – due largely to the clear guidelines and the latitude of the EAR – it proved hard for the organisation to complete the tasks and implement all aspects of the project within the short time-frame. All in all, the processes of applying for and then managing the projects proved a distraction from BSPK's core work, involved a disproportionate amount of resources, and did not develop its capacities, nor did it further the strategic development or the goals and issue campaigns of the organisation. As the president of BSPK noted, 'the big problem for us is the absence of a legal framework [in Kosovo] relating to labour rights and employment . . . the projects did nothing to deal with this issue, whatsoever'.[7] For what amounted to a small proportion of the organisation's overall revenue (BSPK had to enlist partner organisations to run both projects thereby reducing the overall revenue available to the organisation itself), significant time and energy were diverted towards short projects that delivered relatively little in the way of resources. It was reported that the most disappointing aspect of engaging with the EAR was the fact that BSPK did not have sufficient resources nor could it obtain further donor revenue to continue the initiatives beyond the terms of the projects. Although the establishment and continued existence of local BSPK offices in majority Serbian areas of the north stands as a sustainable legacy of the assistance, as a trade union BSPK is committed to long-term development, support and engagement; discrete short-term projects, however successful in achieving their stated objectives, are not deemed by the leadership to reflect the overall strategic goals of the organisation.

Kosova Education Centre[8]

The Kosova Education Centre (KEC) is a locally established and registered NGO committed to working on education policy and issues and providing training and support to teachers and educators. It is a prominent civil society organisation renowned for its work on educational training and provision. KEC has been the recipient of project funding from several bilateral donor agencies, including the Soros Foundation (Open Society), Step-by-Step International, the World Bank and various education foundations and charities. When interviewed in November 2008 the organisation had completed one EU-funded project, and received notification of another award in November 2008. The first EU project, entitled 'Education Participation Improvement Project', which was for €291,000 and lasted for 18 months, involved KEC working with the trade union SBASHK (Union for Education, Science and Culture) and a newly established grass roots community organisation, the Association for Children and Human Rights (ACHR), and also with the international organisation, Step-by-Step. The two core overriding objectives of the project were: to improve access and educational attainment in primary and secondary schools (including attendance, retention and completion); to enhance the access of vulnerable groups (girls, minorities, children from poor families, rural areas, etc.) to education in Kosovo. In terms of policy development and sustainable institutional reform, the project aimed to improve the capacities of schools, state and non-state actors to monitor access and education participation; to strengthen school level education planning; improve the effectiveness of schools in maximising enrolment, attendance and completion; strengthening central and local government capacity to manage projects, monitor system performance and school effectiveness. The latest EIDHR-funded macro grant (funded directly from Brussels) is for a two-year regional education project involving NGOs from Bosnia, Albania, Serbia and Romania. KEC is the main partner.

The completed first project is viewed by both the EAR and KEC as having been a success on the basis that all activities and proposed outcomes were delivered. According to Jehona Shala, the Director of KEC, this was achieved largely due to the fact that the partner organisations with whom KEC worked knew each other well, had established contacts, and had co-operated previously. Under such circumstances it would appear that EU-funded initiatives work particularly well. An initial aspect of the project was to help build the capacity of the partners – particularly SBASHK, the Trade Union, and ACHR, the new local NGO. Particular emphasis was placed on helping to build co-operation between all partners through bespoke training sessions and study visits. Although as an established organisation with, relatively speaking, quite developed internal capacities, KEC was not the main target of the capacity-building training, but the tutelage helped them as an organisation. With regard to the other partner organisations, there was value obtained from learning through a partnership with KEC about project management and internal organisational management.

The second and critical dimension of the project was to provide funding for the various partners to then provide ten days of training for 500 teachers on the delivery of anti-bias teaching, education for social justice (done by KEC); advocacy training sessions (run by SBASHK) and training on children's rights (led by ACHR). The role of KEC was to co-ordinate the training and the various facilitators, manage the project cycle, policy development and advocacy aspects of the project (working with government agencies), as well as monitoring and evaluation. KEC brought quite considerable existing knowledge and capacity to the project. The organisation has run training sessions for a long time in Kosovo and thus has experience in organising sessions, recruiting trainers and producing resources.

Although the main outcome of the project was the facilitation of training sessions, in terms of governance interaction the project generated a limited advocacy role for KEC and the other partner organisations. A representative from the Ministry of Education was on the project steering committee and a memorandum of understanding was signed with the ministry to run the trainings of teachers. KEC also established a working group to develop two education policies in consultation with representatives from the ministry of social welfare. The working group established as part of the project and including ministry officials undertook study visits to Croatia and Slovenia to gather information.

Conclusion

With the closure of the EAR in 2008 and the transfer of responsibility for the allocation of EIDHR and IPA project grants to the ECLO, the provision of EU assistance to Kosovo has entered a new phase of development. Indeed, the emphasis of aid channelled through NGOs has already shifted considerably from the provision of emergency relief and basic development aid in the early years of this decade, towards institutional capacity-building and good governance since 2005. With regard to the latter, the focus has been building the project management capacities of the NGO sector, and engaging the non-governmental sector in training and the dispersal of knowledge in the context, wherever possible, of partnerships with the state. Such an approach is immediately reminiscent of the rationale governing the allocation of EU assistance in BiH and Serbia: supporting NGOs as agents of good governance, triggering an increase in state capacity, and strengthening civil society in the process.

With regard to the extent to which the intervention and aid in Kosovo is comparable to what has been documented in Serbia and BiH, there appears to be more emphasis placed by the EAR and now the ECLO on building the capacity of a particularly weak NGO sector to apply for and access the funds available. Training sessions organised by the ECLO across the territory have provided tutelage in how to prepare submissions and instruction regarding the requirements of managing a project grant. This is in recognition of the fact that NGOs are particularly weak in Kosovo, with the location of expertise and experience in the hands either of the few international organisations operating in the country, or held by a very small number of NGOs with good connections to INGOs and with project management experience. In other words, there is a pressing need to extend know-how and to engage more NGOs. As it stands, the absorption capacity for IPA funds is extremely low and it will prove difficult to allocate project grants to what amount to less than ten organisations in the country with the capacity to manage a small project.

The research undertaken for this study suggests that to an extent the strategy seems to be working. Funded projects run by, for example, the Kosova Education Center (KEC) have successfully engaged and built the capacity of small enmeshed organisations; the emphasis placed on building partnerships and empowering key organisations to act as conduits for project management know-how and assistance is greater than has been the case in BiH or Serbia.

On the basis of this objective in particular, it would appear that some of the lessons of a decade or more of supporting NGOs in the other locations have been learnt. Yet the basic strategy remains the same – 'capacity-building' in Kosovo means developing the ability of a core of NGOs to manage grants; to engage them in essentially apolitical activities that support, at a decidedly ephemeral and peripheral level, bureaucratic and policy change in accordance with EU norms; and to build their capacities to deliver much-needed services and training in communities. Whilst no funding is available for more overtly political or advocacy-oriented organisations, for the small cohort of self-styled professional NGOs in Kosovo this support is clearly enabling; for other indigenous organisations, such as trade unions, the assistance delivered through short-term project grants would appear to provide little dividend and it remains to be seen whether the EU aid that is trickling down to the grass roots will empower organisations at this level.

As discussed throughout this study, the assistance strategy of the EU is built around the logic that good governance can be developed through supporting non-state actors to engage with the state and government. The embedded assumption that state capacity is deficient and that partnership with NGOs will maximise policy outputs, implementation and the overall effectiveness of governance, is sufficiently contentious in Serbia and particularly controversial in BiH. The specific political context of Kosovo – an embryonic state with very limited capacity, the over-arching political prominence of relations with Belgrade, a non-state sector that emerged against a background of hostility towards the state and in the context of post-war reconstruction – further complicates the impact of the 'good governance' aspect of EU intervention. The extent to which, as a strategy for building good governance, empowering the non-state sector is achievable whilst the state sector remains immensely weak is highly contentious insofar as it runs the risk of further undermining the state.

There is still insufficient data available to make a worthy assessment of EU assistance in Kosovo, at least in terms of the resources channelled through NGOs. Nevertheless, certain aspects of the empirical data included above raise pertinent issues regarding the impact of this form of intervention. The first quite obvious point is that not all organisations elicit the same degree of benefit from managing an EU project. The aid generates governance and capacity-building best where established relationships are already in place, in the context of less contentious policy and issue areas, and where the provision of services is most needed by the state and communities. What is also critical is the extent to which recipient NGOs are able and willing to work across issue areas and on short-term projects that do not contradict or constrain long-term and overriding strategies of the organisation itself. Access to other sources of foreign donor support – whether it be the provision of top-up resources or the availability of experts to help in the preparation of applications – also seems to be a critical determinant of impact. The ECLO in Pristina, like the Delegations in Sarajevo and Belgrade, places great emphasis on partnerships and co-operation between NGOs as a means of diffusing know-how and ensuring that smaller community organisations with little existing capacity are brought into the process of project grants and assistance. As already mooted in previous chapters of this study, such an objective depends on the extent to which existing hierarchies within NGO communities can be challenged and the degree to which funds and knowledge can move beyond a narrow core of professional project management experts within the NGO community.

Conclusion

In terms of framing the conclusions reached within this study, a recent article by Thomas Carothers published in the *Journal of Democracy* (2009) is particularly helpful insofar as it articulates and sets out a clear distinction between the two broadly competing interpretations of civil society assistance delivered by foreign donors. Many of the negative assessments of development aid channelled through NGOs in post-socialist, transitional and post-conflict states fail to recognise as politically relevant or simply reject the development aspects of this form of intervention. There is a tendency to privilege the value of engaging NGOs with government in the context of policy development, in the contestation of planning or investment decisions, and in terms of such organisations providing agency for civil society and marginalised communities in the context of political spaces. If donor aid fails to deliver such heady objectives then it is deemed to be politically deficient and its impact superficial or even inconsequential. What Carothers' article reminds us is that both NGOs and donors rarely conceptualise their intervention in such narrow terms.

A 'development' framing of donor assistance for NGOs and CSOs views democratic transformation less in terms of procedures and institutions and more as a long-term process dependent upon social and cultural as well as economic and political change. Formal democratic procedures are not seen as an end in themselves, but as an initial and important aspect of the installation of justices and rights, governance and the liberalisation of the state. The role of NGOs in such an eclectic process cannot be reduced to political challenge in the context of policy development or the overt defence of particular interests in the realm of formal politics. Rather, a critical aspect of their role is to act 'behind the scenes' and to work with civil society actors rather than focus on political elites. Such a perspective immediately validates and enhances the role of donor-supported NGOs in development-oriented projects and service provision. It also captures the value of other aspects of NGO activities in the context of donor projects, namely helping to empower sections of the community, encouraging further engagement and the articulation of interests prior to any formal interaction in the context of policy and political development.

This marks a distinct contrast to the more conventional perspectives on such intervention, adopted mostly by political scientists, whose focus tends to be formal politics and the institutionalisation of interest group or social movement organisations. Perhaps the most potent – or even pernicious – legacy of what is described as the *Transitions to Democracy* approach to studying regime change and the development of civil society is the overriding emphasis placed on democratic procedure and the institutionalisation of democratic mechanisms. Indeed, beyond elections and constitutionally enshrined procedures for political deliberation – elections plus rights – there is little else considered as being indicative of fundamental change. Support for NGOs and CSOs is framed in terms of first encouraging transition during the last days of the authoritarian regime and then helping to bed down democracy and extend pluralism after the transition has occurred, or during the so-called phase of 'consolidation' (Diamond and Plattner 1996).

The difficulty with such a framing of civil society is that it confines civil society and NGO activity to the political sphere as formal interest or lobbying groups, with their role, post-transition, deemed to be purely supportive and essentially apolitical (Baker 1998; Ottaway and Carothers 2000). The overriding sense is of democratic civil society engaged in liberal policy deliberation rather than direct action or any anti-system mobilisation. Whilst the more ostensibly political organisations or manifestations of civil society are tolerated, this is in the interests of diversity and liberal pluralism. In contrast, the so-called 'development' perspective accredits NGOs and civil society with a more sustained political role, and one that is not confined to participation within the narrow confines of policy development and formal politics, but a 'behind the scenes' role which thus delivers a far more political outcome in helping to transform societies and to instigate the liberalisation of states.

By distinguishing between the two frameworks, Carothers alerts us to the importance, when drawing conclusions regarding the impact of EU assistance, of not viewing such intervention too narrowly. Not only must we acknowledge the intrinsic democratic value of associational life, of a plurality of non-governmental organisations expressing divergent and disparate views, but any evaluation of donor intervention must also be sensitive to the critical, longer-term development objectives and outcomes of aid channelled through NGOs.

EU assistance channelled through NGOs:
a summary of the findings

It is imperative to begin any summary of the findings of this study by emphasising the extent to which the provision of funding channelled through NGOs
in post-conflict, crisis-ridden states with the ultimate objective of political, economic and social transformation on a large scale is an ambitious and significant
endeavour. If the findings of this study are to be believed, what it seemingly
delivers is the provision of an array of social and educational services, training
programmes, relief efforts and socio-economic development projects in communities. In most cases the services would not otherwise be provided and this
is particularly significant in a region in which both state provision and market
proliferation are depleted or simply absent. Despite concerns regarding waste
and duplication of donor resources and the suggestion that funding benefits
organisations and the individuals within them more than the poor and needy,
the findings of this study suggest that the services described above, most of
which are typically delivered for sums of money in the region of €50–100,000
represent, on the whole, good value for money.

The emergence of a contingent, albeit small and narrow, of professional
NGOs that have increased capacity to manage projects effectively represents a
positive outcome of EU intervention. Teachers can be successfully trained,
detailed reports on human rights abuses can be drafted, and the skills of the
unemployed can be improved for relatively small amounts of money. More significantly, this study has revealed evidence in BiH and Serbia of projects delivering sustainable outcomes, of NGO initiatives engaging municipalities and
government agencies, raising awareness of issues and the need for policy
change, and mobilising and empowering sections of communities. Such outcomes, however limited, are seemingly driving a shift in perceptions of the status and purpose of NGOs amongst the public and policy makers.

The EU dominates the aid sector in all three locations, and the number of
other donors and the amounts of money they commit to the region is declining. However, in aligning its assistance to the SAp and harnessing its aid for
NGOs to clear, albeit rather general, development goals, the Commission has
brought a degree of coherence and focus.

However, there is also much revealed in this study to suggest that EU assistance is failing to deliver adequately or effectively on its objectives and, importantly, the aims or ambitions of the intervention are somewhat unrealistic,
over-ambitious, and do not reflect the reality of what is being realised. From
the qualitative and quantitative data in this study, there is a clear and evident

disconnect between the grand strategic aims of the Commission for the PCC states and the impact of aid on the ground. This is particularly the case with regard to developing regional co-operation, where there is virtually no evidence of assistance triggering genuine co-operation between NGOs across the region. More generally, not only are broad development objectives translated poorly into funded projects, but the mechanism of short-term project cycles and discrete initiatives detract from realising long-term strategic goals unless there is extremely rigorous co-ordination and evaluation. In reality the focus of assistance projects is necessarily general in order to accommodate local realities and contexts, but this results in excessive latitude in terms of which initiatives are funded by the local Delegations. The allocation of grants ends up being based on the capacity of organisations to manage projects and thus the absorption capacity of a particular NGO sector, rather than on the development needs or the most worthy projects.

There is a fundamental tension between the desire of the Commission in Brussels to devolve responsibility and autonomy to local Delegations and allow them to set funding priorities, manage projects, etc., and the need to keep a close check on the focus and outcome of projects. The Commission lacks the capacity to evaluate the impact of its aid both in terms of short-term impact (the duration of the project), or in terms of long-term sustainable benefit. The Commission relies on reports from local Delegations, which in turn are based on the reports from NGOs and are based entirely on project management evaluations – did the project achieve all its stated aims and were the financial aspects accurate?

The empirical data in BiH and Serbia also reveals the extent to which impact is limited by absorption capacity and the fact that it is proving difficult to diffuse aid and project management know-how beyond a small core of NGOs located in capital cities or large urban areas. Local NGOs and smaller community-based organisations are engaged in projects but as subordinate partners, and because of a lack of basic capacity at this level it is extremely difficult for such organisations to graduate to managing projects themselves. In other words, hierarchies are reinforced as a consequence of assistance. Relying on local assessors also acts as a constraint on the movement of projects beyond a narrow cohort – those 'known' NGOs dominate and set a standard for the sector – they can act as gate-keepers and quickly take control of the flow of donor resources. Several of the assessors encountered during the course of this research were still actively engaged in NGOs, and were also providers of training to applicants. There is thus a potential conflict of interests with these individuals exercising considerable power over the allocation of project funding.

Sustainability of outcomes and the long-term impact of donor assistance is a widespread concern raised by scholars of donor intervention in general. With regard to the Commission's assistance for BiH, Serbia and Kosovo, the process, rules and mechanisms for allocating project grants act as the biggest single constraint on sustainability. There is no possibility for projects to be extended (time period can be, but not the actual project or the money). Recipient NGOs are thus locked in a cycle of short-term projects and are compelled to think in terms of discrete initiatives and short-term goals rather than in terms of the broader outcomes and the sustainable development of schemes. The short-term focus of EU projects can also conflict with the strategic longer-term goals of the organisation itself. Whilst there is much discussion about the importance of building the capacity of NGOs, it would seem that this refers specifically to the project management capacity of an organisation.

The changing focus of assistance also discourages recipients from building up specialist knowledge and instead leads to the creation of professional project management organisations that only connect with communities or the interests they claim to represent fleetingly and in the context of a 12–18-month project. This encourages a sense of mistrust amongst the general public for NGOs and panders to a sense of them as being opportunists.

The rapidly changing focus of funding can be explained partly in terms of the pace of the SAp agenda, which continually identifies issues raised in country reports or by working groups within the Commission or the European Parliament, but it is also a consequence of EU donor assistance existing within a broader global context in which new issues becoming prominent. The Commission is inevitably affected by other donors operating in the Western Balkans and is inclined to take on an issue because, as the main donor and international agency, it feels compelled to be at the forefront of development issues in the region. This leads to duplication and the element of competition between the EU and other donors generates a climate of low co-operation and ultimately the waste of resources.

One of the main reasons that smaller and more marginalised NGOs do not obtain project funding is that the application process is daunting and hugely time-consuming for most potential applicants. Even for the successful NGOs the amount of resources and effort involved is not worthwhile and difficult to justify – it is not unusual at all for the entire organisation to be turned over to preparing the application with all other work put on hold in the final days before the submission deadline. In essence, in order to submit a worthy application and to stand a chance of being allocated a grant, an organisation must have significant capacity – links with other foreign donors to help provide the match funding, access to expertise, and the organisational infrastructure to sustain the momentum of completing the process.

Despite the expressed intention of the Commission and each of the Delegations to extend the dissemination and to engage new smaller organisations in the process, the local Delegations do not provide the right type of training assistance. The help they offer through day-trainings is too basic for organisations that stand any real chance of gaining a project, and too inaccessible for those organisations that really stand little chance. The training sessions are held either in Sarajevo, Belgrade or Pristina, and focus essentially on explaining the application form and what documentation is required – information readily available on the websites of the Delegations. Once an organisation has made a successful application such tutelage is of little value – what such an NGO requires is invariably more specific; how to increase their success rate, apply for larger grants, or engage international or regional partners.

The support during the project, particularly in BiH, is very good and the Delegation field work staff provide a great deal of assistance and are apparently readily available for advice, but this is not the case during the application stage when it would seem that communication with the Delegations in Serbia and BiH is constrained and limited to formal requests regarding procedural issues.

A further critical finding, and one that in many ways gets to the very heart of what is wrong with EU assistance, is the significant disparity in terms of what funded projects actually delivered. Essentially, the same resources were being granted to projects producing environmental leaflets for a small number of high-school students as projects delivering psycho-social support for victims of torture. However, a survey of more recent projects in all three locations suggests that a tightening up of procedures and a narrowing of the focus of project calls has dealt with this issue to such an extent that the vast majority of projects surveyed represent good value in terms of the provision of cost-effective services.

The impact of projects on both the society and the organisation itself varies considerably between actors in each of the three locations. It would appear from the analysis of case studies that the key variables are: the existing capacity of the recipient organisation; the specific relationship between partner organisations – whether they have worked together before and how well they interact; the availability of resources from other international donors; and the extent to which the organisation can draw on existing knowledge of the issue and the political or public prominence of the issue. The case of Kosovo in particular suggests quite clearly that projects do not impact on all organisations in the same way; trade union organisations that may have established themselves as NGOs find it harder to absorb short-term projects within their day-to-day schedules and longer-term development goals. What might be termed semi-non-governmental organisations, such as CESD in BiH, have the advantage of existing capacity to apply for and manage projects, but because of their link with scientific institutes or other specialist departments they are somewhat restricted to particular types of projects. In the case of CESD the dearth of project calls with a specific environmental focus in BiH recently has meant that the organisation has not been able to apply for projects. It would appear that the organisations that benefit most are relatively newly established lean NGOs, not particularly committed to working on a set issue, with a flexible internal structure, able to quickly mobilise resources around a project proposal. Whilst such organisations may well be able to benefit most from project grants, their capacity to graduate from small grants to larger projects is seemingly constrained. This is a very significant concern because it would appear that one of the weaknesses of EU assistance is that while it is perhaps effective at delivering discrete projects, plugging training gaps, it cannot deliver grander political objectives such as governance and the empowerment of civil society.

The most important finding of the study, and in a sense the most damning critique of the assistance, is that projects designed to enlist state and non-state actors and to lay the foundations of governance partnerships, bar a few notable exceptions, fail to deliver wholeheartedly on this objective. Where cross-sectoral interaction does occur in the context of an EU-funded project it does so at a very superficial level indeed, and is usually conditioned by members of the NGO knowing personnel from, for example, the ministry of education or the local authority. Such interaction is thus based on informal relations and personal favours rather than the institutionalisation of formal interaction that lays down the foundations for good governance.

One of the most significant concerns related to the changing focus of aid and the short-termism of project funding is the extent to which EU assistance appears to have stalled, or at least has become somewhat entrenched in the provision of low-level maintenance aid that delivers only modest results. The research in Serbia and BiH reveals little sense of recipient NGOs graduating from managing small projects to becoming engaged in large-scale development initiatives involving significant resources deployed over a longer period of time. Most recipient NGOs remain locked into applying for and managing short-term projects, which takes them from issue to issue and keeps them engaged in small projects that deliver small amounts of resources for the effort involved.

Whither the future?

The question is thus raised as to how the EU should deploy its assistance henceforth, whether it should continue to channel its scarce resources through small projects, or whether it needs to consider alternative mechanisms as the pressure to move these countries on more quickly becomes greater. One scenario is that the focus of the assistance will need to be increasingly tightened and that NGOs will have to align their projects much more closely to working with government agencies around specific policy or enforcement issues. A slightly different scenario sees a shift from aid being channelled through NGOs to a situation whereby the EU works more overtly and closely with governments. In other words, if the accession agenda gains momentum and the capacities of the region's states starts to increase, the Commission may find it more expedient to bypass NGOs, or at least approach the building of governance partnerships from the perspective of the governmental rather than the non-governmental sector. There is certainly evidence in Kosovo of donors, including the EU, prioritising state administrative reform and direct engagement with government agencies that was not the case in BiH or Serbia a decade or so ago.

Whichever scenario becomes the reality, EU assistance for Kosovo, BiH and Serbia beyond 2010 will be conditioned, of course, by the dynamics of the accession or enlargement agenda. But the Commission will also be forced to consider whether funding NGOs to deliver short-term projects is an appropriate means of delivering ever more complex and ambitious changes in terms of state capacity and good governance. Critics would argue that the current mechanism of funding NGOs at best delivers slow and patchy change and runs the risk of encouraging the 'agency capture' of key services and functions by NGOs. At worst, the intervention maintains the status quo of depleted state capacity, the empowerment of corrupt and impenetrable elites, and the provision of skeletal services.

In terms of relating the findings of this study to more general discussions within political science regarding the limits and impact of donor intervention and support for NGOs a number of points need to be raised. First and foremost, the study has yielded even more evidence to suggest that NGOs are not necessarily the institutional incarnations of civil society, and that despite the discourse of 'civil society promotion' that encases much donor intervention globally, it needs to be acknowledged that supporting NGOs is primarily concerned with delivering various objectives in transitional and post-conflict states of which promoting civil society is merely one aspect. What is striking from the evidence presented here is that whilst assistance tends to be based on the tacit assumption that an indigenous civil society is not in existence and that a strata of relatively new NGOs offers the best prospect through which to channel development aid, the effectiveness of such intervention is ultimately conditioned by the extent to which recipient organisations are connected to existing civil society networks and can generate social capital. Evidence from BiH, Serbia and Kosovo would suggest that partnerships between NGOs, and between the government and organisations, work best when there is an established relationship and a history of interaction, rather than where this is being built from scratch.

The second issue raised by the study concerns the difficulties in generating new modes of governance and the dynamics of power at the heart of the partnership between state and non-state actors (Börzel 2007). If there is one overriding point raised by this study it is that the importance of *state* capacity and the ability of government and state elites to enforce outcomes and orchestrate partnerships with NGOs is critical and cannot be over-estimated, particularly in contexts where the sovereignty of the state is in dispute or seriously compromised. It seems, from the perspective of these Western Balkan case studies, that whilst much is made of the importance of governance and the value of engaging state and non-state sectors, there is little attempt in practice to identify the contexts in which this is most likely to occur, to recognise the difference between wildly contrasting forms of such interaction, and to learn how to instrumentalise support for NGOs in terms of ensuring a balance of power between the two sectors. Whether this occurs because of a deficiency in the theoretical literature on governance, or because the vital power dynamics of the interaction get lost in the context of practical application, is hard to discern. However, unless assistance targets the capacity deficiencies of government agencies, so that states become relatively empowered and possess capacity to enforce and to manage the interaction with NGOs (to cast a 'shadow of hierarchy'), then, as illustrated throughout the empirical sections of this book, outcomes are likely to be modest and unsustainable.

The third and final issue that has wider resonance concerns the practical and theoretical limits of what this form of intervention can deliver. The development perspective on intervention and assistance channelled through NGOs encourages us not to overlook the importance of democratisation and the engagement of NGOs in that process, but to focus on a broader set of goals, on changing values and attitudes, and on the climate in which politics takes place. Yet the case of Serbia in particular reminds us of the fundamental tension with this approach: can such development-focused aid realise its heady and multifarious objectives in the context of difficult political circumstances – illiberal regimes, incomplete transitions – without a direct political challenge? From the perspective of the human rights organisations in Belgrade, or those working with displaced persons in Bosnia, engaging professional NGOs in apolitical projects that predominantly side-step causes and focus instead on ameliorating the effects, or making changes at the margins without directly challenging nationalist elites or existing hierarchies, are destined to have limited impact in climates of corruption and intimidation.

Conversely, advocates of the development approach would contend that whilst there are obvious limits to what NGOs and civil society assistance can achieve, a decade of EU aid and intervention has, in a piecemeal way, already changed the way states function in the region and transformed the process of policy-making and enforcement. Through an engagement with NGOs, a preparedness to work with elected elites and in the context of conditionality, the Commission has helped to deliver change and, despite certain difficulties along the way, will continue to do so. Indeed, from such an optimistic viewpoint, channelling aid through NGOs, as an approach, has the capacity to tackle all obstacles in the path of regime change, and will ultimately deliver Bosnia, Serbia and Kosovo full EU membership.

Notes

Introduction

1 For the most part, this book is concerned specifically with the European Commission's assistance to and initiatives for BiH, Serbia and Kosovo. It is fully acknowledged by the author that the Commission's perspectives and position on these states and the region may differ, and has differed, quite considerably from individual member states within the EU. This is particularly the case, of course, in the context of Kosovo.

2 http://ec.europa.eu/europeaid/who/about/index_en.htm (accessed 3 April 2008).

1 The EU and the Western Balkans

1 Kosovo is included within this group under UN Security Council Resolution 1244. Until the final status of Kosovo is resolved, formal membership of the EU is not technically possible. EU aid (CARDS/IPA) is delivered to Kosovo on the basis of regional assistance.

2 http://ec.europa.eu/enlargement/the-policy/countries-on-the-road-to-membership/index_en.htm (accessed 10 October 2008).

3 Ibid.

4 World Bank report, 2008.

5 http://ec.europa.eu/enlargement/financial_assistance/cards/index_en.htm (accessed 3 April 2008).

6 Co-operation with the International Criminal Tribunal for the Former Yugoslavia (ICTY) is particularly important for Croatia, BiH and Serbia.

7 SAA negotiations with Serbia were suspended between May 2006 and June 2007 because of the regime's reluctance to co-operate with the ICTY.

8 http://ue.eu.int/ueDocs/cms_Data/docs/pressdata/en/er/Declang4.doc.html (accessed 4 November 2008).

9 CARDS Assistance Programme to the Western Balkans: Regional Strategy Paper 2002–2006, Brussels, October 2001.

10 http://www.rcc.int/ (accessed 3 November 2008).

11 The annual budget of the RCC Secretariat is €3 million, a third of which comes from the countries of South Eastern Europe, a further third from the European Commission and the remaining third from other RCC members and international partners.

12 Progress report, October 2008.

13 Communication from the Commission to the Council and the European Parliament: 'Instrument for Pre-Accession Assistance (IPA) Multi-annual Indicative Financial Framework for 2008–2010' (copy of document obtained from the European Commission).

14 European Commission (2005), *Evaluation of the Implementation of Regulation 2666/2000 (CARDS assistance to the Western Balkans)*. http://ec.europa.eu/europeaid/evaluation/response/cards/951651_resp.pdf (accessed November 2008).

15 EU Commission (2007) 'IPA Programming Guide' (p. 7).

2 Theorising EU assistance and intervention in Bosnia-Herzegovina, Serbia and Kosovo

1 For example, Zene za zene International, a local NGO.

2 For example, Pomozino djeci, Visegrad.

3 Transaction cost theory (cf. Eppstein and O'Halloran 1999; Heritier 2003) argues that delegation and co-operation between state and non-state actors takes place to reduce the costs imposed by lengthy negotiations and discussions, thus provising an incentive for both sides to co-operate. Principal–agent theory argues that the lack of time and expertise on the part of policy elites and government officials (principal) to deal with increasingly complex problems acts as an incentive to engage non-state actors who will provide knowledge and expertise (cf. Moe 1987).

3 The EU in Bosnia-Herzegovina

1 The 'Bonn Powers' refers to the conclusions of the 1997 PIC meeting in Bonn. It was agreed that the High Representative would be able to make unilateral binding decisions in matters such as passing legislation and removal of intransigent elected officials.

2 CEC, European Partnership for BiH, 2007 (on-line version).

3 The Body includes the Prime Ministers and Finance Ministers from the state and entity levels.

4 Miroslav Lajčák interviewed by Toby Vogel, *European Voice*, 4 March 2008.

5 The scenario painted across the western media and amongst certain academics was that political leaders of the RS would, as threatened, totally withdraw their co-operation with the state-level institutions as a precursor to breaking away entirely; in response the Bosnian Croats would also break their links with the state

authority and join Croatia, and then Bosnia would no longer exist as a state. In other words, Dayton unravelled. Such concerns were widely voiced by representatives from NATO as well as by commentators and regional specialists at a conference held at Chatham House in London in December 2007, which the author attended and contributed to.

6 Interview with official in the Directorate for European Integration, 13 February 2008, Sarajevo.

7 Interview with Tuzla Reference Group, 9 November 2004, Tuzla.

8 For example, Sarajevo Canton made KM 1 million (approximately £300,000) available to NGOs in 2004. Although currently the bulk of the money goes to sports clubs and old established apolitical organisations, the hope is that this will change as NGOs become more adept at advocating for the available funds. Yet even in the case of Sarajevo, where the authority is clearly inclined to support NGOs, no announcement is made of projects to be funded, and details regarding the process of application are not clearly displayed. (Interview with Milan Mirić.)

9 EESC Western Balkans Civil Society Forum, Brussels: March 2006.

10 http://ec.europa.eu/europeaid/where/worldwide/eidhr/index_en.htm (accessed 12 May 2008).

11 http://ec.europa.eu/enlargement/potential-candidate-countries/bosnia_and_herzegovina/eu_bosnia_and_herzegovina_relations_en.htm (accessed 12 May 2008).

12 EESC Western Balkans Civil Society Forum Report, Brussels: March 2006: 16.

13 European Commission, 2006 'Communication from the Commission to the Council and the European Parliament: Instrument for Pre-accession Assistance (IPA) Multi-annual Indicative financial Framework for 2008–2010': 5–6.

14 http://ec.europa.eu/enlargement/pdf/key_documents/2007/nov/bosnia_herzegovina_progress_reports_en.pdf (accessed 12 May 2008).

15 World Bank Country Brief, 2007.

16 http://ec.europa.eu/bulgaria/finance_business/pre-accession/index_en.htm (accessed 12 May 2008).

17 See the Delegation to the European Commission website, available at: http://www.europa.ba/?akcija=clanak&CID=19&jezik=2&LID=34 (accessed 1 October 2007).

18 Interview with Paolo Scialla, Team Co-ordinator, Democratic Stabilisation Programme, Delegation of the European Commission to BiH, Sarajevo, 24 March 2004.

19 Interview with Vlado Pandurević, 9 February 2007.

20 Interview with Vlado Pandurević, 12 February 2008.

21 Information obtained from the Delegation in Sarajevo.

22 Interview with Zvjezdana Dragović and Irena Hadžiabdić, AEOBiH, 8 February 2007, Sarajevo.

23 Interview with AEOBiH, 8 February 2007, Sarajevo.

24 The organisation that has organised trainings with the Delegation is the Civil Society Promotion Centre (Sarajevo).

25 Interview with Aida Doguda (Director), Civil Society Promotion Centre, 11 April 2007, Sarajevo.

26 The successful applicants include: Vive zene (Tuzla); CTV (Centre for Torture Victims – Sarajevo); Bureau for Human Rights (Tuzla); Step by Step (Sarajevo).

27 Interview with Vlado Pandurević, 9 February 2007, Sarajevo.

28 Interview with Halida Vuković, Fondeko, 8 February 2007, Sarajevo.

29 The law in the Federation stipulated that women victims of rape had to submit documentation in support of their claim within six months of the incident allegedly taking place. This meant that crimes against Bosniak women that occurred during the war could not be registered and thus victims were unable to gain justice, support or legal recognition from the state. A similar law, originating from the socialist era, had been amended in Serb-held territories at the start of the war in an attempt to document cases of rape and torture committed against Serbian women.

30 Interview with Selma Begić, Fondacija lokalne demokratije, 11 April 2007, Sarajevo.

31 The problem they are dealing with relates to the Bosnian phenomenon of 'two schools under one roof', whereby two ethnically distinct schools use the same building. For returnees, having the name of an indicted war criminal as the name of the school, or to have such people named on the school board, is offensive and upsetting. The project sets out to gather information on the extent of the problem.

32 Interview with Anka Izetbegovic (Executive Director), Duga, 12 April 2007, Sarajevo.

33 Information obtained from interview with Anka Izetbegovic (Executive Director), DUGA, 12 April 2007, Sarajevo.

34 Interview with Vesna Bajšanski, Programme Co-ordinator, Step-by-Step, 11 April 2007, Sarajevo.

35 Interview with Zvjezdana Dragović and Irena Hadžiabdić, AEOBiH, 8 February 2007, Sarajevo.

36 Interview with Rijad Tikvesa (Director), Ekotim, 7 February 2007, Sarajevo.

37 Four documents were produced: 'Compact between the BiH Council of Ministers and the NGO sector'; 'Compact between the BiH Council of Ministers and the NGO sector on standards of service provision'; 'Code of conduct for NGOs in BiH'; 'Strategic courses for the development of the NGO sector in BiH'.

38 The concern here is that a high proportion of local government funding available for NGOs and the non-profit sector goes to sports clubs rather than to civic associations and NGO networks.

39 The project is entitled: 'Anti-Xenophobia: Rights-based campaign to support reconciliation and promote minority returnee re-integration'.

40 Interview with Aida Doguda (Director), Civil Society Promotion Centre, 11 April 2007, Sarajevo.

4 The EU in Serbia

1 The powers of the Federal President were limited to the domains of foreign policy and defence.

2 Ramet and Pavlaković (2005), p. 108.

3 Kesić (2005), pp. 115–16.

4 International Crisis Group, 'Serbia's New Constitution: Democracy Going Backwards', Policy Briefing n.44, November 2006.

5 The US Government suspended financial support to Serbia in response to the adoption of the law that granted state support for war crimes suspects.

6 *B92*, 'EU: Karadzic arrest important step' 22/07/2008. http://www.b92.net/eng/news/politics-article.php?yyyy=2008&mm=07&dd=23&nav_id=52102 (accessed 22 July 2008).

7 Reported in *The Guardian*, 23 July 2008.

8 Helsinki Committee for Human Rights in Serbia (2007), *Serbia 2006: Human Rights – Hostage to the State's Regression*, Belgrade: Zagorac, p. 16.

9 OECD (2006), *Investment Policy Co-operation with non-OECD Economies*, Annual Report 2006, p. 58.

10 SEIO – 70 per cent of respondents supportive of EU membership for Serbia.

11 Helsinki Committee for Human Rights in Serbia (2006), *Serbia 2005: Human Security in an Unfinished State*, Belgrade: Zagorac; Helsinki Committee for Human Rights in Serbia (2007), *Serbia 2006: Human Rights – Hostage to the State's Regression*, Belgrade: Zagorac.

12 The EU has only recently focused on the issue, which is surprising considering the importance of NGOs in aid and assistance. The recently appointed head of the local Delegation to Serbia, Josep Lloveras, took up the issue and placed it on the list of 15 priorities that Serbia has to deal with as part of the SAp.

13 *Danas*, 'Hronika najavljenog zlocina'('Chronicle of a Foretold Crime'), 12 July 2005.

14 See, for instance, the annual reports published by the Helsinki Committee for Human Rights.

15 For instance, the vicious personal attacks on Sonja Biserko, president of the Helsinki Committee and a leading human rights activist in the former Yugoslavia, in mainstream and respected publications such as *Politika* (3 September 2006), *Ogledalo* (6 July 2006), *Srpski nacional* (19 June 2005). Biserko, a Nobel Prize nominee in 2005, was physically attacked outside her home in Belgrade and was repeatedly castigated in the media for speaking out against human rights abuses and the issue of Srebrenica in particular.

16 *Time Magazine*, 'Blast from the past', 19 April 2007.

17 See *Vreme*, vol. 604 to 621, from 1 August to 28 November 2002.

18 *B92*, 'O inicijativi nekih NVO' ('About the initiative of some NGOs').

19 Ibid.

20 Interview with European Movement, Belgrade.

21 'Letter to the Governments of the EU Member States' issued on 18 January 2008 and available at www.helsinki.org.yu/index.html.

22 The Zagreb Summit of November 2000 formally established a new relationship with the Federal Republic of Yugoslavia. The Summit marked the start of the SAp, and in its declaration stated that: 'the prospect of a stabilisation and association agreement is now established in accordance with the invitation issued by the Council on 9 October 2000. A decision has been taken to set up a "EU/FRY consultative task force". The Commission will work on a feasibility study with a view to negotiating directives for a stabilisation and association agreement.' http://www.delscg.cec.eu.int/en/documents/24-11-2000-zagreb-declaratione.htm (accessed 26 July 2007).

23 The Agency continues to distribute aid to Kosovo, but via its Pristina office.

24 http://www.ear.eu.int/news/news.htm (accessed 6 July 2007).

25 Interview with John White, EAR, 23 March 2007, Belgrade.

26 EAR Annual Report, 2006: 18.

27 Ibid: 15.

28 Most EU support for NGOs comes from CARDS, via the EAR. Whilst a few NGOs have obtained funding directly from Brussels, usually as part of global EIDHR macro project initiatives, EIDHR micro grants have not been made available to the NGO sector in Serbia.

29 EESC Western Balkans Civil Society Forum briefing paper, March 2007.

30 Interview with Vassilis Petrides, The European Agency for Reconstruction (EAR), 23 March 2007, Belgrade.

31 Ibid.

32 Ibid.

33 EuropeAid/123857/L/ACT/CS (2006).

34 Interview with Delegation, Belgrade.

35 Interview with Jelena Radojković, Belgrade Centre for Human Rights, 22 March 2007, Belgrade.

36 For example, projects run by International Aid Network (Belgrade) and Srpski savetza izbeghce (Serbian Refugee Council).

37 Srpski demokratski forum and International Aid Network (Belgrade).

38 Grupa 484 (Belgrade).

39 Interview with Jelena Radojković, Belgrade Centre for Human Rights, 22 March 2007, Belgrade.

40 For example, Royal Norwegian Ministry of Foreign Affairs, Olaf Palme International Centre, OSCE, Council of Europe, Royal Danish Embassy, Canadian International Development Agency (CIDA), Open Society Institute in Belgrade (Soros Foundation).

41 Interview with Jelena Miloradović (Coordinator), Srpski demokratski forum (Serbian Democratic Forum), 22 March 2007, Belgrade.

42 Interview with Ljiljana Vasić Pomoc deci, 8 June 2007, Belgrade.

43 Interview with Nikola Jasmina, Victimology Society of Serbia, 8 June 2007, Belgrade.

44 Interview with Jelena Miloradović, Srpski demokratski forum, 22 March 2007, Belgrade.

45 Interview with Anika Krstić, Srpski savetza izbeghce (Serbian Refugee Council), 22 March 2007.

46 Interview with Tanja Pavlov, Grupa 484, 22 March 2007, Belgrade.

47 Interview with Svetlana Vukomanović, Centre for Democracy foundation, 19 July 2007, Belgrade.

48 Ibid.

49 Interview with Miljenko Dereta, Centre for Civic Initiatives, 20 July 2007, Belgrade.

50 www.siepa.sr.gov.yu/investment/investor_guide/foreign_investment/tax_legislation.htm (accessed 1 April 2008).

51 Regional Environmental Center.

52 www.siepa.sr.gov.yu/investment/investor_guide/foreign_investment/tax_legislation.htm (accessed 1 April 2008).

53 Interview with Ljiljana Vasić, Pomoc deci, 8 June 2007, Belgrade.

54 Interview with Miljenko Dereta, Centre for Civic Initiatives, 20 July 2007, Belgrade.

55 Interview with the European Movement, Belgrade.

56 Interview with Anika Krstić, Serbian Refugee Council (Srpski savet za izbeghce), 22 March 2007, Belgrade.

57 Interview with Stefan, Education Centre of Roma, 20 July 2007, Belgrade.

5 Quantitative analysis of EU assistance to Bosnia-Herzegovina and Serbia

1 Information obtained from questionnaire completed by the organisation and also from an interview with Zoran Puljić, Mozaik, 13 February 2008, Sarajevo.

2 Interview and questionnaire with Azra Nuhić, CTV Most, 10 April 2007, Sarajevo.

3 The Bosnian organisation Fondacija lokalne demokratije was able to secure match funding from the state on the basis that the organisation provided various services for victims of domestic violence as part of the project initiative.

4 For example, the Danish Embassy, which had provided match funding to organisations such as the Serbian Refugee Council (Srpski savet za izbeghce), no longer offered such assistance from 2008.

5 For instance, the Serbian organisation Pomoc deci run support projects for Roma citizens and IDPs across the country; the organisation operates entirely from Belgrade and field offices and local partner organisations co-operate only to facilitate the provision of services within communities.

6 The organisations awarded both EIDHR and CARDS grants during 2006 were: Fondacija lokalne demokratije; Zdravo da ste; Vesta; Crveni kriz Tuzlanskog Kantona; and Bospo. All are based either in Sarajevo or Tuzla.

7 Interview with Vlado Pandurević, 13 February 2008, Sarajevo.

8 http://ec.europa.eu/environment/enlarg/enlargement_en.htm (accessed 6 March 2008).

9 Respondents were asked to tick statements with which they agreed and were instructed that they could tick more than one box.

6 EU assistance and intervention in Kosovo: lessons learnt?

1 The example being the Sarajevo-based NGO Fondacija lokalne demokratije.

2 Interview with Arnaud Pierre, 31 October 2008.

3 Interview with ECLO, Pristina.

4 http://ec.europa.eu/enlargement/archives/ear/kosovo/kosovo.htm (accessed 24 February 2009).

5 Interview with Carole Poullaouec, ELO, 7 November 2008, Pristina.

6 Interview with Bujar Hoxha, Care Netherlands, 6 November 2008, Pristina.

7 Interview with Dafina Mehaj (International Department) and Haxhi Arifi (President), BSPK, 5 November 2008, Pristina.

8 Interview with Jehona Shala, Kosova Education Center, 6 November 2008.

References

Anastasakis, O. and Bechev, D. (2003) 'EU conditionality in South-East Europe: bringing commitment to the process', *European Balkan Observer* 1/2: 3–4.

Andersson, M. (2002) 'Poland', in H. Weidner and M. Janicke (eds), *Capacity Building in National Environmental Policy*, Berlin: Springer.

Baker, G. (1998) 'The changing idea of civil society: models from the Polish democratic opposition', *Journal of Political Ideologies*, 3/2: 125–145.

Baker, G. (1999) 'The taming of the idea of civil society', *Democratization* 6/3: 1–29.

Barclay, A. H. (1979) *The Development Impact of Private Voluntary Organizations: Kenya and Niger*, Washington, DC: Development Alternatives Inc.

Barnett, M. and Duvall, R. (2005) 'Power in global governance', in M. Barnett and R. Duvall (eds), *Power in Global Governance*, Cambridge: Cambridge University Press, pp. 1–32.

Batt, J. (2007) 'Bosnia and Herzegovina: politics as "war by other means" challenge to the EU's strategy for the Western Balkans', *Journal of Intervention and Statebuilding* 1: 65–67.

Belloni, R. (2000) 'Building civil society in Bosnia-Herzegovina', Human Rights Working Papers, No. 12 (January).

Bernard, N. (2002) *Multi-level Governance in the European Union,* The Hague: Kluwer International Law.

Biserko, S. (2006) *Human Security in an Unfinished State*, Belgrade: Helsinki Committee for Human Rights in Serbia.

Börzel, T. A. (2003) *Environmental Leaders and Laggards in the European Union. Why There Is (Not) a Southern Problem*, Aldershot: Ashgate.

Börzel, T. A. (2007) 'State capacity and the emergence of new modes of governance', NEWGOV Deliverable 12/D8.

Börzel, T. A. and Buzogany, A. (2008) 'New modes of governance in accession countries: the role of private actors', Paper presented at the NEWGOV Cross-Cluster Workshop on 'Civil Society, New Modes of Governance and Enlargement', Berlin, 3–5 July 2008.

Bose, S. (2002) *Bosnia after Dayton: Nationalist Partition and International Intervention*, London: Oxford University Press.

Bose, S. (2005) 'The Bosnian state a decade after Dayton', *International Peacekeeping* 12/3: 322–335.

Bretherton, C. and Vogler, J. (2006) *The European Union as Global Actor* (2nd edition), New York: Routledge.

Bunce, V. (2000) 'Comparative democratization: big and bounded generalizations', *Comparative Political Studies* 33/6–7: 703–734.

Burnell, P. J. and Calvert. P. (2004) *Civil Society in Democratization*, London: Frank Cass.

Caddy, J. and Vari, A. (2002) 'Hungary', in H. Weidner and M. Janicke (eds), *Capacity Building in National Environmental Policy,* Berlin: Springer.

Caplan, R. (2002) *A New Trusteeship?: The International Administration of War-torn Territories,* Oxford: Oxford University Press.

Carmin, J. (2010) 'Civil society capacity and environmental governance in Central and Eastern Europe', *Acta Politica* 45/1.

Carmin, J. and Jehlicka, P. (2005) 'By the masses or for the masses? The transformation of voluntary action in the Czech Union for Nature Protection', *Voluntas* 16/4: 397–416.

Carmin, J. and Vandeveer, S. D. (2004) 'Enlarging EU environments: Central and Eastern Europe from transition to accession', *Environmental Politics* 13/1: 3–24.

Carothers, T. (2002) 'The end of the transition paradigm', *Journal of Democracy* 13/1: 5–21.

Carothers, T. (2009) 'Democracy assistance: political vs. developmental?', *Journal of Democracy* 20/1 (January): 5–19.

Cellarius, B. A. and Staddon, C. (2002) 'Environmental nongovernmental organisations, civil society and democratization in Bulgaria', *East European Politics and Societies* 16/1: 182–222.

Chandler, D. (1999) *Bosnia: Faking Democracy after Dayton*, London: Pluto Press.

Chandler, D. (2000) *Bosnia: Faking Democracy after Dayton* (2nd edition), London: Pluto Press.

Chandler, D. (2005) 'From Dayton to Europe', *International Peacekeeping* 12/3 (Autumn): 336–349.

Chandler, D. (2006) 'State-building in Bosnia: the limits of "informal trusteeship"', *International Journal of Peace Studies* 11/1: 17–38.

Chandler, D. (2007) 'Introduction: Inside the Bosnian crisis', *Journal of Intervention and Statebuilding*, Special Online Supplement, 'Inside the Bosnian Crisis', 1 December 2007.

Commission of the European Communities (CEC) (2005) Annual Action Programme for Bosnia and Herzegovina, http://ec.europa.eu/enlargement/pdf/financial_assistance/cards/publications/ap_bih_2005_en.pdf

Crawford, G. (2003a) 'Promoting democracy from without – learning from within (Part I)', *Democratization* 10/1: 77–98.

Crawford, G. (2003b) 'Promoting democracy from without – learning from within (Part II)', *Democratization* 10/2: 1–20.

Dangerfield, M. (2004) 'Regional co-operation in the Western Balkans: stabilisation device or integration policy?', *Perspectives on European Politics and Society* 5/2: 203–241.

Deacon, B. and Stubbs, P. (1998) 'International actors and social policy development in Bosnia-Herzegovina: globalism and the new feudalism', *Journal of European Social Policy* 8/2: 99–115.

Delegation of the European Commission to Bosnia-Herzegovina (2005) *Mapping Study of Non-State Actors in Bosnia-Herzegovina*, http://www.europa.ba/?akcija= clanak&CID=33&jezik=2&LID=52

Delevic-Djilas, M. (2007) *Regional Co-operation in the Western Balkans,* Paris: Institut d'Études de Sécurité.

Diamond, L. (1996) 'Rethinking civil society: towards democratic consolidation', *Journal of Democracy* 7/3: 3–17.

Diamond, L. and Plattner, M. F. (1996) *The Global Resurgence of Democracy*, Baltimore and London: Johns Hopkins University Press.

Doherty, B. (2002) *Ideas and Actions in the Green Movement*, London: Routledge.

Donais, T. (2002) 'The politics of privatization in post-Dayton Bosnia', *Southeast European Politics* 3/1 (June): 3–19.

Du Pont, Y. (2000) 'Democratisation through supporting civil society in Bosnia and Herzegovina', *Helsinki Monitor*, No. 4.

Edmunds, T. (2008) 'Intelligence agencies and democratisation: continuity and change in Serbia after Milosevic', *Europe-Asia Studies* 60/1: 33–34.

Eppstein, D. and O'Halloran, S. (1999) *Delegating Powers: A Transaction Cost Approach*, Cambridge: Cambridge University Press.

European Agency for Reconstruction (EAR) (2006a) *Annual Report on Serbia*, Belgrade, http://ec.europa.eu/enlargement/archives/ear/serbia/main/ser-annual_ programme_2006.htm

European Agency for Reconstruction (EAR) (2006b) *Kosovo: Annual Report*, Pristina, http://ec.europa.eu/enlargement/archives/ear/kosovo/main/kos-annual_ programme_2006.htm

European Bank for Reconstruction and Development (EBRD) (2002) *Transition Report 2002: Agriculture and Rural Transition*, London: EBRD.

European Stability Initiative (ESI) (2006) *Bosnia-Herzegovina: Country Report*, http://www.esiweb.org/misc/search.php?cx=009383585810117201492%3Acbs stwl2yaw&cof=FORID%3A10&ie=iso-8859-1&q=bosnia+2006&lang=en&sa= Search

Evans, P. B. (1995) *Embedded Autonomy: States and Industrial Transformation*, Princeton, NJ: Princeton University Press.

Fagan, A. (2001) 'Environmental capacity-building in the Czech Republic', *Environment and Planning A*, 33/4: 589–606.

Fagan, A. (2005) 'Taking stock of civil-society development in post-communist Europe: evidence from the Czech Republic', *Democratization* 12/4: 528–547.

Fagan, A. (2006) 'Trans-national aid for civil society development in post-socialist Europe: democratic consolidation or a new imperialism?', *Journal of Communist Studies and Transition Politics* 22/1 (March): 115–134.

Fagan, A (2008) 'Global-local linkage in the Western Balkans: the politics of environmental capacity building in Bosnia-Herzegovina', *Political Studies* 56/3 (October): 629–652.

Fagan, A. and Sircar, I. (2010) 'Compliance without governance: the role of NGOs in environmental impact assessment processes in Bosnia-Herzegovina', *Environmental Politics* (forthcoming).

Freizer, S. and Kaldor, M. (2002) 'Civil society in Bosnia-Herzegovina', unpublished paper.

Glasius, M. and Kostovicova, D. (2008) 'The European Union as a state-builder: policies towards Serbia and Sri Lanka', *Suedosteuropa* 58/1: 84–114.

Gligorov, V. (2004) 'European partnership with the Balkans', *European Balkan Observer* 2/1 (May): 2–14.

Gligorov, V. (2005) 'Balkan Transition', *European Balkan Observer* 3/2 (October): 10–17.

Grabbe, H. (2006) *The EU's Transformative Power: Europeanization through Conditionality in Central and Eastern Europe*, Basingstoke: Palgrave Macmillan.

Green, A. T. and Kohl, R. D. (2007) 'Challenges of evaluating democracy assistance: perspectives from the donor side', *Democratization* 14/1: 151–165.

Grindle, M. S. (ed.) (1997) *Getting Good Government: Capacity-Building in the Public Sector of Developing Countries*, Cambridge, MA: Harvard University Press.

Grindle, M. S. (2004) 'Good enough governance: poverty reduction and reform in developing countries', *Governance* 17/4: 526–548.

Hall, J. A. (ed.) (1995) *Civil Society*, Cambridge: Polity.

Hann, C. (1996) 'Introduction', in C. Hann and E. Dunn (eds), *Civil Society: Challenging Western Models*, London and New York: Routledge.

Hann, C. M. (2002) *Postsocialism: Ideals, Ideologies and Practices in Eurasia*, London: Routledge.

Harrison, G. (2004) *The World Bank and Africa: The Construction of Governance States*, London: Routledge.

Hellman, J. S., Jones, G. and Kaufmann, D. (2000) *Seize the State, Seize the Day: State Capture, Corruption and Influence in Transition*, Washington, DC: World Bank.

Henderson, K. (2002) *Slovakia: The Escape from Invisibility*, London: Routledge.

Héritier, A. (2003) 'Composite democracy in Europe: the role of transparency and access to information', *Journal of European Public Policy* 10/5: 814–833.

Hix, S. (1998) 'The study of the European Union II: the "new governance" agenda and its rival', *Journal of European Public Policy* 5/1: 38–65.

Howard, M. M. (2003) *The Weakness of Civil Society in Post-Communist Europe*, Cambridge and New York: Cambridge University Press.

Hughes, J., Sasse, G. and Gordon, C. (2004) *Europeanization and Regionalization in the*

EU's Enlargement to Central and Eastern Europe: The Myth of Conditionality, New York: Palgrave Macmillan.

Hurrell, A. (2005) 'Power, institutions, and the production of inequality', in M. Barnett and R. Duvall (eds), *Power in Global Governance,* Cambridge: Cambridge University Press.

Hyde-Price, A. G. V. (1996) *The International Politics of East Central Europe*, Manchester and New York: Manchester University Press.

ICVA (International Council of Voluntary Agencies) (2002) *Guide to Civil Society in BiH: Directory of Humanitarian and Development Agencies in Bosnia and Herzegovina* (Vol. 1), Sarajevo: ICVA.

Ilić, D. (2005) 'Jugoslovenska Komisija za Istinu I Pomirenje 2001–?' ('The Yugoslav Commission for Truth and Reconciliation 2001–?'), *Rec* 73/19.

Inotai, A. S. (1997) *What is Novel about Eastern Enlargement of the European Union?; The Costs and Benefits of Eastern Enlargement of the European Union*, Budapest: Institute for World Economics, Hungarian Academy of Sciences.

Jachtenfuchs, M. (2001) 'The governance approach to European integration', *Journal of Common Market Studies* 39/2: 245–264.

Janicke, M. (1997) 'The political system's capacity for environmental policy', in M. Janicke and H. Weidner (eds), *National Environmental Policies: A Comparative Study of Capacity Building*, Springer: Berlin, pp. 4–24.

Juncos, A. E. (2005) 'The EU's post-conflict intervention in Bosnia and Herzegovina: (re)integrating the Balkans and/or (re)inventing the EU?', *Southeast European Politics* 6/2: 88–108.

Kaldor, M. (2003) 'Civil society and accountability', *Journal of Human Development* 4/1: 5–27.

Keane, J. (ed.) (1988) *Civil Society and the State*, London: Verso.

Kenis, P. and Schneider, V. (1991) 'Policy networks and policy analysis: scrutinizing a new analytical toolbox', in B. Marin and R. Mayntz (eds), *Policy Network: Empirical Evidence and Theoretical Considerations*, Boulder, CO: Westview Press.

Keohane, R. O. and Hoffmann, S. (1991) *The New European Community: Decisionmaking and Institutional Change*, Boulder, CO and Oxford: Westview Press.

Kesić, O. (2005) 'An Airplane with Eighteen Pilots', in S. P. Ramet and V. Pavlaković, *Serbia Since 1989: Politics and Society Under Milošević and After*, Seattle: University of Washington Press, pp. 95–124.

Kohler-Koch, B. (1996) 'The strength of weakness: the transformation of governance in the EU', in S. Gustavsson and L. Lewin (eds), *The Future of the Nation State: Essays on Cultural Pluralism and Political Integration*, Stockholm: Nerenius & Santerus, pp. 169–210.

Kooiman, J. (1993) *Modern Governance,* London: Sage.

Kopecky, P. and Mudde, C. (eds) (2003) *Uncivil Society? Contentious Politics in Post-Communist Europe*, London: Routledge.

Kostovicova, D. and Bojičić-Dželilović, V. (2006) 'Europeanizing the Balkans: rethinking the post-communist and post-conflict transition', *Ethnopolitics* 5/3: 223–241.

Kostovicova, D. and Bojičić-Dželilović, V. (2008) *Transnationalism in the Balkans*, London: Routledge.

Krastev, I. (2006) 'Democracy's "doubles"', *Journal of Democracy* 17/2 (April): 52–62.

Krnjevic-Miskovic, D. (2001) 'Serbia's prudent revolution', *Journal of Democracy* 12/3: 96–110.

Lazic, M. (2005) *Promene i Otpori* (Changes and Resistance), Belgrade: Filip Visnjic.

Leftwich, A. (1994) 'The developmental state', Working Paper No. 6, University of York, Department of Politics.

Lijphart, A. (1984) *Democracies: Patterns of Majoritarian and Consensus Government in Twenty-one Countries*, New Haven, CT and London: Yale University Press.

Linz, J. and Stepan, A. (1996) 'Towards consolidated democracies', *Journal of Democracy* 7/2: 14–22.

Loza, T. (2007) 'Bosnia: condition serious but stable', Transitions on Line, 11 December, http://www.tol.cz/look/TOL/

MacDonald, N. (2007) 'Bosnia prime minister resigns amid tension', *Financial Times*, 2 November. Accessed at: http://www.ft.com/cms/s/088de29c-88c5-11dc-84c9-0000779fd2ac,Authorised=false.html?_i_location=http%3A%2F%2Fwww.ft.com%2Fcms%2Fs%2F0%2F088de29c-88c5-11dc-84c9-0000779fd2ac.html

McMahon, P. C. (2004) 'Building civil societies in East Central Europe: the effects of American NGOs on women's groups', in P. Burnell and P. Calvert (eds), *Civil Society in Democratization*, London: Frank Cass.

McMahon, P. C. (2007) *Taming Ethnic Hatred: Ethnic Co-operation and Transnational Networks in Eastern Europe*, Syracuse, NY: Syracuse University Press.

Malcolm, N. (1994) *Bosnia: A Short History*, London: Pan Books.

Mandel, R. (2002) 'Seeding civil society', in C. M. Hann (ed.), *Postsocialisms: Ideals, Ideologies and Practices in Eurasia*, London: Routledge.

Mayntz, R. (2003) 'New challenges to governance theory', in H. P. Bang (ed.), *Governance as Social and Political Communication*, Manchester: Manchester University Press.

Mayntz, R. and Scharpf, F. W. (1995) 'Steuerung und Selbstorganisation in staatsnahen Sektoren', in R. Mayntz and F. W. Scharpf (eds), *Gesellschaftliche Selbstregulierung und politische Steuerung*, Frankfurt and New York: Campus, pp. 9–38.

Meyer, D. S. and Tarrow, S. (eds) (1998) *The Social Movement Society: Contentious Politics for a New Century*, Lanham, MD: Rowman & Littlefield.

Migdal, J. S. (1988) *Strong Societies and Weak States: State-Society Relations and State Capabilities in the Third World*, Princeton, NJ: Princeton University Press.

Minic, J. and Dereta, M. (2005) 'IZLAZ 2000: an exit to democracy in Serbia', in J. Forbrig and P. Demes (eds), *Reclaiming Democracy: Civil Society and Electoral Change in Central and Eastern Europe*, Washington, DC: The German Marshall Fund of the United States.

Moe, T. M. (1987) 'An assessment of the positive theory of congressional dominance', *Legislative Studies Quarterly* 12/4: 475–520.

Muehlmann, T. (2007) 'Police restructuring in Bosnia-Herzegovina: problems of internationally-led security sector reform', *Journal of Intervention and Statebuilding* 1, Special Supplement, 1 December.

Murphy, Dale (2000) *The Structure of Regulatory Competition: Corporations and Public Policies in a Global Economy*, Oxford: Oxford University Press.

OECD (Organisation for Economic Co-operation and Development) (1992) *Market and Government Failures in Environmental Protection: The Case of Transport*, Paris: OECD.

OECD (1994) *Capacity Development in Environment*, Paris: OECD.

OECD (1995) *Developing Environmental Capacity: A Framework for Donor Involvement*, Paris: OECD.

OECD (2006) *The Challenge of Capacity Development: Working Towards Good Practice*, Paris: OECD.

Ottaway, M. (2000) 'Social movements, professionalization of reform, and democracy in Africa', in M. Ottaway and T. Carothers (eds), *Funding Virtue: Civil Society Aid and Democracy Promotion*, Washington, DC: Carnegie Endowment for International Peace.

Ottaway, M. (2002) 'Think again: nation building', *Foreign Policy* September/October: 16–24.

Ottaway, M. (2003) 'Rebuilding state institutions in collapsed states', in J. Milliken (ed.), *State Failure, Collapse and Reconstruction*, Oxford: Blackwell.

Ottaway, M. and Carothers, T. (2000) *Funding Virtue: Civil Society Aid and Democracy Promotion*, Washington, DC: Carnegie Endowment for International Peace.

Papadimitriou, D. (2009) 'Europeanisation, conditionality and state building in Kosovo: the elusive pursuit of EU actorness', unpublished paper for Workshop: EU Enlargement and Institutional Reforms in Southeast Europe (February 2009), Freie Universität Berlin.

Papadimitriou D., Petrov, P. and L. Greicevci, L. (2007) 'To build a state: Europeanisation, EU actorness and state-building in Kosovo', *European Foreign Affairs Review* 12/2: 219–223.

Pearce, J. and Howell, J. (2001) *Civil Society and Development*, Boulder, CO: Lynne Rienner.

Peters, B. G. and Savoie, D. J. (2000) *Governance in the Twenty-first Century: Revitalizing the Public Service*, Montreal: McGill–Queen's University Press.

Phinnemore, D. (2003) 'Stabilisation and Association Agreements: Europe Agreements for the Western Balkans?', *European Foreign Affairs Review* 8/1: 77–103.

Picciotto, S. (2005) 'The WTO's appellate body: legal formalism as a legitimation of global governance', London: School of Public Policy, University College London.

Pierre, J. (2000) *Debating Governance: Authority, Steering and Democracy*, Oxford: Oxford University Press.

Pierre, J. and Peters, B. G. (2005) *Governing Complex Societies: Trajectories and Scenarios*, Basingstoke: Palgrave Macmillan.

Pond, E. (2008) 'The EU's test in Kosovo', *The Washington Quarterly* 31/4: 97–112.

Preston, C. (1997) *Enlargement and Integration in the European Union*, London: Routledge.

Pugh, M. (2002) 'Postwar political economy in Bosnia and Herzegovina: the spoils of peace', *Global Governance* 8/4: 467–482.

Pugh, M. (2005) 'Transformation in the political economy of Bosnia', *International Peacekeeping* 12/3: 448–462.

Quigley, K. F. F. (2000) 'Lofty goals, modest results: assisting civil society in Eastern Europe', in M. Ottaway and T. Carothers, *Funding Virtue: Civil Society Aid and Democracy Promotion*, Washington, DC: Carnegie Endowment for International Peace, pp. 191–216.

Radaelli, C. M. (2003) 'The Europeanization of public policy', in K. Featherstone and C. M. Radaelli (eds), *The Politics of Europeanization*, Ch. 2, Oxford: Oxford University Press.

Ramet, S. P. and Pavlaković, V. (2005) *Serbia since 1989: Politics and Society Under Milošević and After*, Seattle: University of Washington Press.

Rangelov, I. (2006) 'EU war crimes policy in the Western Balkans', in D. Kostovicova and V. Bojičić-Dželilović (eds), *Austrian Presidency of the EU: Regional Approaches to the Balkans*, Vienna: Renner Institute.

Rhodes, R. A. W. (1997) *Understanding Governance: Policy Networks, Governance, Reflexivity, and Accountability*, Buckingham and Philadelphia: Open University Press.

Riddell, R. (2007) *Does Foreign Aid Really Work?*, Oxford and New York: Oxford University Press, pp. xxvi, 505.

Risse-Kappen, T. (1996) 'Collective identity in a democratic community: the case of NATO', in P. Katzenstein (ed.), *Culture of National Security: Norms and Identity in World Politics*, New York: Columbia University Press, pp. 357–399.

Rootes, C. A. (2003) *Environmental Protest in Western Europe*, Oxford: Oxford University Press.

Rosenau, J. N. (1992) 'Governance, order and change in world politics', in J. N. Rosenau and E. O. Czempiel (eds), *Governance without Government: Order and Change in World Politics*, Cambridge and New York: Cambridge University Press, pp. 1–29.

Rosenau, J. N. (1995) 'Governance in the twenty-first century', *Global Governance* 1/1: 13–43.

Rosenau, J. N. and Czempiel, E. O. (1992) *Governance without Government: Order and Change in World Politics*, Cambridge and New York: Cambridge University Press.

Salamon, L. M. and Anheier, H. K. (1997) *Defining the Nonprofit Sector: A Cross-national Analysis*, Manchester: Manchester University Press.

Sali-Terzic, S. (2002) 'Civil society', in Z. Papic (ed.), *International Support Policies to South-East European Countries: Lessons not Learned in B-H*, Sarajevo: Muller, pp. 175–194.

Sampson, S. (1996) 'The social life of projects', in C. Hann and E. Dunn (eds), *Civil Society: Challenging Western Models*, London: Routledge.

Scharpf, F. W. (1978) 'Interorganizational policy studies: issues, concepts and perspectives', in K. Hanf and F. W. Scharpf (eds), *Interorganizational Policy Making. Limits to Co-ordination and Central Control,* London: Sage, pp. 57–112.

Scharpf, F. W. (1997) *Games Real Actors Play: Actor-Centered Institutionalism in Policy Research*, Boulder, CO: Westview Press.

Schiff, J. A. (2006) *Labor Market Performance in Transition: The Experience of Central and Eastern European Countries*, Washington, DC: International Monetary Fund.

Schimmelfennig, F. and Sedelmeier, U. (2004) 'Governance by conditionality: EU rule transfer to the candidate countries of Central and Eastern Europe', *Journal of European Public Policy* 11/4 (August): 669–687.

Schimmelfennig, F. and Sedelmeier, U. (2005a) *The Europeanization of Central and Eastern Europe*, Ithaca, NY: Cornell University Press.

Schimmelfennig, F. and Sedelmeier, U. (2005b) *The Politics of European Union Enlargement: Theoretical Approaches*, New York and London: Routledge.

Schimmelfennig, F. and Wagner, W. (2004) *External Governance in the European Union*, London: Taylor & Francis.

Schmitter, P. C. (1991) 'The European Community as an emergent and novel form of political domination', Madrid, Instituto Juan March de Estudios e Investigaciones, Centro de Estudios Avanzados en Ciencias Sociales.

Sergi, B. S. (2004) 'Understanding the "EU factor": the Balkans regions as recipients of FDI and industries', *South-East Europe Review* 4: 7–20.

Sergi, B. S. and Bagatelas, W. T. (2004) *The Slovak Economy and EU Membership*, Bratislava: Iura edition.

Share, D. (1987) 'Transitions to democracy and transition through transaction', *Comparative Political Studies* 19/4: 525–548.

Sissenich, B. (2007) *Building States without Societies: European Union Enlargement and the Transfer of EU Social Policy to Poland and Hungary*, Lanham, MD: Lexington Books.

Smillie, I. and Todorovic, G. (eds) (2001) *Patronage or Partnership: Local Capacity Building in Humanitarian Crises*, Westport, CT: Kumarian Press, 2001.

Smith, J. (2005) 'Enlarging the European Union', *Journal of Common Market Studies* 43/1: 127–130.

Smouts, M. C. (1998) 'The proper use of governance in international relations', *International Social Science Journal* 50/155: 81–89.

Sorensen, J. S. (1997) 'Pluralism or fragmentation', *War Report,* May.

Stubbs, P. and Gregson, K. (1998) *Social Policy, Protection and Practice: The Care of Vulnerable Groups in Bosnia-Hercegovina*, papers and proceedings from a conference held in Sarajevo, 10–12 December 1997, Sarajevo: Svjetlost.

Sugar, P. F. (1963) *The Industrialization of Bosnia-Herzegovina, 1878–1918*, Seattle: University of Washington Press.

Swyngedouw, E. (2005) 'Governance innovation and the citizen: the Janus face of governance-beyond-the-state', *Urban Studies* 42/11: 1991–2006.

Tomasevich, J. (1955) 'Peasants, politics, and economic change in Yugoslavia', Palo Alto, CA: Stanford University Press.

Van der Heijden, H.-A. (1997) 'Political opportunity structures and the institutionalisation of the environmental movement', *Environmental Politics* 6/4: 25–50.

VanDeveer, S. and Dabelko, G. D. (2001) 'It's capacity stupid: international assistance and national implementation', *Global Environmental Politics* 1/2: 18–29.

VanDeveer, S. and Sagar, A. (2005) 'Capacity building for the environment: North and South', in E. Corell, A. Churie Kallhauge and G. Sjostedt (eds), *Furthering Consensus: Meeting the Challenges of Sustainable Development Beyond 2002,* London: Greenleaf.

Vasic, M. (2005) *Atentat na Zorana,* Beograd: Politika, B92, Vreme, Narodna Knjiga, pp. 16–30.

Vermeersch, P. (2003) 'Ethnic minority identity and movement politics: the case of the Roma in the Czech Republic and Slovakia', *Ethnic and Racial Studies* 26/5: 879–901.

Vogel, T. (2008) 'Bosnia's long goodbye', *European Voice*, http://www.european-voice.com/article/imported/bosnia-s-long-goodbye/59436.aspx 19/3/2008

Wedel, J. (2001) *Collision and Collusion: The Strange Case of Western Aid to Eastern Europe, 1989–1998*, New York: St. Martin's Press.

Weinthal, E. (2002) *State Making and Environmental Co-operation,* Cambridge, MA: MIT Press.

Weiss, L. (1998) *The Myth of the Powerless State*, Oxford: Polity Press.

Weller, M. (2008) 'Negotiating the final status of Kosovo', Chaillot Paper No. 114 Paris: Institute for Security Studies.

White, G. (1994) 'Civil society, democratization and development (1): Clearing the analytical ground', *Democratization* 1/3: 379–395.

World Bank (2008) *Western Balkan Integration and the EU: An Agenda for Trade and Growth*, http://web.worldbank.org/WBSITE/EXTERNAL/COUNTRIES/ECAEXT/0,,contentMDK:21797167~pagePK:146736~piPK:226340~theSitePK:258599,00.html

Yanacopulos, H. (2005) 'Patterns of governance: the rise of transnational coalitions of NGOs', *Global Society* 19/3: 247–266.

Zaum, D. (2005) 'Economic reform and the transformation of the payment bureaux', *International Peacekeeping* 12/3: 350–363.

Index

www.ingramcontent.com/pod-product-compliance
Lightning Source LLC
Chambersburg PA
CBHW050433280326
41932CB00013BA/2101